10/01

Visual Thinking for
Architects and Designers

Visualizing Context in Design

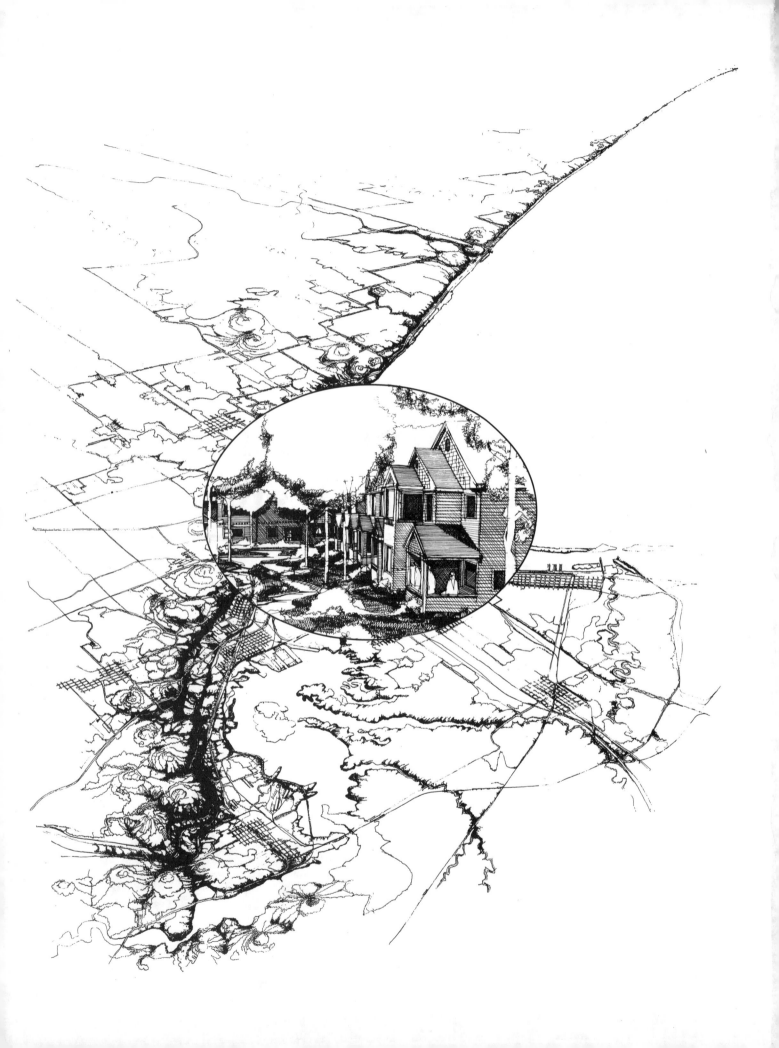

Visual Thinking for Architects and Designers

Visualizing Context in Design

Ron Kasprisin • **James Pettinari**

VAN NOSTRAND REINHOLD
I(T)P ™ A Division of International Thomson Publishing Inc.

New York • Albany • Bonn • Boston • Detroit • London •Madrid • Melbourne •
Mexico City • Paris • San Francisco • Singapore • Tokyo • Toronto

Van Nostrand Reinhold Staff
Editor: John Griffin
Production Editor: Carla M. Nessler
Production Manager: Mary McCartney
Designer: Theo Coates Design

Printed in the United States of America
For more information, contact:

Van Nostrand Reinhold
115 Fifth Avenue
New York, NY 10003

Chapman & Hall
2-6 Boundary Row
London
SE1 8HN
United Kingdom

Thomas Nelson Australia
102 Dodds Street
South Melbourne, 3205
Victoria, Australia

Nelson Canada
1120 Birchmount Road
Scarborough, Ontario
Canada M1K 5G4

Chapman & Hall GmbH
Pappelallee 3
69469 Weinheim, Germany

International Thomson Publishing Asia
221 Henderson Road #05-10
Henderson Building
Singapore 0315

International Thomson Publishing Japan
Hirakawacho Kyowa Building, 3F
2-2-1 Hirakawacho
Chiyoda-ku, 102 Tokyo
Japan

International Thomson Editores
Campos Eliseos 385, Piso 7
Col. Polanco
11560 Mexico D.F., Mexico

1 2 3 4 5 6 7 8 9 10 BAW 01 00 99 98 97 96 95

Library of Congress Cataloging-in-Publication Data
Kasprisin, Ronald J.
    Visual thinking for architects and designers/
    Ron Kasprisin and James Pettinari
            p.   cm.

    Includes index
    ISBN 0-442-01641-7
    1.Architectural drawing.   2.Architecture—Composition, proportion, etc.
    I. Pettinari, James.   II. Title.
NA2700.K37   1995
720'.28'4--dc20

95-30325
                                                            CIP

Acknowledgments

The publication of this book was supported in part by a grant from the
Johnston/Hastings Publications Support Endowed Fund, established by Professor
Norman Johnston and Architect Jane Hastings, of Seattle, Washington.

The authors also wish to acknowledge the support of the University of Oregon
Department of Architecture and the University of Washington Department of
Urban Design and Planning.

All of the drawings in the book are part of the authors' creative work that has
grown out of their practice and teaching. The authors acknowledge the assistance
of students and staff in the preparation of certain base mapping and information
visualizations on a number of projects presented in the book and the support and
challenge of the many communities, public and private institutions, including the
National Endowment for the Arts that provide the basis for the work.

Contents

Part 1 Understanding Place in Context

Part 2 Case Studies of Cascadia

Chapter Six: The Tlingit Archipelago Case Study Background and Overview

Chapter Seven: Ish River Case Study

Chapter Eight: Cowlitz-Willamette Case Study

Chapter Nine: Clark Fork: Bitterroot, Missoula, Montana Case Study

Index...271

Foreword

This book is about particular techniques and methods used in the documentation of the region as a physical place. Hence, it is both a method and a theory of regional descriptive analysis. The work is unique in the sense that it has no peer as a comprehensive methodology and, as such, is a pioneering work. Books have been published on a variety of media types, but none have integrated their techniques into a broader methodology/theory to this extent. The result is a tremendously significant work for urban and regional design practice and teaching.

In developing this book, Pettinari and Kasprisin have drawn upon many years of experience working with community groups in small-town public-space design. Their work has had profound and lasting effect on how leaders and citizens in those places envision the future of their communities. In many cases, this work has led to both policy and environmental development which has enriched and greatly improved the quality of the public environment. To this extent, the work in this book is more than an academic analysis of descriptive methodology. It is a vital, effective, and practical approach which has led to significant change in creating the kinds of nurturing environments that help sustain and enhance community life.

Much of this work is located in the Pacific Northwestern part of North America, in an area called the Cascadia bio-region. This region runs roughly from the Pacific Ocean in the west to the eastern slopes of the Cascade Mountain Range, and from the Oregon/California Border to, and including, Western British Columbia and Alaska. Several different urban areas within this zone are documented in a variety of ways with the goal of providing a broad view of the region as a physical place.

Designers, policy/decision makers, and the public will immediately see the value of these techniques for understanding and describing a region. While these examples will enhance the reader's understanding of the Cascadia region, it should be pointed out that the techniques illustrated in this book are models which can be used to facilitate regional comprehensive analysis anywhere in the world.

This book proposes special ways to envision place at the scale of the region. It presents illustrative techniques, using both diagrammatic and orthographic drawing types, with the goal of creating a comprehensive understanding of place. Such materials are developed, improving professional and public knowledge, regarding significant physical elements of a region, and their meaning for local planning and design decisions. In addition to presenting understandings of existing places, this methodology allows for growth and development testing of future scenarios, thus providing an image of the region's future.

Planning and design professionals must understand the impact of population growth on the physical environment of a region in order to deal with issues concerning the quality of human life within that region. In a democratic society, community investment decisions based on public vote are a fundamental part of implementing intelligent development strategies. These decisions provide relevant and useful information to the public regarding the impact of alternative policy scenarios: a crucial part of the planning process. The techniques presented in this book will be of great assistance to those seeking ways to improve communication between professionals and the public about their community, and illustrate the impact of policy and design decisions on the regional environment.

In a broader context, the ability of the environment to sustain human life is a great concern to us all. Environmental planners and designers are on the forefront of the intense debate concerning how public policy and the designed environment can develop and still contribute positively to sustaining life on earth. At the most fundamental level, sustainability is an issue that requires us to understand specific local and regional environments. From the perspective of sustainability, there are no generic places. This book is not about sustainability; it is about techniques of describing real and specific places. However, such techinques are fundamental to our ability to understand place and to make intelligent decisions about the future of the places in which we live.

With this book, Pettinari and Kasprisin have provided us with an extremely useful methodology which contributes to the professional's improving ability to meet the regional, planning, and design challenges of the twenty-first century.

Jerry V. Finrow, AIA, Dean
College of Architecture and Urban Planning
University of Washington
Seattle, Washington
April, 1995

Former Dean
School of Architecture and Allied Arts
University of Oregon
Eugene, Oregon

Introduction

Visual Thinking

We have experimented with visual thinking methods in design and planning projects for over two decades, leading to a substantive body of urban design work marked by extensive visualization. The work is characterized by pen and ink drawing methods and techniques, by the use of drawing as a visual thinking process in urban design, and by a public communication orientation in the types and formats of drawings used in the urban design. We propose, in the examples of this book, that visualization is inherent to the conduct of urban design, not as a representative media, but as a direct connection between the designer and the three dimensional reality of human settlements; and that drawing is perhaps the most direct cognitive process useful in exploring spatial relationships.

Preferred Drawing Style

For us, at the heart of the work is a love for drawing, a process that in and of itself is enjoyable; and a love for the complex physical patterns of cities and towns. We hope to share that enjoyment and methods and techniques with professionals, students, and laypeople. We will demonstrate, in a time of significant technological change, that drawing offers even more potential in design than ever before, given the need to spatially test ideas and policies and the growing community demand for increased access to the design process.

We began using pen and ink drawings as a means of preparing long lasting high-resolution visualizations suitable for multiple reproduction and for the lasting quality of line work. Over the years, we developed fast sketch qualities that are highly durable and public-friendly, based on numerous three dimensional formats and viewpoints. The technical pen with India ink and high-quality felt tip pens have be-

come part of the signature of our work. These tools, methods, and techniques can be integrated into and complement the computer graphics of contemporary professional practice. The drawing methods may even offer a therapeutic relief from high-tech practices. They are shared in the examples and case studies of the book with the emphasis that drawing is a learned process, not an in-born talent, achieved through motivation, confidence building, practice, and application.

Drawing as Visual Thinking

Two points made by Rudolph Arnheim in *Visual Thinking* (1969) establish a fundamental base for the use of drawing in the exploration of complex urban patterns: **1.** that "...cognitive operations called thinking are not the privilege of mental processes above and beyond perception but the essential ingredients of perception itself ... active exploration, selection, grasping of essentials, simplification, abstraction, analysis and synthesis, completion, correction, comparison, problem solving, ... combining, separating, putting in context"; and **2.** "Shapes are concepts ... What matters is that an object at which someone is looking can be said to be truly perceived only to the extent to which it is fitted to some organized shape." Drawing is a way of speaking, a versatile language for spatial thinking that enables the designer/planner to not only *represent* an idea or policy but to structure and organize the idea through the *shaping* process. The use of drawing as a cognitive process is generative (i.e., by its act, spatial relationships are formed and evolved as a result of the process). Drawing enables designers to work with the shape and content of the built form, to assess historic and contemporary form, and to assess the opportunities and implications of new forms. In many ways the shapes and patterns of cities and towns are spatial metaphors for underlying cultures, economies, and politics, all with their needs and resultant imprints on the built form. The book explores ways to visually differentiate many of these imprints without removing them from the larger context. It develops graphic diagrams and viewpoints that both highlight and integrate issues, constraints, and opportunities. The act of shaping a building, a city block, or a neighborhood is an intentional act of integrating culture, biological environs, artifact, and functional needs. It is assisted by drawing methods that permit the planner/designer/public to visually perceive changes and underlying conditions.

Drawing as Design Communication

An additional ingredient in urban design is the communication role of design drawing, not as presentation but as an ongoing visual story for designers and communities of their conditions, directions, and options. The design process has been challenged by the increasing demands of citizens for more ownership of decision-making in the remaking of their communities. This challenge can alter the ways in which designers communicate and assist towns and cities in dealing with change. This can be both intimidating and liberating. It is an evolution that we believe can lead to more involvement and design input for the designer, not less. The more the public is aware of what is happening in and to their environment, of the connections to past actions, and of the spatial or form implications of new inevitable actions, the more direct their participation as "authors" of change. The changes are more effective because the public, not the experts, implement the actions and live in the results.

We demonstrate drawing formats and types, ranging from regional aerial oblique perspectives to show a community's location in a larger geographical area, to before and after or historic time patterning sequential drawings of changes in the community's built pattern. It is not drawing versus words or text but the use of drawing as a means of integrating complex information into relational drawings, viewed by the public in a context, orientation, and referencing that is familiar and direct. Like a fine piece of painted art, the viewer is asked to explore the visual shapes and patterns in the drawing, guided by light to dark value structures and other principles and elements of drawing to discern the messages and meanings told in the shapes and patterns.

Drawing as a Testing Mechanism

The policies and guidelines used in urban planning and design are developed separately and insulated from the context within which the issues and/or project are located. Using drawing visualizations as a part of the urban design process can be the testing mechanism that spatially *demonstrates* the on-the-ground implications of proposed policies, regulations, guidelines, private agendas, and plans. Articulating in a *public language* the connections between increments means thinking of increments as interlocking built form pieces that perform with others to make the reality of place. Much of the work in this book reflects a conscious effort to develop testing methodologies as a part of a larger design process that not only involve the public more but are designed to provide them with more direct input through increased design opportunity arising out of a more understandable visualization of their particular context and place.

Visualizing Context and Place

We use *context* and *place* throughout the book, two terms that are commonplace in the urban design professions but, we argue, can be accorded greater use and understanding through improved visualization methods.

Place

"Place" is a statement of value associated with a localized or smaller physical space, defined in differing ways by planners and designers. It is often assigned a special quality based on the combination of culture, social interaction, politics, function, climate, and/or physical design. Place can be primarily architectural, defined as the "physical form of the public realm" (Gosling/Maitland, 1984) and distinguished as artifact for a portion of a settlement (town or city). We treat place as urban form that resulted from cultural and other human interactive behaviors.

Place can take different scales, ranging from the drama of settlements in powerful natural settings to the room scale. Standing on Ptarmigan ridge on Mt. Baker in Washington state and looking at the mountain at the end of alpine meadows and steep rock slopes produces an awesome sense of being somewhere special without a "building" in sight, devoid of human culture yet recognized by the human observer as a territory of value (for the observer). It is also the intimate, bustling, and entirely human-made colorful complexity of a multi-tiered Pike Place Market above Seattle's waterfront. "People need an identifiable spatial unit to belong to" (Alexander, 1977), as an aspiration for territorial "place," that special area where identity, structural clarity, and involvement all come together. Place is also viewed as a physical space with some social and/or cultural meaning, a space where the type and expression of activity adds to the dimension of "place." It is defined by the quality of the interaction of the space and the society that occupies it, many variations of a theme with multiple interpretations by planners, designers, and laypeople (Lynch, 1984). All have validity as a basis for understanding the differentiated parts of the city. Each place and its value have creative differences that can be better distinguished through co-participation of designer and community. When designers assume the sole role of place-definer, the integrity of the dynamics of the placemaking process may be compromised, comparing place to place as equals and losing the design opportunity of the difference.

Context

Context is defined in this book as the larger present spatial outcome or physical watershed of human activity. It has multiple scales and time frames and is *not* a backdrop, setting, or background. It is *place* connected to other places and places within larger places. Connected, influenced by one another, exchanging information, and all constantly changing. The term "place" is often used by the design professions as a valued space as opposed to less valued space, separating one place from another and losing the importance of context: places within places. How about assuming that all spaces have value to somebody or some other organism, all dependent on the nature and well being of the next space for its place-value. Each either has an aliveness based on its relationships to other places or it has symptoms of decline. That aliveness is a part of the definition of context and can be identified and described, in many cases as a part of the extent and well-being of the

spatial outcome. It is a third condition that encompasses both qualitative and quantitative expression of context, not a compromise or merging of the two. All physical (urban or settlement) forms of context are continually changing, redefining interior parts and external edges and limits based on the activities within and among its places.

Principles of Visual Thinking in Urban Design

The book is illustrated with the authors' drawings, reflecting their own work in public participation-design endeavors with more than seventy communities. Part I is composed of six chapters and constructs a theoretical approach to visualizing connected places within the environment. Part II contains case studies of urban planning and urban design projects that are organized according to the Cascadia Bio-region and its ecoregions, further connecting these individual community studies to one another. Part I, Chapter One outlines fundamental elements, principles, constructs, and techniques common to art and design and the language of drawing that are useful in expanding the visual cognitive process as applied to context. We discuss drawing techniques useful in the communication of a hierarchy and value of information rather than pure illustration techniques. Chapter Two discusses the means to visualize the components of context, from landform and settlement patterns to bio-physical and cultural information. Chapter Three addresses the Scale Ladder, the means of assessing context and place through scale changes. Chapter Four describes Time Patterning as a means of assessing change rather than only artifacts. Chapter Five summarizes the multiple ways to assist the public in envisioning their "place" by extending it back to context, increasing everyone's awareness of the interconnections within the environment.

This book is one way of understanding place and context through visualization. It is not the only way. We focus on the physical reality of place and context. The act of visually thinking in a hands-on drawing process within a framework of place and context as a means of understanding that there are underlying forces in individual behavior and cultures that are integral to the creation of physical context and place. The act of visually thinking within a framework of place and context as a means of expanding the boundaries of the design process is an underlying message.

References

Alexander, Christopher. 1977. *A Pattern Language.* New York: Oxford University Press.

Arnheim, Rudolph. 1969. *Visual Thinking.* Berkeley and Los Angeles: University of California Press, p. 13, par. 1.

Arnheim, Rudolph. 1969. *Visual Thinking.* Berkeley and Los Angeles: University of California Press, p. 27, par. 1.

Cullen, Gordon. 1961. *Townscape.* New York: Reinhold Publishing Corporation.

Gosling/Maitland. 1984. *Concepts of Urban Design.* New York: St. Martin's Press/London: Academy Editions

Lynch, Kevin. 1984. *Good City Form.* Cambridge MA: The MIT Press.

Visual Thinking for Architects and Designers

Visualizing Context in Design

Part One

Understanding Place in Context

Introduction

Designers require a language of design, visualization of verbs and nouns in the form of drawing. This part of the book describes and discusses fundamental principles, elements, and techniques useful in visualizing context and place as the overall containers for design. The authors have concentrated on those aspects of the visual language that they have found to be effective in exploring design opportunity in ways that are threefold in purpose: design aids, communication images, and quickly executed.

This part also lays the foundations for the case study examples in Part II by identifying various aspects of context that help the designer work through the complexity of information and identify design opportunity. These include the bio-physical and jurisdictional aspects of context; the scale ladder as a means of associating the concept of place with a larger complex web of places, referred to as context; time as a measure of change in context; and the role of public awareness and understanding as an active ingredient in changing place and context

1 Principles, Elements, and Techniques of Drawing Visualization

Introduction

Guidelines and techniques for drawing provide the designer with a set of tools that form a language useful in exploring and participating in the design process. If guidelines are ignored or not learned and practiced, the process can be very frustrating and unproductive. Having them as a basic foundation provides more freedom in expression, not less.

This chapter provides the basic principles (the actions as relationships) and parts (the objects put into action) for students and professionals to use in constructing an individualized language for effective communication. These basic principles represent the most effective techniques found useful by the authors in the context of the design and communication process discussed in this book; they are by no means all-inclusive and readers are encouraged to supplement reading on special techniques.

These principles and elements are the fundamental building blocks used in art. They are the critical elements upon which craftsmanship is based; and craftsmanship is an integral part of design and design-communication. Hopefully, the reader will experience an expansion of design capacity as his/her drawing-as-communication skills expand.

Principles

When experimenting with the principles, elements, and techniques in this book, be mindful of the following principles:

Principle One
- shapes are concepts: in the perception of shape

is the initiation of the concept *formation* (Arheim, 1969).

Principle Two
- patterns are shapes in relationship: each pattern can be a relationship that occurs over and over again; or, a pattern can change each time it occurs, adding or subtracting as adaptation requires.

Principle Three
- shapes can be made into patterns intentionally using the principles and characteristics of graphic communication to capture emerging patterns as design opportunity.

Principle Four
- fear of drawing is natural to the creative process, a reflection of intimidation (self-imposed or other), lack of confidence, fear of success/failure, or simply due to a lack of familiarity with basic rules of the process; the very act of drawing (without intellectualizing the process) can overcome the fear of starting.

The tools of communication used in this book and the focus of the principles and characteristics, with few exceptions, are pen and ink, limited to black, grays, and white.

Relationships and Elements

Relationships and elements help organize and make a communication. Relationships are the co-participating interactions between and among elements or building blocks of a communication.

Relationships

The following terms and their definitions are used to represent relationships in visual communication:

balance
harmony
gradation
dominance
repetition
variety
alternation
patterning

Balance

The state of equilibrium of a total work—the harmonious proportion of its elements. It is the total effect of the elements and their relationships that exhibits equality in weight, color, temperature, value, intensity, and so on. Balance is not two equal halves; for example it may describe a graphic with a small dark-valued shape in an upper corner and a larger light-valued shape in a lower opposite corner, creating a balanced affect.

Harmony

The combination or arrangement of elements into an agreeable whole. It is the feeling of *fit*. With harmony, the values of a work may be distributed throughout, creating a sense of harmony among the arranged shapes.

Gradation

The change within a given shape of the value, color, temperature, or other component. When portraying light on a surface, ink lines increase or decrease in density and separation in a manner that suggests light to dark or dark to light. Scribble techniques are effective in

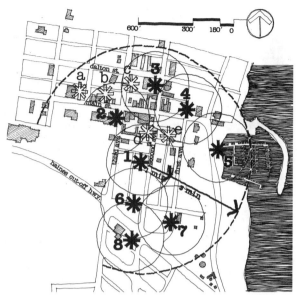

1-1 Repetition. Repetition is effective in attracting the eye of the observer. In *Haines Parking Diagram,* walking distances from key activities are reinforced in two ways: repeating the asterisk (*) symbol for the location of key activities; and repeating the same walking radii, indicated by circles, around each activity asterisk.

portraying light gradations on round or curved objects such as trees.

Repetition

The recurrence of a shape, pattern, or other element in a graphic communication. It can produce movement or direction; it can be combined with *variety* to create similarity using the same object with a difference in size, color, or other property. For example, a

1-2 Dominance. The USS Missouri shape and symmetrical placement on the page contribute to an intentionally dominating effect; the mid-dark value assigned to the primary shape reinforces *domination* to emphasize the message of powerful war ma-chinery.

circular shape can be repeated over and over with a different size or characteristic in each repetition.

Dominance

Emphasis of one feature or affect of an element over others in the same graphic. A graphic may be *dominated* by circular shapes such as many trees in a landscape drawing or by many and larger light valued shapes combined with fewer and lesser dark and middark values.

Variety

The difference between or among elements that avoids monotony or sameness.

Alternation

The repeated use of two or more shapes, or two or more sizes of one shape in regular patterns. Variety (and repetition) can be added to alternation for additional affects.

Patterning

Patterns are both elements and relationships. A pattern-element is a result of relating and repeating various shapes. A pattern-principle is the act of placing shapes in relationship. Patterning is a formative process, using lines, dots, and values as shapes to construct an image.

Elements

An *element* in graphic communication is a conventional symbol that represents a substance in physical matter. It is a basic unit of description used to portray objects in space. In pen and ink work, the elements of a graphic are the building blocks or units for graphic construction. When mixed with *principles*, they produce wholes that are indeed greater than the sum of the parts (or elements).

Basic elements of graphic communication are:

shape

1-3 Shape. In pen and ink drawing, shapes are composed of outlines as in these rectangular and angular building shapes; as curvilinear columnar shapes composed of both outlines and shadow lines; and as organic loops in perspective composed of outlines, curvilinear smaller shapes within the outlines, and loose line-hatching. Each shape connects to others to form a larger pattern of shapes, communicating a waterfront viewpoint.

size
dot
line
direction
texture
color
value

Shape

The form of an object distinguished by its outline and/or value *extent*. Shapes are delineated by rectangular, angular, and curvilinear outlines. When drawing shapes, remember that shape is normally "involved" with light, and consequently the point of view of the observer and the direction of light alter the appearance of shape. The example has most shape types.

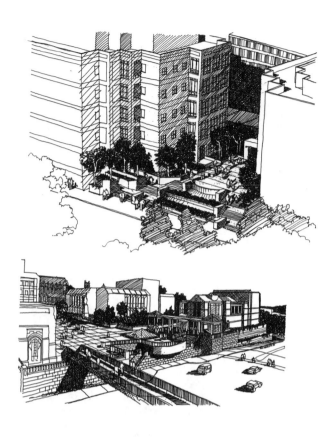

1-4 Line. Use lines as the basic building component of shapes and value patterns, both as outlines and as overlain patterns. In *University of Washington Sketches,* a Pentel Sign pen (felt tip-type) was used for all line types: diagonal hatchings for lighter values (farther apart) and darker values (closer together); cross hatchings for darker values; curving lines for organic outlines such as trees; and, tightly spaced scribbled lines for organic and textured effects such as the interior of trees, which also produce darker values due to increased line-per-square-inch density.

1-5 Line Value. Line value can have a clear hierarchy that is selectively used to emphasize specific spatial ideas. Value is used selectively to highlight the walls of trees that this building design plays off of. In the top drawing a quick, vertical hatching emphasizes the mountain backdrop and outlines building profile. In the lower drawing, similar vertical strokes are used to build up a framed tree wall that is penetrated by a funicular through the building proposal.

Size

That quality of a shape that determines how much space it occupies. It is also the relative extent of a shape in relation to other shapes: equal, larger, or smaller.

Dot

A point, a small diameter circular shaped mark resembling a sentence period. It can be manipulated in clusters to form shapes without line boundaries; it can be grouped in densities to establish value; and it can be varied over distance to represent distance-effects.

Line

A thin mark made by a pen, pencil, or other graphic tool. A line is a dot extended; a thin shape with a discernable beginning and end. In pen and ink techniques, the line is the basic unit of construction. It can be altered by width; it can be placed next to and over other lines to form patterns. It can be used to create value through contrast by increasing its density (lines per square inch) in a given shape more than the line density in nearby shapes. Lines can be composed of continuous straight or curved thin marks; they can also be composed of adjacent separated and repetitious marks such as dots, asterisks, etc.

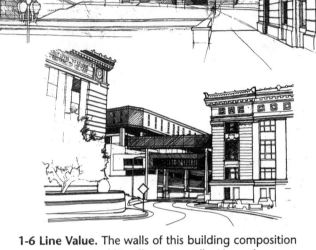

1-6 Line Value. The walls of this building composition are not treated literally nor equally. Line value emphasizes certain walls and building elements that define the space and connections between buildings. In the top drawing, freehand, diagonal strokes are used to emphasize the background enclosing wall of the urban space. The pedestrian connections that tie the existing courthouse to its proposed expansion are the focus of the lower drawing.

1-7 Texture. Texture in pen and ink drawing can be accomplished using the basic elements such as dots, lines, scribbles, and hatching. In Omak, dots are used in white tree shapes to provide the effect of blossoms or fruit; scribbling is used in dense patterns in the trees for foliage, varying the density to achieve value differentiations among trees; and, scribbling is used on the church facade for fieldstone texture. White or no linework can represent smoothness.

...*guest cabins*   *boardwalks*...

1-8 Value. In the *Waterfall Cannery* series, a fine-point technical pen produced varied value patterns using loops, straight lines, scribbling, hatching, and no lines (white). All of the darks are achieved through dense hatching rather than solid darks. Dark values are intentionally placed behind and/or around white primary shapes to increase the contrast be-tween dark and light. Rounded shapes such as foothills in perspective and trees in plan are given shape through value variations by increasing line density. The shapes on the foothills are made larger and more apart for lighter values and smaller and closer together for darker values. In the plan view, the water shape was assigned to a mid-dark value to dramatize the buildings and land shapes as the primary focus.

1-9 Value and Composition. The one-point perspective view creates an inherent focus around the single vanishing point in the center of the drawing. Drawing value given to the road further strengthens sense of movement towards the horizon.

Direction

A way of travel or viewing; it is an orientation for pointing or moving. Three orientations for direction include: horizontal, vertical, and oblique. Direction in a graphic has a dominance in the composition, as in a built design, and is determined by the use of linear shapes, line placement, and value patterns. Simply by aligning your working paper vertically (portrait format) or horizontally (landscape format), you establish a dominant direction, assuming that the working graphic format coincides with that of the paper. Direction has certain conventions of expression in art: horizontal represents repose and stability; vertical represents dignity and growth; and, oblique is the energizer, representing movement in two-dimensions and depth in three-dimensions (Webb, 1990).

Texture

The appearance of the sense of touch, the surface quality of objects that affect touch or sight, characterized by:

rough
smooth
slick
dry
wet

In graphic visualizations, texture is identified by sight rather than touch, requiring the use of line patterns that replicate surface qualities associated with touch. Slick or wet surfaces can be drawn using reflections of objects onto ground plane surfaces.

Value

The key element in graphic visualizations, above and beyond shapes, patterns, and composition. Value is the structuring element of a graphic: it emphasizes and deemphasizes shapes and patterns; it makes one shape dominate and others supportive; and, it places other elements in relationship. This is why it is also listed under Principles.

Value is the light to dark relationship of a graphic, between the extremes of white and black, where variations of lightness and darkness are placed in ways to create contrast, for example. A value scale from black to white with nine intervals is recommended for pen and ink work; a five interval scale is also effective, producing sharp contrasts. For a helpful tool, draw a value scale using fine line hatching

techniques. Keep the scale handy as a guide for graphics visualizations.

Guides for the use of value follow:

- values are shapes: avoid making values lines or scattered pieces; use values in shadow shapes, building planes, vegetated clusters or edges, and land masses;

- develop a value plan: allocate one value per shape; make each value different from adjacent values; resolve all values; distribute the values throughout the graphic, not just in one location or at the center of interest;

- placing the lightest value next to the darkest value (i.e., white next to black) provides the strongest contrast and emphasis, attracting the viewer's eye;

- build value foundation through the effective placement of the values in a graphic: usually with the white or lightest value at or near the center of interest supported by darkest values in the vicinity of the center of interest; if the contrast is too strong with the opposite values immediately next to one another, separate the values with a light to mid-light value; use mid-light, mid, and mid-dark values throughout the rest of the graphic in supporting roles; and

- experiment with a *light pattern:* use values to layout and structure a value pattern using light as the focus.

Edges

Edges are the limits of all shapes and patterns. They are also the connecting elements among shapes; the transitions between materials, colors, values, and textures. Edges are energy, generated by the meeting, joining, or repelling of two entities.

In graphics, edges are categorized as:

hard
soft
interlocking
merged
lost and found

1-10 Hatching and Scribbling. In *Mill Square*, the left-side building plane facing the viewer is composed of four levels of hatching: level one or the first application is a one-direction diagonal hatching, closely spaced; level two (second application) consists of two diagonal directions that "carve out" the face from the application one; level three consists of a horizontal hatch over the second application, darkening the "mill square" letter shapes; and level four, "PRODUCE FROM THE SOUTH," has all four hatching directions—two diagonal, one horizontal, and one vertical. All hatchings are freehand and *consistently applied.* Consistently applied scribbling can be an effective and fast technique for texture and value. Any scribbling can be effective by maintaining uniform application. In *Wilsonville Spire*, the background trees are given a texture, value variation pattern, and shape all with a consistent scribble technique. Ground shadows are dark scribbles achieved by layering scribble upon scribble.

Hard Edges

Hard edges are the most commonly recognized: they attract attention due to contrast and immediacy of the change between two shapes. The edge is clearly recognized as the beginning of one shape and the end of another. Hard edges have more contrast than other types due to the abrupt nature of the change from shape to shape. Edges that face a light source are characterized as hard or sharp. Shadows that fall on flat smooth surfaces tend to be hard. They are effective when mixed with other different edge conditions, but can become monotonous when over-used, losing the ability to connecting shapes and patterns.

Soft Edges

Soft edges have a blurry quality, less attracting to the eye with more of a connecting role than hard edges. They are used to join two shapes as if they flowed or melted together. This melting is easy to accomplish with techniques such as scribbling and hatching. Too many hard edges in a graphic can create a mosaic effect: Many pieces located next to one another with little interaction except through value and color. Soft edges help blend and join shapes, connecting the parts into a larger whole.

Interlocking Edges

Interlocking edges occur when two shapes penetrate one another like interlocked fingers. Look around any environment and you will see countless examples of one shape interlocking another: the edge of one photograph jutting into the rectangular "window" of another; a piece of paper (shape) penetrating the page (shape) of an open book. These edge conditions are methods of connection, integrating visual information so that the viewer's eye moves smoothly from shape to shape, rather than stopping at a hard edge.

Attitude and Work

Why discuss attitude and work? The authors subscribe to the thesis that *talent* does not exist as an inherent quality in people. Talent is the result of motivation, comfort, confidence, and the ensuing effort or work that results from the interest generated by the motivation. Usually, if someone wants to work at a type of drawing, and is comfortable and capable of dealing with the natural fears of trying something different, the *time-logged on drawing, pen to paper,* increases dramatically with an proportionate

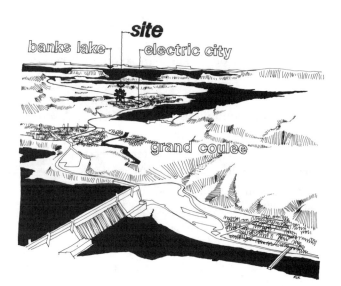

1-11 Opaqueing. Where high contrast is desired between shapes (e.g., land masses and water bodies), a solid or opaque application can dramatize major patterns. In *Grand Coulee,* the network of river-lakes associated with the dams on the Columbia River is the focus and was made black for maximum contrast with the white land forms.

increase in ability, skill, and eye–resulting in "talent."

Drawing is a personal experience once the pen touches the paper. No one else can do it for you; no style but your own can result. Drawing is an act of craftsmanship, of developing the skills associated with working with certain materials to the point that the artist transcends skill. Learning only comes through interaction with the tools, their use, not their intellectualization; thus the necessity for motivation and work.

Basic Techniques of Pen and Ink

Hatching and Cross-hatching

Hatching is achieved with straight lines (freehand or with a straightedge) drawn close together to form a field or screen. The individual lines are not the message, the screen is the message. Spacing the lines too far apart will create a "stripe" effect; spacing lines closer together increases the "screen" or "field" effect. Three basic principles to remember:

1. The more lines per square inch the stronger the "field" effect and the darker the value.

2. Additional value is created by overlaying

additional screens with the same density and line weight at different directions, usually in this order: diagonal, opposite diagonal, horizontal, vertical.

3. Hatch lines always meet or overrun the shape edges; lines that do not meet edges create an additional shape in the gap.

Hatching technique is transparent. Shapes can still be observed under multiple layers of hatching, which is useful in visualizing ground plane shapes within building shadows, for example.

Dotting or Stippling

Dots and stipples are essentially the same technique, using period-like marks (.) at varying densities per square inch to achieve value, texture, and field or screen. Dots take longer to implement but are effective for textures when the dot pattern is varied, clustering dots more densely in some areas and dispersing them in others.

Scribbling

Scribbling patterns are effective for texture, value, and gradation. Almost random, it has a free-form quality, yet the technique is most affective if the type of scribble pattern is kept consistent so that it does not call attention away from the field and overall visualization. Some designers use a leaf-like pattern, others a curly-type; consistency is the key. When scribbling, work in layers with darker values added to initial layers that define the shape.

Opaqueing

When a shape permits no light or underlying color to show through it, it is opaque. Light is the key: it can pass through a cross-hatched image, strike the paper's surface, and reflect back but it is completely absorbed with no reflection by an opaque image. In pen and ink drawing, solid black ink is opaque.

Outlining

Outlining is the simple line boundary defining a shape, without additional in fill within the shape. Most base maps, the drawings with the fundamental shapes for reference and orientation, are outline drawings. Value can be achieved on an outline drawing by using different pen weights to create contrasting line thicknesses. A principle of outlining in varying line widths is based on the shape's closeness to the ground plane: water edge, topography, curblines, etc. are narrow widths (light) and buildings (farther

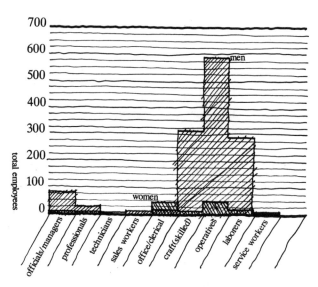

1-12 Colored Markers. Colored markers can be made into effective black and white reproductions after they serve their colorful purpose in public meetings. For charts and graphs, colored fine-point markers (such as Sharpie pens) are used for blue horizontal x-axis bands and wide markers are used for the data relationship lines in red and purple, etc. These diagrams have dual use: as colored charts for public communication and as effective and less expensive black and white reproductions in reports.

away from ground) are wider (darker).

Colored Marker Techniques

Colored markers can be used effectively in graphics intended for black and white reproduction. Color principles are not discussed in this book; readers are encouraged to refer to the numerous quality books on the subject. Of importance here are the use of color markers, both wide and narrow, for diagrams and other visualizations, and the ability to reproduce them into clean replications through the printing process.

Type of Line

Colored markers come in wide/narrow sharp edged points, fine and medium rounded points, and chiselled or caligraphic points. The same principles that apply to pen and ink line weight apply to colored markers: fine lines represent lesser emphasis and heavier or wider lines represent greater emphasis. Contrast is achieved by putting a finer line in close relationship to a heavier one. The degree of contrast is dependent upon the separation between the fine and the heavy line. The power of contrast cannot be overstated as it is the basic *structure* of a visual communication.

Wide lines or strokes with colored markers are most effective when the entire width of the marker edge, whether the wide or narrow edge, is kept flush to the paper continuously and consistently. A squiggly line is not noticeable when the entire line is squiggly. Only when you vie for perfection—a perfectly straight line—and mars it with an accidental squiggle will the viewer notice the difference: the squiggle. Be consistent. Be loose.

Marker strokes that are combined to form a *field* filling up a shape such as a land use area or a building elevation wall surface are most effective when they are kept consistent in their vertical or horizontal alignment. Think of when you cut the family grass: you cut it in rows and you overlap each cut just a bit so as not to leave any strips of un-cut grass. Do the same with the markers: "cut the grass" in an overlapping technique. If you miss a section and white paper does show through, *leave it alone—do not go back over it.* A small white piece is less obvious than the result of trying to fix it by going over previously applied marker.

When coloring shapes, regardless of configuration, an outline stroke can be applied prior to or after the vertical or horizontal strokes to connect the edges of the strokes into a unified whole.

Visualization Constructs

Semi-Abstract and Real Constructs

Semi-abstract Visualization Constructs

Throughout this book, semi-abstract and real drawings are used in combination as complementary communications in a continual back and forth study process, passing on information from one communication type to the other. Semi-abstract drawings are graphics that selectively emphasize certain qualities, filtering out layers of details and visualizing the essential organization, structure and movement patterns of a given context. Diagrams are constructs that are semi-abstract in nature and are used extensively as a visual thought process in planning and design. Semi-abstract diagrams seek to demonstrate the relationships between the place of study or focus and the context of place.

Real Visualization Constructs

Real graphic images are commonly defined as drawings that represent the actual or true object or context, a pictorial depiction. Visualizing three dimensional *reality* can be important to the public participation process in that the layperson often feels secure in the recognition of clearly identifiable scenes and settings. Because they can be difficult to deliver with constructed perspective views in a short time, students and professionals often avoid creating them. The approaches described in this chapter will assist you to quickly visualize realities early in the design process as a form of research, revealing the physical complexities of a context. The nature of the techniques that are demonstrated in this section are meant to facilitate the useful blending of real and semi-abstract, avoiding a dependence on one or the other. Semi-abstract diagrams then permit the designer to select and separate certain aspects or relationships from the complexities of the real view and manipulate them on a conceptual level.

Perspective and Paraline Drawing Shortcuts

There are excellent books on the market describing the techniques for constructing perspectives and paraline drawings. The intention of this book is to describe the characteristics and relationships of place and context, not construct elaborate perspectives; hence, this section on shortcuts.

Perspectives

Perspectives are often associated with presentation drawings and less used as visual thinking tools for study and exploration because of their time consuming nature. Orthographic views, such as plans, elevations, and sections are quick and easily understood. These mechanical views isolate planar components; this is both their advantage and disadvantage. We see the world through perspective rather than ortho view. Inherent in perspective visualization is the integration of plan, elevation, section, parts organization, and structure. In our approach, a perspective drawing

framework can be quickly made from a few simple rules of thumb and/or with the help of photographs and slides.

You only need a few vanishing points to create an accurate perspective framework within which detail can be approximated. The purpose of the chart, **Vanishing Points Within the View,** is to shortcut the tedious process of laying out perspective from a plan drawing. **Plan Projection** illustrates the traditional method of locating vanishing points from plan projection. Three different viewing angles are used; 30/60, 45/45 degrees (two point perspectives) and 0/0 degrees (one point perspective). From the plan of a cube rotated at each viewing angle, a perspective is developed along a horizon line. The first series of perspectives locates one to two critical vanishing points in terms of D, the distance one is standing from the picture plane. The second line of drawings takes the same perspectives, connects corners along the cube's surfaces, and projects those lines to fine diagonal vanishing points for lines at 45 degrees. Again, all vanishing points are given in terms of D, the distance between the viewer and the picture plane. Many times D is difficult to determine when starting a perspective. **Vanishing Points in Relation to Picture Plane** summarizes the location of the key vanishing points found in plan projection. The vanishing points are given in terms of D, the distance one is standing from the object being viewed, or X, a dimension along the x or y axis of the picture plane. The relationship, D=1.7x comes from the triangle formed by a person viewing perpendicular to the picture plane with a cone of vision of 60 degrees. X is the distance from the center of vision, along the x or y axis of the picture plane, to the farthest edge of the picture one wants to include in the drawing. Knowing D or X gives a couple of key vanishing points to set up a perspective thus eliminating plan projection.

One–Point Aerial Perspective Structure

The one-point perspective (0/0 case), perspective structure consists of one vanishing point within the drawing along the horizon line and at the center of vision, and four other diagonal vanishing points at distance D or 1.7x, east, west, north, and south from

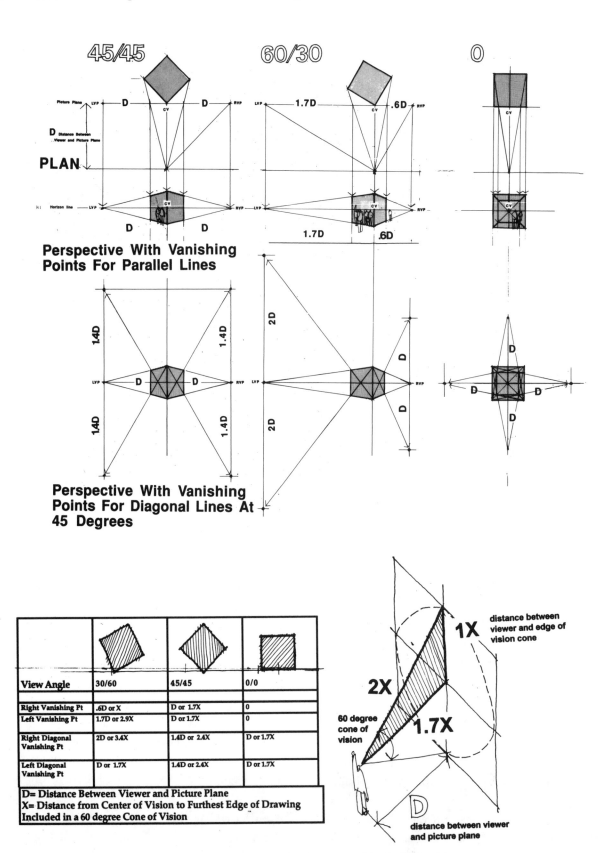

45/45   **60/30**   **0**

PLAN

Perspective With Vanishing Points For Parallel Lines

Perspective With Vanishing Points For Diagonal Lines At 45 Degrees

View Angle	**30/60**	**45/45**	**0/0**
Right Vanishing Pt	.6D or X	D or 1.7X	0
Left Vanishing Pt	1.7D or 2.9X	D or 1.7X	0
Right Diagonal Vanishing Pt	2D or 3.4X	1.4D or 2.4X	D or 1.7X
Left Diagonal Vanishing Pt	D or 1.7X	1.4D or 2.4X	D or 1.7X

D= Distance Between Viewer and Picture Plane
X= Distance from Center of Vision to Furthest Edge of Drawing Included in a 60 degree Cone of Vision

distance between viewer and edge of vision cone

1X

2X

60 degree cone of vision

1.7X

distance between viewer and picture plane

1-13 Locating Vanishing Points Within the View. Perspectives created by traditional plan projection can be tedious and time consuming. Plan projection does not lend itself to exploratory, three-dimensional visualizations throughout the design process. By knowing the distance one is standing from an object, and/or the limits of the vision cone, one can locate the few necessary vanishing points to set up a three-dimensional structure within the view.

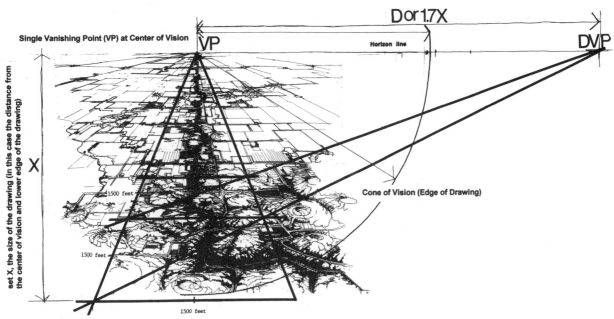

1-14 One-Point Perspective Structure (0/0 degrees). Perspective structure can be created from two vanishing points, one at the center of vision, another diagonal vanishing point at D or 1.7x due north, south, east, or west from it. In the case of the above aerial perspective, a diagonal vanishing point has been chosen east of the first vanishing point at the center of vision.

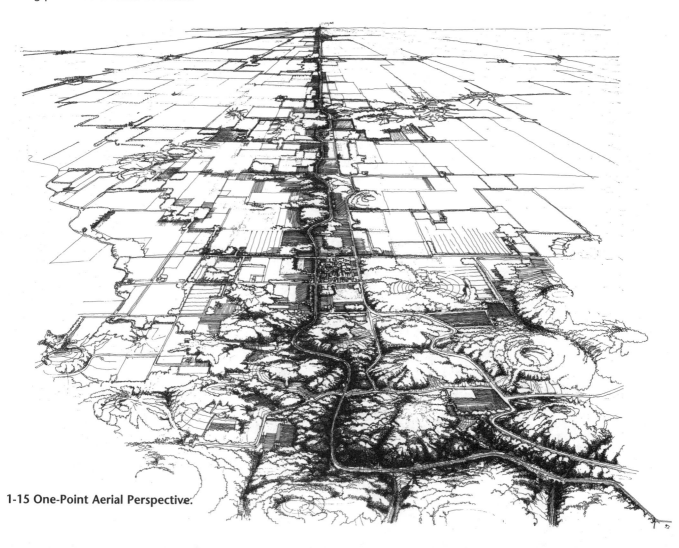

1-15 One-Point Aerial Perspective.

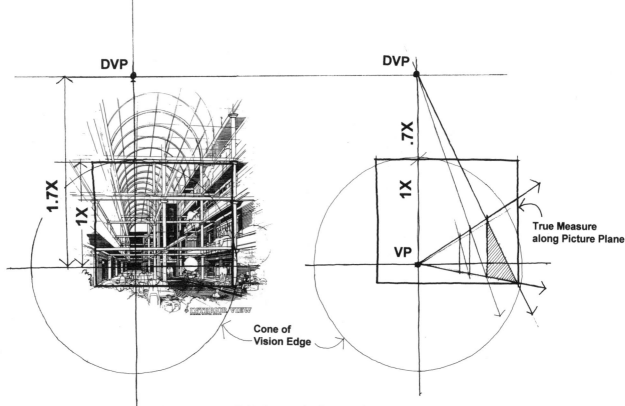

1-16 One-Point Interior Perspective Structure (0/0 degrees). Perspective structure created from two vanishing points, one at the center of vision, the other at D or 1.7x due north from it.

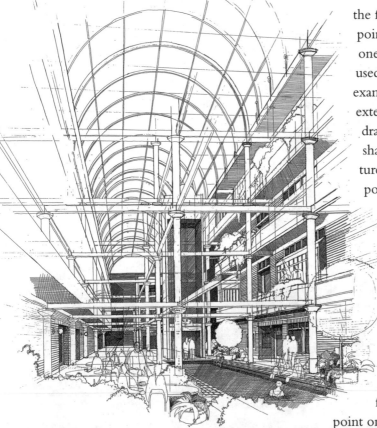

1-17 One-Point Interior Perspective.

the first vanishing points. We only need the first points and one of the others to create a simple one-point perspective structure that can be used to visualize many different situations. For example, the two drawings, one interior, one exterior are at two different scales, yet the drawing of the room and the aerial perspective share the same one-point perspective structure. They begin by locating a single vanishing point within a picture plane and an approximate cone of vision (how big the drawing will be). This first vanishing point is along the horizon line and at the center of vision. In the case of the room, the picture plane is four floors high and two 20-foot bays wide, or 40 feet. The center of vision is at eye level (more or less six feet) and in the middle of the left bay. In the case of the aerial perspective, the picture plane is roughly a 1500- by 2000-foot rectangle with the single vanishing point on a horizon line along the top and center of the composition.

1-18 Spokane Sketches. Begin with a scaled site plan with building footprints. Establish the one vanishing point on the site plan. Extend the corners of all vertical elements outward (upward or toward the viewer or downward away from the viewer if depressed below the ground plane). Establish the desired roof plane points, connecting the corners with lines parallel to the equivalent ground plane lines. Add detail and retrace, eliminating the construction lines. As an alternative to eye-balling the changing floor heights, use the intersecting angle method: since the vertical lines are vanishing to a point, they are no longer parallel as they would be in elevation. By using the same angle from a horizontal line intersecting each vertical level, the space between levels is increased (moving toward the viewer) or decreased (moving downward or away) due to the vanishing vertical lines.

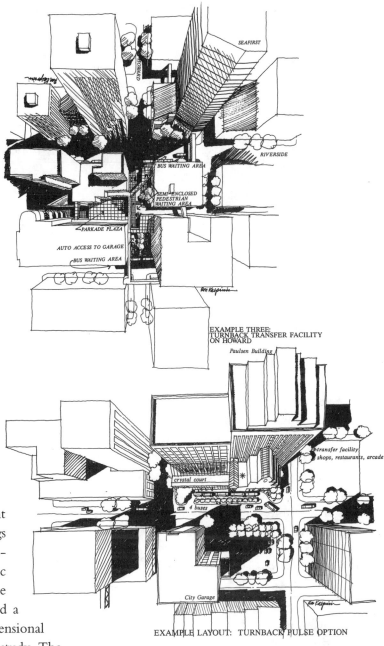

One-Point Birds-eye Perspective

A transit transfer facility feasibility study in downtown Spokane, Washington required a number of alternative concepts for a public involvement process and staff review. The study drawings were prepared in a manner suitable for display and discussion purposes at public meetings and workshops. A short time frame and budget restrictions necessitated a fast, effective approach to the three-dimensional diagrams deemed appropriate for the study. The drawings are on yellow flimsy tracing paper drawn with a black Pentel Sign pen, mounted on foam core and photographed in slide format.

The downtown building scale of Spokane, Washington contains a number of high rise office and department store buildings that form the enclosures for the study areas and a critical part of the pedestrians' view. As the sense of *place* is defined and redefined throughout downtown, the total enclosure or walls of the *place* in context need to be communicated rather than what an illustrated site plan can display: the ground plane with shadowed building footprints and any existing and/or proposed features.

The one-point birds-eye study drawings were purposefully drawn to articulate the vertical surfaces of the pedestrian place using *walls as reference and orientation information*. These drawings were supported by shadowed plan diagrams of the larger downtown core for larger scale reference, orientation, and *place-connection*. A two-dimensional street plan with building outlines can leave out critical information for the property owners, merchants, and staff people who attend the workshops.

Spokane Sketches, One and *Two* are products of a method that is intended to be fast and loose, done without parallel rules or T-squares, estimating the heights of buildings. It is valid as a study tool and proportionately accurate with the estimation of building heights based on their heights relative to one another. If the buildings become more prominent to the study, with changes to their volumes and shapes, an alternate method of determining the heights can be employed such as using diagonals to establish floor lines.

Determine an appropriate site plan scale, large enough to draw from with sufficient visual impact. The site plan requires building footprints and street elements (curbs, utility poles, etc.). Determine the desired focal point on the ground plane that best centers the viewer's eye and shows the most information horizontally and vertically. This is a judgment decision. Locate the focal point on a sheet of flimsy tracing paper laid over the site plan to assist in making a decision on the most appropriate location.

Using a straight-edge, extend all of the ground floor corners of the buildings along a line connecting each corner with the focal point, radiating these lines out from the ground plane in a direction away from the ground plane (up). Repeat for all the surrounding buildings necessary for the information base. Include enough of the background buildings to adequately establish a scale and intensity of buildings for the definition of place. View photographs and elevation drawings to determine the heights by numbers of stories of the buildings. Assume ten feet per story on the average, with a ground floor height of fifteen feet.

Using your judgement, select a key building and establish a height limit that looks proportionately correct. Selecting the upper limits for the highest building in the image sets a boundary that can be used to estimate the proportionate heights of lower buildings. Remember that since this is a perspective, all lines going to the vanishing point are distorted equal distances between you and the vanishing point. Spaces that are equal in reality become incrementally smaller as they approach the vanishing point. If a building is twenty stories, begin drawing a reasonable second floor line and make each succeeding line slightly farther away from the ground plane. The issue here is the ground plane information in relation to the building heights. The building heights can be approximate but proportionately reasonable.

Based on photographs, additional detail for facades and the ground plane can be sketched in as desired. A sepia print or black line print or bond copy can be made for the addition of color.

Related Techniques

Shadow shapes are value shapes. They can be either solid and opaque (black) or transparent. In the Spokane sketches, a near opaque black shadow technique is used to create high contrast in order to call attention to the building shapes. There is an element of transparency with the opaque shadows accomplished by outlining the curb lines (leaving the actual line as a negative shape—-not blackened) and by making the trees negative shapes within the shadow area, so that they stand out against the blackened ground plane.

Hatching and cross-hatching on the building vertical planes applies mid-values to each vertical shape, changing to darker values the more the plane is turned from the light source. The hatchings are close enough together so as not to read as stripes but as a field or screen of value. Shadow lines on the ground plane are parallel in the same manner that the ground plane building footprint edges are parallel.

Still working on the flimsy tracing paper, add whatever additional secondary facade articulation, ground plane elements, and textures you deem necessary for the level of information being communicated. Retrace the drawing onto another clean piece of flimsy; draw only those lines that are desired for the graphic communication, eliminating construction lines, study lines, "goofs," etc. until a clean image is made. Add any additional features.

Add shadows to the buildings, particularly on the ground plane. Shadows should be the darkest value and have enough contrast to set the buildings and other elements apart. Make the shadows transparent using the following options:

- use cross-hatching over previously drawn ground plane elements and textures; the hatching will permit a hint of the ground plane information to be seen; and

- if black or near solid shadows are desired, leave the curb lines white in the shadows and permit trees and other elements to show through by not darkening them. Instead, hatch them with a gray value and they will be attached to the shadow but lifted up from the ground plane.

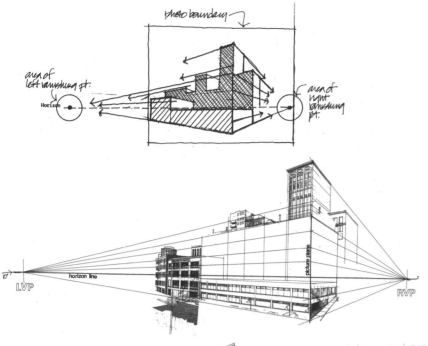

1-19 Perspective Structure from Photographs. Vanishing points can be found in any photographic view. Here, two vanishing points are found along the horizon line of a slide of an existing building context. The lower view develops a building proposal within a three-dimensional framework created by the right and left vanishing points and a corner picture plane from which all dimensions can be understood.

1-20 Building In-fill Developed Within a Two-Point Perspective Framework.

1-21 Interior Room Perspective. The interior perspective is developed along the single vanishing point from a photographic slide of the exterior context.

Trace the final image onto mylar or good quality tracing paper, either free-hand following the study underneath as a base or with a straight edge. The free-hand style is recommended as a work-saving technique and as a means of adding line character to the drawing. If a straight edge is used without a T-square or parallel rule, errors will be more noticeable due to the attempted perfection of the straight-edge.

Diagonals or other selected angles can be used to effectively determine the proportional separation of equal distances between the center of vision and the viewer. To determine the distorted separation of

equal building floor levels emanating out from the ground plane is similar to selecting the separation between equal sized floor tiles on a one-point eye level perspective: remember that due to the *vanishing* of the lines between the vanishing point and the viewer's location, that equal distances that are transferred from the view plane to vanishing lines will be incrementally intercepted closer and closer to the vanishing point, creating an incremental shortening in perspective of equal distances in plan.

Steps in the process are as follows: from the ground plane, extend vertical lines from each build-

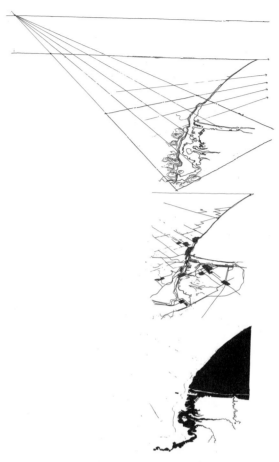

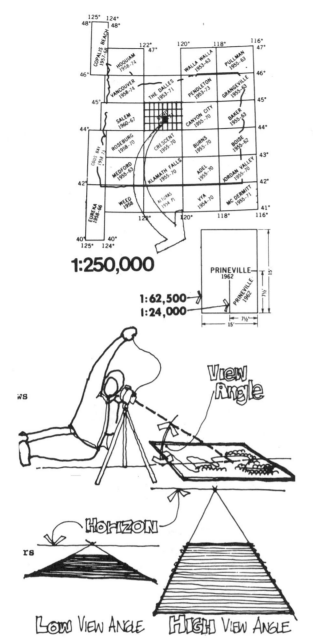

1-22 Aerial Perspectives With the Aid of Map Photography.

1-23 Duluth Aerial Perspective. Aerial perspective structure begins with the photographic slide of USGS maps. To complete and extend the aerial, two vanishing points are found by extending grid lines to the horizon line. Topography, settlement, and water surface as separate line values are drawings in themselves. The final perspective emphasizes the settlement pattern and concentrates line value on the interface of land and water.

ing corner using the focal point as in the methods above. From a corner of the key building, using an adjustable triangle (preferred) or a 45, 30, or 60 degree triangle if suitable, place the horizontal *base* of the triangle on the horizontal ground plane line of the building (i.e., front line or line facing you). Draw a line along the designated angle (i.e., 30 degrees) from one corner of the base line until that line intersects with the extended vertical line from the other corner of the same vertical plane. This indicates the height of the next story. Return to the corner of the new story line and repeat the process all the way up the vertical plane until the correct number of stories

is achieved. If closer separations are desired between each floor line, decrease the angle used from 30 to 5 degrees or increase it to 45 degrees for more separation. Your eye will need to determine the appropriate relationship based on experimentation.

Repeat the other steps from the preceding example.

Combining Slide Tracing and Perspective Shortcuts

A slide of a real scene, an eye-level urban street view or a river valley photographed from the air, can provide vanishing points and a perspective as a base upon which to build alternatives and ideas. Usually, the horizon is visible on eye-levels and low angle aerial obliques so you don't have to establish an artificial horizon. Once the horizon line is identified

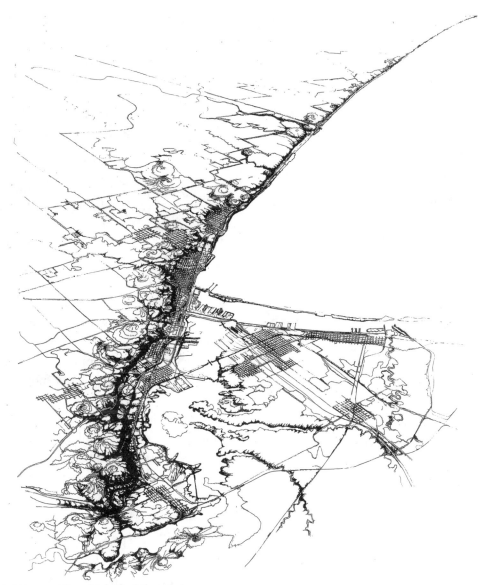

1-24 Aerial Perspective; Duluth, Minnesota.

and traced, the dominant grid lines or building edges, or parallel street directions, can be extended to the horizon to establish vanishing points. Another critical element is the establishment of some grid system (farm fields, city grid system, road network, etc.) to provide a grid-in-perspective so that assumptions on proportions can be made to apply information and generate concepts and ideas. Once this perspective framework is drawn, modifications, alternatives, and explorations are easily done.

Drawing from Existing Built Context: Duluth

In this case, new building infill is studied in a drawing of historic built context. First, the historical building block has been traced from a slide of the study area. From the parallel building lines in the existing view the right and left vanishing points are found along the horizon line. The visualization provides a built context and a perspective structure within which to study the infill design proposal. This visualized historic building context provides a reference for massing, proportion, and scale decisions in the making of a new building. The surrounding context has been visualized first, not added after the building proposal is completed. Through the perspective structure, existing floor lines, window proportions, and roof profiles are carried into the study site for reference.

Room Interior Connected to Exterior Context

Within the building proposal, the same process has been used to study an interior room. First, the view of the exterior context, paramount in this proposal, is traced from a slide panorama taken from an adjacent building. Since the infill site is a block within the existing city grid, a common vanishing point is found in the panorama and used to construct a simple one-point perspective that explores room design. The value of the final perspective is given to the exterior sky, not the room itself.

Photographing Maps for Aerial Perspectives

Aerial perspectives represent a unique way of perceiving the whole and revealing connections. There are few other opportunities to visually experience large contextual areas at a sitting. The act of visually recording this information provides the designer with a special comprehension of a place that goes beyond the simple reading of maps and computer printouts. The aerial perspective view simultaneously places one over an immediate foreground while referencing and connecting that foreground to the infinity of the horizon. Land form unfolds in a continuous pattern and settlement becomes revealed not as an isolated entity, but as part of a connected system.

The structure of aerial views can be traced from photos or slides photographed from maps. The United State Geological Survey has standard maps covering the entire United States. Cultural features (roads, railroads, cities, and towns), land features (hills, mountains, valleys, tree cover), and water features (rivers, lakes, ponds, salt water bodies) are all color coded for easy reference. Even updated information is color coded.

The contour maps differ according to the scale of the map and the relief of the landform. Raised contour maps are available for certain portions of the country, including Alaska. The scales available include: 1:250000, 1:62500, and 1:24000, the most common.

Photographing Maps

A 35mm camera with a standard lens is sufficient to photograph maps. However, a good, clear image is critical to the quality of shapes on the slide. When one map contains the area in question, it is advisable to enlarge the area to be photographed by including at least one other map in each direction for a larger field. More maps are preferable in the direction of the photograph. Include key elements for reference and orientation such as mountains, rivers, and other communities, even if they are not the subject of the project. Remember, context and connection. Maps can be taped or tacked together and laid out on a horizontal surface or a vertical wall or fence. The most effective and simple way to photograph a map is outside using natural light, but not bright, sunny light which can cause shadows from small wrinkles. Use the largest depth of field (f stop) possible for the best sharpness. If you use low speed film you should also use a tripod.

The horizon line is important in aerial perspectives done in this manner. It gives any view a reference point on the earth's surface, avoiding a cut-off or disconnected image. The horizon line can be found by extending any two parallel lines (three provide better accuracy) until they meet. The higher the angle of view, the more removed the horizon line will be, the lower the angle, the more visible the horizon line. Don't try to find the perfect photographic angle when taking the slides: take a lot of slides using a descending spiral approach to the map. Start with a high angle and shoot slides in a spiral around and closer to the map, changing the angle often to get a variety of positions. The slides can be projected at a variety of scales for selection and tracing. They also provide excellent references for public meetings.

Example: Two-Point Aerial Oblique Perspective

In this aerial perspective, the basic organization of water edge, generalized topography, and city grid pattern have been traced from a slide of a United States Geologic Survey (USGS) map. From a square traced in perspective, the two vanishing points that structure this view were established by extending the two parallel edges representing the depth lines to the horizon line. This line was artificially established at a selected point to control the size of the drawing and create a sense of curvature of the ground plane. In this case, the viewer is at an angle to the grid of the photographed map. This gives two sets of parallel lines, one vanishing to the right and the other vanishing to the left. Both points are along the horizon line. If you look directly parallel to the grid of the map, you see one, single vanishing point along the horizon line.

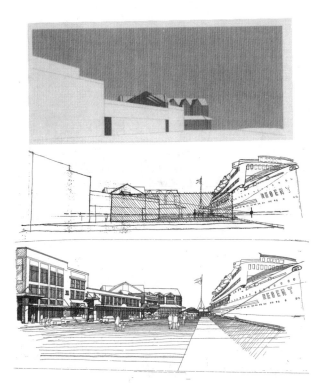

1-25 Perspective from Computer Layout. Combining Sketching, Computer Printouts, and Photography. A single vanishing point and a picture plane combine a computer printout of a building design and a sketch done from a photo of a ship. The proposed building facade is developed through freehand sketching within the composition.

Drawing delineation focuses on the following systems in order of their priority:

• the border of land and water—Lake Superior and its tributaries;

• major topography of the hill edge; at first, topography lines are traced flat, on the ground plane, with rendering techniques used later along the bottom of the hill line to suggest depth; at this height, the literal differences in topography have little relevance to the drawing's content; and

• the settlement pattern, city grid, and railroad lines.

In this visualization, the border of water and land shapes receives the darkest value. The linear edge formed by this interface gives this settlement its character; this, rather than the surface of Lake Superior, is the focus of the drawing.

Perspective Principals, Computer Work, and Photography

The natural and built elements comprising the phys-

ical world exist in infinite combinations and are often seemingly impossible to visualize three dimensionally. Computers can quickly print out perspective structure making it possible to produce perspectives without an understanding of perspective theory. With some knowledge of perspective theory the possibilities of combining freehand drawing, photography, and computer work are unlimited. However, it is possible to combine different media to quickly modify and explore changes without the computer. The perspective of a waterfront proposal in Ketchikan, Alaska was done by combining a computer printout of proposed building massing, freehand exploration of the block elevation, and a photograph of a cruise ship that will frequent the area. All three ingredients are held together by a one-point perspective framework that allows scaled dimensional comparison between the three elements and the picture plane.

Sectional Perspective Connected to Context

Sectional perspectives are usually limited to visualizations through buildings. They can also be used in urban design at the site and district scales. Sectional perspectives are essentially one-point perspectives using the same two vanishing points; one at the center of vision and the other at D or 1.7X north, south, west, or east from it. In this cannery renovation example, the concept of sectional perspective allows the integration of building decisions regarding structure, materials, and spatial organization. The single building space is visualized as well as the adjacent building elevation and its connection to the working waterfront pier activity.

Axonometric Paraline Drawings from a Plan

An axonometric drawing is a paraline construction where all projections of the object intersect the picture plane at right angles and are parallel to one another. An axonometric drawing has multiple vertical faces occurring in the same orthographic image on the picture plane; essentially, you can see at least three surfaces from where you, the observer, are standing (through the picture plane). Only one view is seen in most plans, elevations, or sections. There are four types of axonometric paraline drawings: *isomet-*

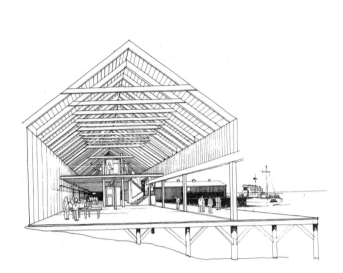

1-26 Klowok Sectional Perspective. Sectional perspective includes context of external building elevation and the workings of a cannery pier. Darkening the section cut itself would emphasize the traditional building section view. Instead, line weight emphasizes the three-dimensional interior spatial aspects of the building cut.

rics, dimetrics, trimetrics, and *transmetrics*. Three are illustrated as guides for quick studies.

The Fast and Loose Method. When conducting quick studies, there is a fast and loose trimetric method. It is not completely accurate in heights, but when doing conceptual studies it can be useful for raising axonometric sketches directly from plan studies. Here are the steps:

Step One: Select a suitable base map usually between 1" = 20 feet and 1" = 100 feet.

Step Two: On your desk, arrange the base map (or your plan study) at a 30/60 degree angle from the horizontal or x-axis; choose which orientation best exposes the most of the vertical planes that are to be raised up from the map (i.e., the object in plan can be rotated back and forth at 30 or 60 degrees for the best view); tape the base map or plan study to the table.

Step Three: Tape flimsy tracing paper over the base map for the first drawing effort.

Step Four: *Remember,* in an axonometric paraline drawing, all vertical projections from the plan are perpendicular to the horizontal x-axis (the pic-

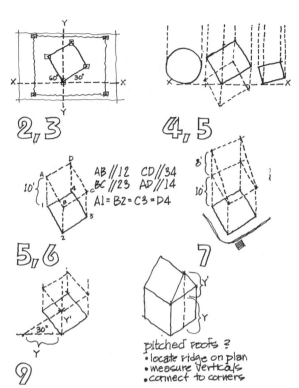

1-27 Axonometric. *Isometric*: a (dimetric) drawing where each horizontal axis or line is rotated away from the 0/180 degree picture plane line at equal angles, usually a 30/30 angle for direct projection. *Dimetric:* an axonometric with equal angles between the 0/180 degree picture plane and the rotated horizontal lines, usually at 45/45 or 15/15 degrees. The 15/15 shows less of the roof plane. *Trimetric:* has two different angles between the 0/180 degree picture plane and the rotated horizontals, usually 30/60 degrees interchangeably. The height of the object is proportionately reduced by measuring the exact height onto the 0/180 picture plane away from the point touching the plane; and extending a 30 degree angle line back to and intersecting the vertical extending from the point.

ture plane)—-no exceptions regardless of the orientation of shape footprints on the plan; similarly, all horizontal lines parallel to one another in plan are still parallel to one another in the axonometric; and, horizontal lines raised up off of the plan, such as roof shapes and ridge lines, are parallel to the lines of the footprint. Making pitched and slanting roofs is easy once you find the upper and lower points of the pitches or slopes.

Step Five: Project or raise up all vertical heights from each building corner perpendicular to the x-axis or horizontal on your first piece of tracing paper (raising up all corners at this time can save

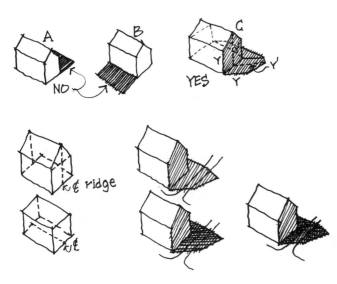

1-28 Axonometric Shadows.

confusion later, do not try to do too much of a finished drawing in the first effort).

Step Six: For most flat building shapes, one measurement of height is all that is necessary; make the height measurement with your scale, mark the height on the vertical extension from the plan corner, then extend the next parallel line from the mark over to the next vertical extension and so on until you have come back around to the first mark; all roof lines are now parallel to the ground or plan lines. Estimate heights from drawings, photographs, field observation (assume nine feet height per floor for residential buildings, ten feet for commercial, and twelve to fourteen feet for retail first floors).

Step Seven: Ground plane or plan features that are not elevated remain exactly as they are in plan; curb lines, sidewalks, grates, etc. are drawn in as they appear in plan.

Step Eight: On the flimsy overlay, add trees as vertical lines (measure up the vertical to the bottom and top of the tree shape), cars (a smaller box on a larger box), shadows, and other features.

Step Nine: On quality tracing paper or mylar, trace the final drawing (freehand is effective), excluding all of the construction lines from the flimsy:

- use finer pen weight to do all outline traces
- use finer or medium weight to add hatches and cross hatches
- work from lighter to heavier weights and values, adding darker or heavier values last

The weights that you assign lines, patterns, etc. tell the observer something of the hierarchy of information—-think it through. If you measure the actual height of the building on the vertical lines in the axonometric the verticals will be slightly distorted. However, in fast studies the distortion is minimal. On a building shape with a flat roof, you can always measure the height out on the x-axis from the building corner and use a 30 degree angle from the measured point extended to intercept the height of the corner on the vertical.

Shadows. A basic principle for shadows is to use them in any direction that best highlights the building shapes (unless you are doing a shadow study on adjacent buildings). Place shadows so that the angle of shadow cast does not coincide with a dominant length or width orientation of key shapes, or just shadow one vertical face.

Step One: Select a shadow angle that is not at the 30/60 degree orientation of the shape and not dominant (where all vertical faces in the view are in shadow); for ease of effort, use the 0/180 degree or 90 degree directions for shadowing building shapes in a 30/60 orientation; project all corners of the building at the ground plane out in the selected direction and measure the vertical height of that building corner out on the shadow line; mark its length; do it for each corner including the hidden corners to the rear of the building; from each mark, draw lines that are parallel to the ground plane lines even if there is a pitched roof (that is the next step).

Step Two: For pitched or sloping roofs, make it easy on yourself by drawing in the shadows for every aspect of the square or rectangular portions of the building first; then, for a pitched roof, find the highest point (ridge line by looking at elevation, photograph, etc.) and mark on the plan; extend a vertical line from that mark and measure the distance from the ground to the height of the pitch and mark; do the same thing on the ground plane from the plan mark and measure and mark; connect the highest point of the pitch to the upper corners of the underlying square or rectangular shape and the sloped roof and its shadow are complete.

When in doubt, break up the building shape into basic components and project those first, adding the more complicated ones later.

Shadow Values. When adding value to shadows, remember: create enough contrast between shape and shadow. Make the ground plane shadow shape darker than vertical plane that is in shade. Make hatching consistent and close together by layering hatches for all exposed shapes at one time (the ground plane, and vertical surface in shade read better if the hatch lines go through all of them as if they are one aggregate shape, adding the next layer to only a portion of that aggregate. If you make hatches go in different directions for each shape, the viewer's eye can become confused. Remember, this is a language, use the characters correctly.

Before/After or Either/Or Same View Perspectives

Before and after or either/or same-view perspective studies are useful in public involvement pro- cesses to give the layperson an integrated image of change within a recognizable reference and orientation. Slide and photographic print methods can provide the inexperienced planner or designer with an effective tool for constructing a perspective and adding changes. Techniques consist of tracing a slide image of the existing view (or reconstructing the view from a photographic print or field sketch), establishing the size of drawing and the amount and composition of three-dimensional context that can aid in reference and orientation for the viewer. Proceeding with flimsy tracing paper, and referring to background information and plan diagrams, the designer can explore various changes to the existing contextual three-dimensional image until a preferred alternative is selected. Use this method to try multiple alternatives quickly and effectively. Once the concepts are selected, a final

1-29 Wilsonville Bank Block. Different views of the same site, similar to before and after sketches for comparison views, using technical pen and india ink hatching line work. Background buildings are left as masses with shading and little if any architectural detail.

tracing paper or mylar overlay can be made for presentation to the public in drawing and/or slide format. In **Wilsonville Bank Block**, a fictitious urban setting, a perspective grid was constructed for the study block and surrounding streets. This example is a part of a public awareness visual and written story-telling methodology (AIA, 1992), demonstrating alternative developments within a given block in a smaller town. A bank development was imagined on the block constructed as it often is in smaller communities, placing the bank away from the retail facade and in the middle of the block surrounded by parking. The second image located the bank and retail buildings in a historic pattern, along the street, with a town square and housing in the block interior.

Two important aspects of design occur using this type of methodology: **1.** the designer makes form decisions using programmatic/contextual assessments, exploring the spatial implications of data in an integrated context frame, not unlike working with a hologram where the pieces can be observed in relation to one another and the whole; and, **2.** the final graphic becomes a language of communication for the participating public.

Three-dimensional contextual information is a visual resource for both creating new building and measuring the impact of building removal. In the **Tongass Highway Study,** the effects of widening of a state highway through the entire length the historic district of Ketchikan, Alaska were visualized at key points. The three drawings describe the proposal at an entrance to the city, where one lane of the road must pass between two historic buildings and the other lane must tunnel through a massive rock outcropping. From the drawing of the existing situation, an extension of the rock outcropping was massed and traced over the first view to simulate a third view of replacing the building with a widened highway.

Panoramic Elevation Studies

Panoramas are effective reference and relational communications tools when the subject includes adequate vertical dimension. The vertical dimension can be built form, land form, or a combination of both. Numerous examples are provided in the case studies, demonstrating their value as reference frameworks. They offer an opportunity to stand back and take a look.

1-30 Wilsonville Town Green. Visualizing the existing conditions of a site, complete with local artifacts and debris, gives a perspective on the cultural treatment of the site prior to redevelopment as a town green. The "after" view adds scale, vegetative scale (leaving out detail), and sidewalk activity as a way of expressing changes in physical conditions and neighborhood use of the area.

In **Pelican,** the City of Pelican, Alaska (population 125 in winter and 600 in summer) undertook a Coastal Zone Management Plan wherein the context of the area was assessed from the bio-physical aspects to built form and culture. The city is unique in its structure and setting: comprising a cluster of homes and canneries along a 12-foot wide wooden boardwalk that follows the base of steep forested mountains. This relationship of linear town/high mountain form was demonstrated for the townspeople through the use of a panoramic elevation taken from one view point.

A series of eleven slides were taken from on top of a gravel pile jutting out into the water on a land

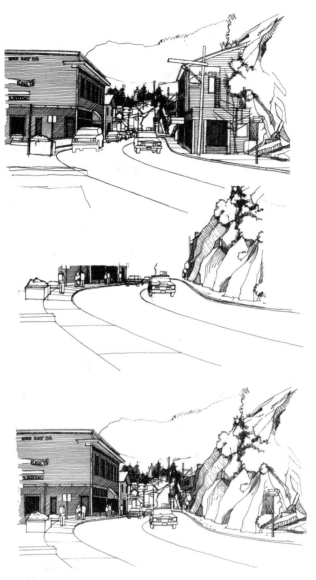

1-31 Ketchikan Tongass Highway Study. These drawings were done first in light pencil on butcher paper. Pieces of the view were inked, cut out with scissors and Xeroxed to accurately portray before and after views of historic building removal along the one way "narrows" entrance into the city.

fill, providing a view of the entire boardwalked portion of town. A pencil tracing was made from each slide by the projection method. The tracings were taped together in a manner that flattened out the ground line, eliminating any curved ground line distortions that occurred as a result of the long panorama. Once taped together, measuring nearly eight feet in length, the drawing was overlaid with mylar and technical pen techniques were added to complete the finished product.

The basic process on the original drawings consisted of three to four layers of ink application:

- an outline drawing of all major shapes;
- determining on flimsy overlays where values are located, roughly slashing in broad strokes of dark and medium dark shapes;
- adding a first layer of texture and shape characteristics (i.e., in the forefront tree shapes); and
- adding one or more layers of dark values to push out the negative or lighter value shapes.

Drawing techniques used for the final presentation included:

- fine point outline shapes for buildings along the boardwalk;
- individual brush tree techniques for foreground and midground tree shapes (a brush tree has a vertical center line with horizontally angled line strokes along it);

1-32 Ketchikan City Entrance. Both views place value and focus on the "framed views" that characterize the restricted narrows place. The bottom view emphasizes the tunnel portal of one lane and the historic building facade that defines the other lane. The window view is from the house above the tunnel, oriented directly along the Main Street Axis.

- curly-Qs for treed slopes more distant and smaller in scale; and
- multiple layers of curly-Qs and scribbles to create graded value patterns.

The final drawing is distorted as it moves in both horizontal directions away from the center, but not enough to detract from the powerful relationship between town form and land form. The mountains in the background on both the left and right sides are critical to establishing a larger context and avoiding a large isolated shape in the center of the drawing.

Blowing Up the Same View

Going deeper and deeper into the same view can be a revealing tool for both the designer and the layperson. Layers upon layers of information accumulate as one progresses down or up the scale ladder until it becomes impossible to comprehend or hold the total sum. For example, it is quite common for designers and planners to record large amounts of contextual information at one scale that is eventually forgotten, or even contradicted, by design actions at following scales. The series of visualization magnifies the same aerial view of Portland, Oregon several times until a building block comes into view. All drawings have been overlaid and traced over the first aerial perspective at the city scale. At the city district scale, the view is abstracted and broken down into understandable pieces and relationships for public discussions regarding design guidelines at the city block scale. This abstract diagram is a reminder, connector, and editor that focuses on selected ideas that will be carried over into the next scale.

Visualizing Programmatic Information

Program information states what and how much is needed for a given project. It occupies space and has

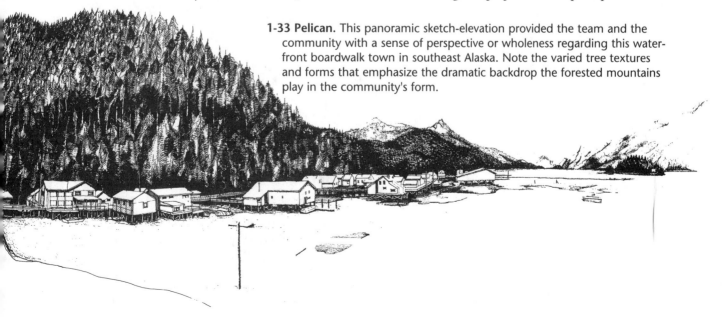

1-33 Pelican. This panoramic sketch-elevation provided the team and the community with a sense of perspective or wholeness regarding this waterfront boardwalk town in southeast Alaska. Note the varied tree textures and forms that emphasize the dramatic backdrop the forested mountains play in the community's form.

spatial implications and impacts. The manner in which this information is explored and incorporated into the design process is an important step in the form generative process. Remember that "information" consists of abstract and isolated distillations of measurement. Putting it together in relationship and reconnecting it to context constitutes a significant design action and re-establishes a sense of reality. Identifying a space program is not absolute but is a starting point for design evolution through design testing. There are many valid methods of graphically communicating and exploring program information ranging from the conventional doodle to the bubble diagram to the axonometric diagram.

Matrices, Charts and Graphs

Matrices are comparison diagrams, usually in a grid format, useful in visually sorting quantitative data. Charts and graphs plot two or more sets of information in a grid-like visual relationship, indicating trends and hierarchies. These types of visuals are most often done with computers. Often the information is

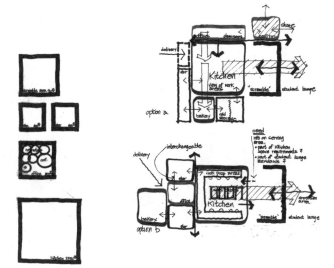

1-35 TVCC Program/Space Types. Multiple colored Sharpie pen diagram on exposed sepia paper for visual thinking and client meetings and workshops. Use grid paper as an underlay for consistency of line spacing and lettering types. This can be done as fast as a computer blow-up and has the advantage of being a hands-on sorting-out process.

Food Technology. Colored Sharpie pens and wide markers are used on gridded tracing paper or some other form of transparent paper (i.e., exposed sepia paper) where roughs and information can be traced onto the presentation sheet.

incorporated into a visual presentation with other graphic displays for the convenient communication of information to the layperson. A utilitarian computer-generated chart is not adequate, but budgets are lean, prohibiting more attractive color computer-generated charts. And time is not available for more sophisticated methods. It may be faster and equally effective to prepare the visualizations by hand, as in the following examples:

Prepared for the Tanana Valley Community College (TVCC) Master Plan in Fairbanks, Alaska, the matrix on *TVCC Program/Space Types* is a preliminary and *working* graphic. It is a process diagram which can be scribbled on, made into slides, or copied in black and white. It is a freehand grid drawn on exposed sepia paper (for transparency-tracing purposes) using colored felt tip pens over a straight-line grid placed under the sepia sheet. Useable for client meetings, the text and numbers were hand-lettered and color coded. The matrix compares academic program types with space facilities, frequency of

request for those facilities, and budgets, and was used during brainstorming sessions with a client task force.

Area requirements

Required facilities and the space needed for activities to adequately function is an integral part of the programming phase of a planning/design process, whether for a city district or one building. In order for the whole to function well the parts need to be adequate in size and placed in compatible relationships. Visualizing these requirements and relationships is another starting point in the formative design process. At this point the quantitative need meshes with the qualitative relationship, forming patterns. Planners and designers can miss opportunity during this phase by relegating the space requirements and relationships to charts and tables or unreferenced bubble diagrams. The following examples demonstrate simple effective ways to explore the relationships of space requirements using dual purpose graphic tools (colored markers that reproduce well in black and white).

Food Technology is a two part area requirements diagram, consisting of: **1.** square area shapes, to scale, representing the designated components of the required kitchen for the TVCC complex, outlined in colored wide-tip marker and noted with title and square footage information; and, **2.** a relationship diagram that explores two options for assembling the components into an integrated part that will eventually be placed in relationship with other parts.

Each diagram is drawn in freehand with colored markers, using a grid underlayment, traced onto a transparent or translucent paper such as tracing paper or exposed sepia paper. The steps between component area shapes and the relationship diagram are a mini-design activity that uses visualization to assess relative sizes, edge relationships among shapes, and activity compatibility arrangements. The edge relationships provide the activity that interlocks or connects part to part. The drawing tools used include wide-tip color markers and medium point color felt tip markers.

TVCC Test Scheme One is a composite area requirement diagram with all of the components arranged in working parts and all of the working parts arranged in compatible connections to make a

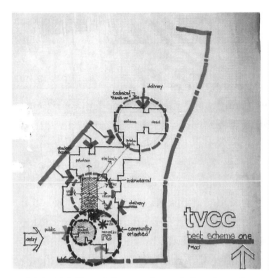
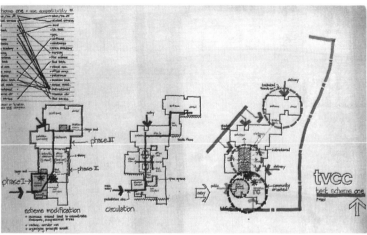

1-36 TVCC Test Scheme One. Colored markers on a transparent base—the beginnings of a spatial organization for client review with preliminary orientation to site-functional conditions.

test diagram. The test scheme is quantifiable, color coded for easier communication, site responsive regarding its overall shape (diagrams not shown here), and form-emergent. It represents three such schemes, each incorporating over 100,000 square feet in area. These diagrams are presentation quality suitable for client and academic program chairpersons review and discussion. Tests were performed on each scheme using a visual graphic methodology. Test drawings included primary interior circulation network, main public access points along exterior perimeter, and service access points. The three-part diagram also generalized technical clusters, instructional clusters, and community-oriented facilities as a means of further testing the workability of each scheme. The graphic dashed circles communicated these general clusters to the lay groups reviewing the diagrams.

Example: Minneapolis Building Block

Visualizing information out of context can be an abstract exercise, especially for the layperson. Visualizing programmatic information within a larger three dimensional context early in the design process puts numerical data into a perspective. Drawings that integrate the documentation of information with its form making opportunities can initiate the design process. In a first step, the square

footage and circulation systems for a Minneapolis development proposal is visualized in plan and section diagram. The next step develops the program in axonometric form within the recognizable context of the surrounding blocks. The surrounding building context is drawn first as a set of reference relationships, not second to decorate the program's massing diagram. From the three dimensional building context, drawn with the help of slides, existing dimensional relationships are extended into the study block to help explore proposed building form. In a final step, pieces of the block proposal are drawn in perspective at critical points; where the block meets the public street and where the block meets the sky to create a new city silhouette. In these perspectives, views are selected to include existing patterns of street frontage and city silhouette to reference new building design.

Diagrams

Diagramming as a Visual Tool: Drawings and Models

A diagram is a graphic that explains the outline of parts and their workings and relationship. Diagrams can be real, semi-abstract, or abstract. Real graphics commonly represent natural appearances; a drawing

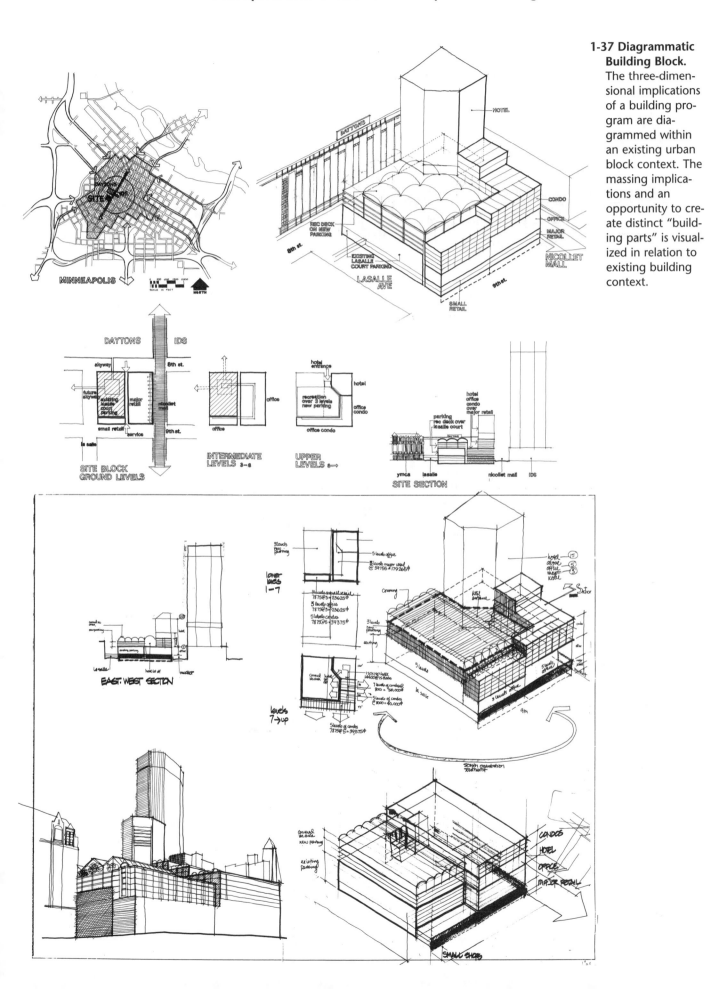

1-37 Diagrammatic Building Block. The three-dimensional implications of a building program are diagrammed within an existing urban block context. The massing implications and an opportunity to create distinct "building parts" is visualized in relation to existing building context.

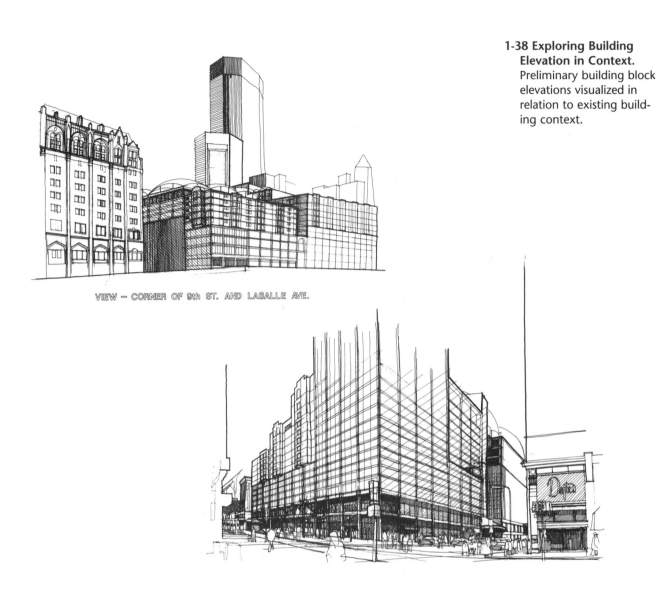

VIEW — CORNER OF 9th ST. AND LASALLE AVE.

1-38 Exploring Building Elevation in Context. Preliminary building block elevations visualized in relation to existing building context.

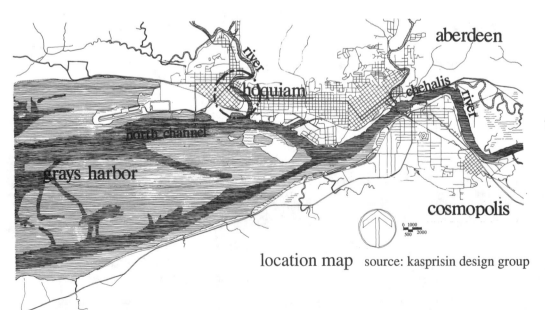

location map   source: kasprisin design group

1-39 Hoquiam Location. Special effort was expended to articulate the mud flats and navigation channels of Grays Harbor as a part of the existing context (circulation).

that closely resembles the actual image, usually in much detail. Semi-abstract and abstract selectively emphasize certain qualities over others, usually with less detail. A significant difference between semi-abstract and abstract is in the degree of connection they have to the realistic frame of reference. Semi-abstract images retain enough identifiable real-frame reference and orientation to make them understandable by the lay audience. The designer selects qualities in a semi-abstract diagram that he or she deems more significant than others, an intentional design decision unimpeded by levels of detail. Selected qualities for diagrams can be defined as organizational structure or order—involved parts and their relationship, and physical characteristics that contribute to the intrinsic worth of the whole—structure plus characteristics. In urban design applications, diagrams are normally real and semi-abstract.

Diagrams can represent the essence of a design. Visualizing context in its differentiated parts in diagrammatic form enables the designer to generate form during the analysis phase. Diagrams in design are the spatial equivalent of diagrams in grammar, the language study dealing with word forms. The graphic language of the designer is a system, like grammar, of shapes and their order or structure, outlined according to the relationship of working parts. Diagramming is a method that assists in distinguishing *things* from *form*; and, helps describe the patterning, differentiation, and evolution of that form.

Kevin Lynch popularized the use of the semi-abstract to abstract diagrams in *Image of the City* (MIT 1960), with his visual form notations, using symbols to represent *path, edge, node, district,* and *landmark*. Planning and design students use his techniques as beginning efforts to spatially understand neighborhoods and city districts. Symbols are combined with value shapes to indicate built form. They are referenced and oriented with scale, direction, and street grid. Absent are detailed forms, filtered out due to his edge-district-node focus. Such diagrams are extensions of the conventional land use bubble diagram.

Perhaps the master of the real-abstract diagram is Gordon Cullen. His techniques are lay-person friendly. In his various works (Townscape, Alcan, City of London), he mixed the real (in three dimensional format) with the semi-abstract, filtering out detail and individual pieces in the townscape, to arrive at a referenced and oriented pictorial diagram that describes selected qualities. Cullen's drawings are executed with a number of consistently related techniques: fine pen point outline of major shapes; selected texture in pen only where necessary for intrinsic character communication; and shading, value shapes, and screening with press-on pre-printed patterns, ink, and/or pencil combinations. His style is loose and informal, yet captures the spatial quality in a thoughtful way, using visual thinking as the path.

The examples that follow combine the real/semi-abstract nature of Cullen's work with the authors' experiential base of fast contextual expressions developed under budget, time, and community participation requirements. Diagrams are the working heart of the pursuit of "context", observing it, recognizing its complexity, saturating oneself with its qualities, selecting an *adequate context* for understanding, and applying a *scale of focus* to it as a means of differentiating its parts.

The diagrams take three major forms: two dimensional plan type formats; three-dimensional perspective sketch formats; and three-dimensional paraline sketch formats.

Two–Dimensional Plan Diagrams

Plan diagrams, as used in these examples, are semi-abstract structural outlines combining parts and their relationships and real characterizations with detailed qualities where the structural and parts relationships are hidden in the realism. This presents an interesting phenomena: do both the designer and the layperson-as-viewer see more in the detailed pictorial or in the abstracted parts-relationship diagram?

Semi-Abstract Plan Diagrams

Location diagrams are commonly used graphics with important reference information for the layperson and public audience. In **Hoquiam Location** a fine point technical pen was used to draw a contextual base for communities clustered on waterfronts in western Washington: three communities on the Washington coast in Grays Harbor where the Chehalis River joins the Pacific Ocean and two

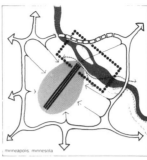

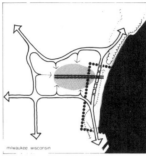

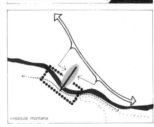

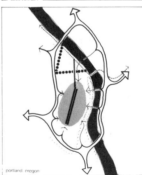

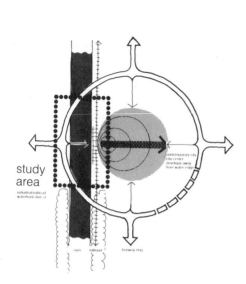

1-40 City/River District Diagram. The diagram describes the reoccurring relationship of river district study areas to their city centers, peripheral freeway system, and urban watercourse. The diagram further suggests potential linkages between the study areas and the city center. The same elements of the generic diagram: city center, main street, peripheral freeway loop, watercourse, and railroad line, are compared in four different cities. Each site composition represents a distinct arrangement of the given elements described in the generic diagram.

tral cores, their major highway systems and connectors, their industrial water-edge zones, and their water bodies. While it is difficult to articulate all these relationships in words, the diagram establishes location, size, orientation, movement, connection, and other relational aspects in a filtered database. It is a basic "guts" drawing. Basic techniques include: fine pen point outline for the water edges and significant open space (looping line technique); medium pen point line for the highway network, using an outlined hollow linear form with arrows for directional movement and solid and dashed line-shapes for existing and proposed segments of the network; a press-on pre-printed dot screen pattern of darker value for the water shapes; a press-on pre-printed dot-line pattern for the industrial areas; and a medium to light press-on dot screen pattern for the central core shapes. The value pattern is an intentional hierarchy of shapes: the water (edge) is the dominant issue followed by the industrial areas, connecting core arterials, and the core shapes—dark shape (water) to dark line patterns (industrial area and core arterial) to mid-dark shape (core area) to mid-dark outline shape (highway system) to light outline shapes (open space).

Footprint Base Plan Diagrams

Adding building footprints (an outline of the area on the ground plane that the building occupies) adds information to a diagram about relative size and area proportions. Adding shadows to the footprints provides height to the surface area proportions, further increasing the information base. Adding block patterns with curb lines (creating sidewalk shapes in the process), major land forms such as water bodies or edges of significant topographical features further enhances the base information communication to

communities on Sinclair Inlet in Puget Sound. USGS maps were used as the base reference, providing waterways and street patterns. In the Hoquiam example, the harbor configuration is critical to the context of the three communities; the channels were differentiated from the shallower tidal flats with line density, using the same pen point. The water treatment uses a consistent horizontal closely spaced line technique in overlayments to increase line density.

Basic Structural Relationship Diagrams

Diagrams can represent circulation and land use in broad semi-abstract formats. The following sequence of four diagrams depicts four different water-edge communities and the relationships among their cen-

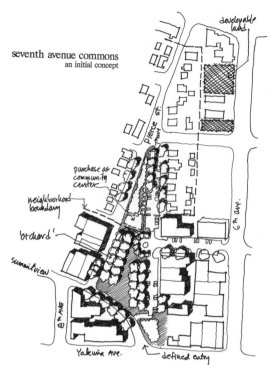

seventh avenue commons
an initial concept

1-41 Seventh Street Commons. A fast diagram done on flimsy tracing paper with Pentel Sign pens for use in workshop meetings. Color marker is added to the back of the flimsy for a muted color effect.

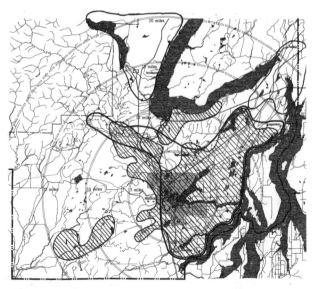

1-42 Shelton Trade Area. A watershed map was used as a base for the trade area designation for Shelton (determined through telephone surveys). Technical pens and Graphos nib pens were used on mylar pin-bar sheets to denote various categories related to the trade area. The pin-bar system permitted other graphic information to be overlaid for comparison purposes.

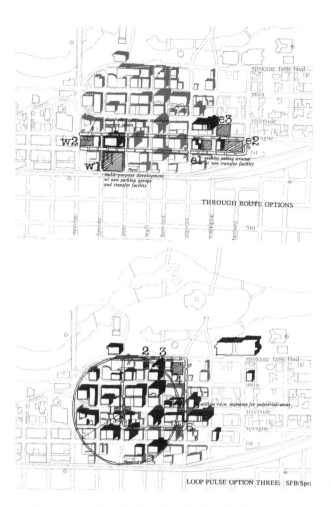

1-43 Spokane Transit Transfer Facility System Diagrams. Three diagrams were each drawn with colored Pentel Sign pens on a base footprint map. Each system option was quickly drawn on yellow trace and photostatted over the base map.

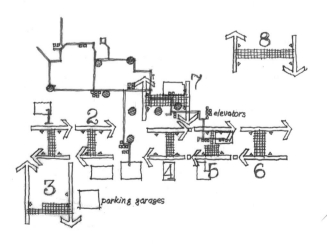

1-44 Spokane Core Options. Loop Pulse Blow-Up. Colored Pentel Sign pens were used on flimsy trace to create this diagram of key buildings, sites, skyway system and options.

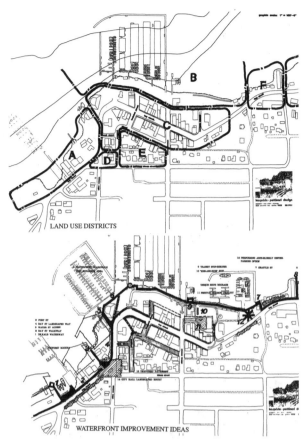

1-45 Port Orchard Activity Districts. Port Orchard Waterfront Access Network.

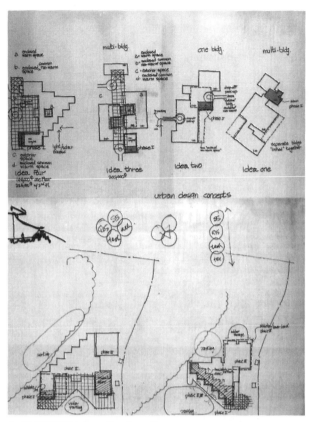

1-46 TVCC Urban Design Concepts.

the layperson as well as to the planner/designer.

Quantitative Spatial Impact Diagrams

Economic, social, cultural, and political activities in human society have spatial manifestations that can be diagrammed to make them accessible to the layperson and more understandable for the planner/designer. In **Shelton Trade Area**, the retail trade area for this Puget Sound waterfront community of 14,000 people was determined through a statistically valid telephone survey conducted by economists and planners for the City of Shelton. The results of that survey were plotted on a two dimensional pin-bar overlay base map containing roads and drainage systems. The overall trade area was outlined first, followed by the hatching of the primary trade area based on a physical capability analysis of the land and existing residential developments. Distance radii added reference to the diagram. The base map for the diagram was drawn with a fine point technical pen. The overlay trade area shapes were made with a heavier pen point for the area outline and a medium

pen point for the hatching to establish enough contrast among the line hierarchies (base map, primary, secondary areas).

In **Spokane**, black Pentel Sign pen outline drawings produced the downtown core and its adjacent block patterns, complete with building footprints in the immediate study area. Shadows were added to core buildings to complete the base diagram. Because the drawings would be presented to lay people, colored Pentels were used to add the overlay information, including transit route option movements within street rights-of-way, study sites for the location of a transit transfer facility, and distance radii from key sites. Provided with the base diagram, the design team was able to quickly produce multiple option diagrams for public comment. The pen work consists of one line weight due to the tight time frame supplemented by colored lines using the same type of pen for line consistency.

Footprint base diagrams are useful for outlining simple boundaries, as in **Port Orchard Activity Districts,** and for indicating simple recommendations, as in **Port Orchard Waterfront Access Network.** The technique of drawing a footprint base with enough reference information (marina includ-

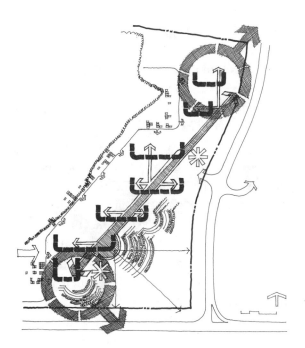

1-47 TVCC Organizing Principles.

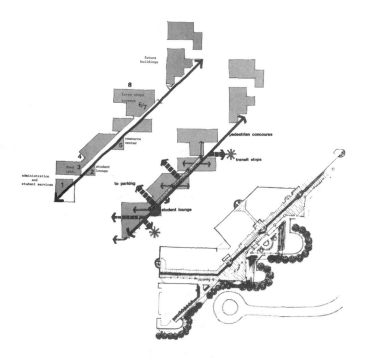

1-48 TVCC Site Circulation Diagrams.

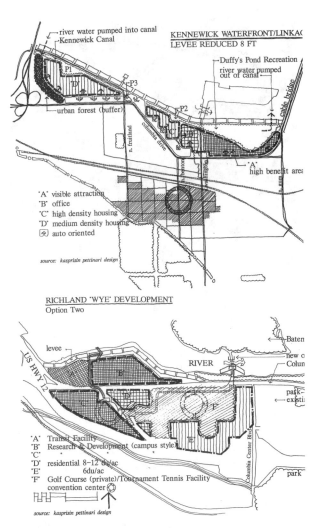

1-49 Tri-Cities Diagrams. Pentel Sign pen drawings representing land activities, development phasing and configurations, and intensity of activities—all in a quantifiable format useful in public workshops. Hatching, arrows, and boundary shapes are all a part of these diagrams presentation conventions.

within a looping (organic) shape representing open space.

Site Study Plan Diagrams

Urban design and architectural site-specific studies can use diagrams as the first major form generative steps, translating program needs, site conditions, area context, and other factors into structural concepts. Steps in the process can range from the use of generic symbols such as circles, arrows, and asterisks to more specific geometry that emerges from program and site analysis. In **TVCC Urban Design Concepts**, based on the space program diagrams previously discussed, basic geometric configurations for parts of the complex have been articulated, but

ing boats for scale, street pattern, and buildings), permits the planner/designer to interchange information with overlays on the same base drawing. The base drawing uses a fine pen point outline technique; the overlays in each case consist of nib type pen point applications (in this case using a Graphos pen nib) with flat, sharp-edge nibs. The value contrast is simple and strong. Mid-values are applied with hatching

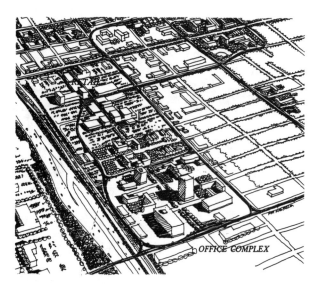

1-50 Office Complex. An aerial oblique diagram of a major diversified center (MDC) or regional shopping center and secondary strip centers with a Personal Rapid Transit (PRT) system traversing the complex. Enough visualization is included to locate existing and possible building developments and the above grade transit system for the readers.

how do they all fit together? Using approaches developed from client meetings, program analysis, and site factors such as increasing daylight and solar exposure, and connecting building groups with protected non-heated areas, two-dimensional diagrams focused on identifying and testing various connecting spaces for the entire complex. In the examples provided, colored medium point felt tip pens were used to outline elements and their relationships, including interior and exterior factors. The academic areas were color coded in black, the circulation areas in blue, and the enclosed non-heated connecting spaces in a red grid pattern representing a translucent or transparent structure. These diagram techniques allowed multiple examples for presentation and discussion with the client group. The markers used also reproduced well in black and white for reproduction purposes. A medium point colored marker permits two line weights: a lighter line when the pen is held near vertically with a fresh tip; and a heavier line when the point is angled closer to 45 degrees from the paper. Heavy weight lines are added with a wide tip marker, kept flat to the paper. These are concept diagrams, meant to be quick studies with a scale accuracy but unimpeded with detail not yet pertinent to the study.

Plan Policy Diagrams

Policies, or action statements or courses, can be explored and summarized in graphics, complementing written policies. The semi-abstract diagram is an effective format to provide a scale and spatial reference and orientation using symbols or specific shapes. Design policy is drawn in symbols so as not to pre-organize an architectural design motif for buildings. The pedestrian concourse and building faces, circulation, and access facilities are the key features located and referenced in the drawing, with highest value given to the concourse and buildings. **TVCC Organizing Principle** and **Site Circulation** continue the diagram style by adding building footprint shapes without further articulation, and focusing attention on the concourse as the complex form-generator. Tri-Cities illustrates city sector activity diagrams.

Three-Dimensional Diagrams

Three-dimensional diagrams use perspective and paraline view constructions. They provide a better opportunity to integrate information into a meaningful context than two dimensional diagrams. As in the case of paraline drawings, where all lines are parallel and to scale, they can be quantitative as well as qualitative.

Three-Dimensional Aerial Oblique Massing Diagram

When dealing with larger land areas or areas with many forms not suited for detail (as on buildings), a massing diagram can effectively demonstrate circulation patterns, settlement patterns, and building and generalized open space characteristics and patterns. In **Office Complex,** a transit-type facility is integrated into an existing and expanded major diversified center (shopping center and peripheral commercial area). The transit system and the shopping center core are key shape elements. At this viewpoint, the shopping center shapes, adjacent commercial, housing, and office buildings all can be articulated without facade detail without losing a sense of scale. The building shapes are hatched on the shade side to provide a value contrast and separate the building shapes from the white ground plane. The transit alignment is pictured as a shadowed hollow

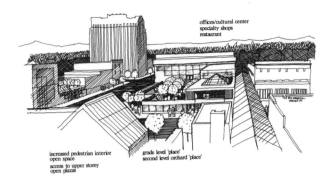

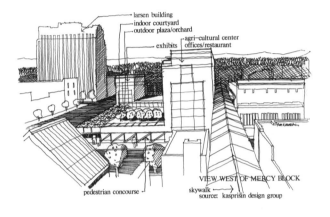

1-51 Yakima Mercy Block Series.

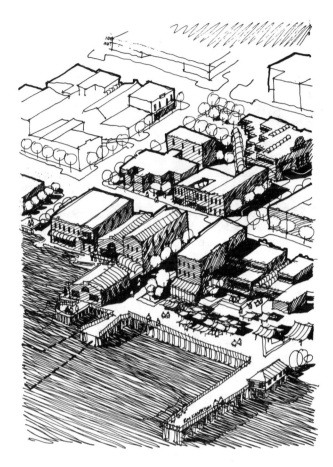

1-52 Port Townsend In-fill. Fine technical pen line drawings of the historic core area with possible in-fill developments.

line representing an elevated structure. Pedestrian areas within the shopping center are a small grid pattern with small units to separate them visually from the larger building shapes. Trees and park areas are represented by small circles, shadowed along the pattern's outer edge. Parking areas are noted by small oval shapes to give the illusion of parked cars rather than striping the surface areas at this scale.

The basic drawing was sketched from a photographic print of the study area. Once the basic grid or street pattern is sketched in, it is easier to fill in buildings and parking lot grids over which new studies can be overlayed.

Multiple Same View Diagrams.

Multiple option massing studies are community- and client-friendly. Once the basic three dimensional

framework is established, multiple massing options are quick to execute using previously established vanishing points and a perspective grid. In *Yakima Mercy Block Series,* eight massing options were constructed for a vacant downtown site in a key block. The visualizations were used in meetings with property owners to discuss ways of distributing preferred square footage in a manner complementary to the site and its adjacent and nearby neighbors. The drawings required a level of detail that aided participants in understanding scale and proportion as well as relationships to surrounding built form. The drawings use black Pentel Sign pen, outline shapes, hatching, and semi-abstract shapes to represent streetscape and mountain background.

Port Townsend In-fill diagrams are drawn with a fine point technical pen using more building artic-

1-53 Port Townsend Precedent. Stitched together from a series of slides and traced, this diagram depicts height precedents influencing new developments, used for demonstrations at public workshops.

ulation than other massing diagrams due to the historic and architectural significance of the buildings. This detail is still minimal, with the primary emphasis on block massing and intra- and inter-relationships. Multiple option sketches for the same site can also act as massing, height, character, and spatial organization diagrams that tell a story in laypeople language.

Eye Level Sketch Diagrams

Port Townsend Precedent is an eye level pictorial or realistic sketch-diagram that uses the camera angle, swivelled from one viewpoint, to achieve a curved panorama. The slide image portrays a block with new buildings, historic construction, and vacant lots. It was traced and inked with a fine point technical pen. The dominant or precedent-setting historic storey heights of adjacent blocks were dashed in with a medium point technical nib in a darker value. This visualization serves as a graphic statement of building height policy based on historic precedent, articulated in a locally familiar reference sketch for easier public comprehension.

Minneapolis Programmatic Diagrams

Background

These diagrams are part of a downtown core study to determine the spatial implications of new office development around the Federal Building in Minneapolis.

Process

These aerial oblique perspectives were initially drawn from a slide tracing. The vanishing point was established by extending the dominant grid to the horizon. With that point established, the drawing was ready for hypothetical perspective volumetric studies proportionately accurate within the perspective grid-block system.

Technique

The perspective was drawn in pencil, traced from a slide aerial oblique view. A fine point technical pen was used to outline building masses and other shapes (block grids, river, highway systems). This provided the basic working tool for volumetric studies: not an end in itself, simply a base tool for visual thinking. The next layer of drawing was, in fact, a visual thinking procedure: outlining in a heavier pen point (in this case a Sharpie pen) the key existing buildings and the potential new buildings superimposed over the existing outline framework.

Planning Opportunity Diagrams

Larger scale opportunity diagrams are useful in depicting initial concepts or directions. Prepared on a dimensioned or scaled base map, they are quantifiable as well as expressions of relationships. In **Point MacKenzie AMSA**, an activity diagram represents eight concepts represented for an area of 30,000 acres and used at a public information meeting in the

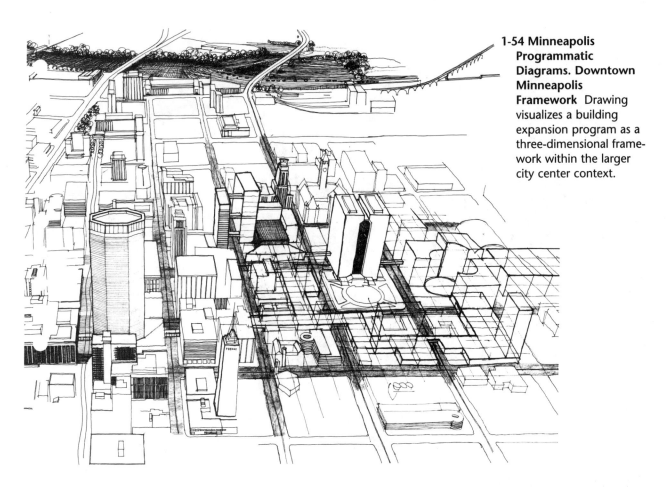

1-54 Minneapolis Programmatic Diagrams. Downtown Minneapolis Framework Drawing visualizes a building expansion program as a three-dimensional framework within the larger city center context.

Matanuska-Susitna Borough in Alaska. Colored markers were the tool of choice for speed and color coding purposes. Both the wide and narrow parts of the nibs proved useful in shaping symbols. A Pentel Sign pen was used for finer line work. In **Takima Opportunities**, diagrams were quickly but accurately drawn with a Pentel Sign pen and colored marker representing land use and circulation/open space schematics, with building footprints again for public information and discussion.

Model Diagrams

Model diagrams are three dimensional constructions, made out of various materials such as cardboard, chipboard, foam board, and illustration board. These model diagrams are discussed here as quick evaluative tools rather than finished presentation models. These models may be used in client meetings but their primary purpose is to aid the planner/designer with the visualization of the form-generative process. Planners can use these model diagrams where circulation components require a three dimensional viewpoint

(vertical separation of pedestrian, auto, and transit facilities, for example), for land value models, for density and/or zoning build-out models, and for built form of larger areas such as downtown blocks or districts. Architects and landscape architects are familiar with using models as study tools. Models can improve the study of context in the following ways:

Quick Study Massing Models/Slide Tracing

The quick study massing model is versatile and relatively simple to assemble. The program requirements are translated into three dimensional forms. A common type is constructed with corrugated cardboard, using the height of each layer of cardboard as a unit of scale (1/8" in height equals twenty feet in elevation, for example). In master plan studies or multiple building complexes, site models are constructed with topography, roads, buildings, and vegetation. The program "pieces" are cut into square units, marked with a colored pen for activity or use code and the area quantity represented by each square (not each square needs to be marked), and readied for "play". Play begins with one or more participants, designers and

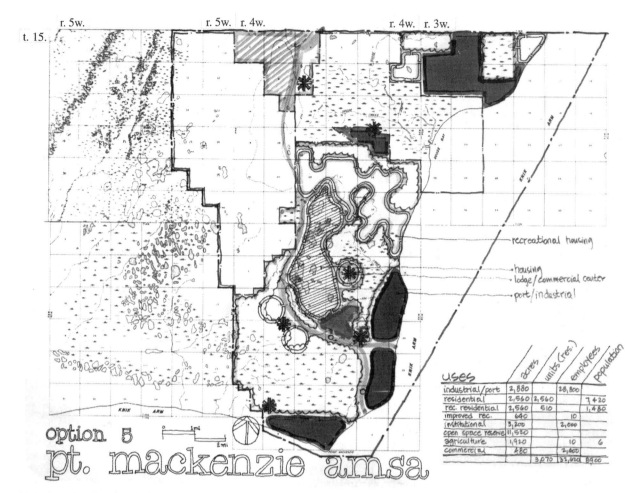

uses	acres	units (res.)	employees	population
industrial/port	2,880		28,800	
residential	2,560	2,560		7,420
rec. residential	2,560	510		1,480
improved rec.	640		10	
institutional	3,200		2,000	
open space reserve	11,520			
agriculture	1,920		10	6
commercial	480		2,000	
		3,070	32,820	8,900

1-55 Point MacKensie AMSA.

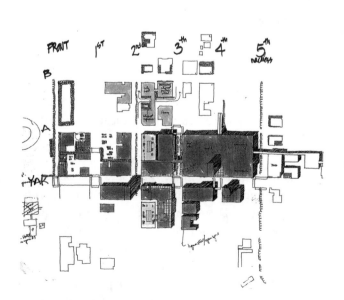

1-56 Yakima Opportunities.

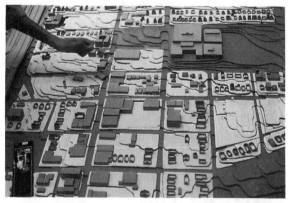

1-57 Roosevelt and Ocean Shores.

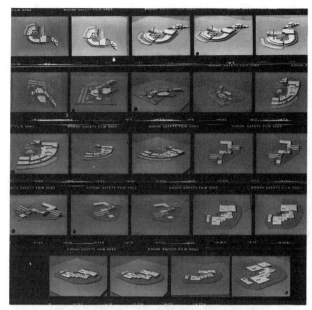

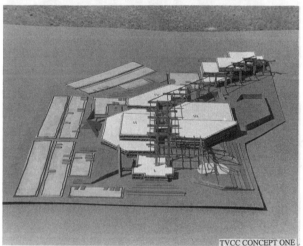

1-58 TVCC Study Models.

1-59 Twenty First Century Production District, Central Eastside Industrial District, Portland, Oregon. Many times city systems are too complicated to readily visualize in three-dimensional drawing form. In this example, several types of circulation systems are overlaid in different colors to represent the existing workings of this intercity industrial district. Existing conditions are portrayed at the district scale, proposed reorganizations at the block scale.

community people, brainstorming around the site or "Monopoly" board, using flip charts or blackboards as doodle pads, and assembling a concept or option or starting point on the board using the cardboard pieces. When a scheme or ideas is clear enough (not necessarily worked out), the massing model can be photographed using a camera on a tripod. The model is disassembled and the play begins again, assembling other models that build on or are stimulated by previous ideas.

After the brainstorming session the slides are developed, reviewed by the participants, discussed, and debated. With an instant slide developer slides can be developed and mounted within ten minutes of their exposure, ready for review and discussion. New study models may be assembled with an additional level of detail as the discussions reach a con-

sensus or the concept slides can be projected, traced onto tracing paper, and used as the basis for more detailed three dimensional graphic diagrams. This process is effective in both studio and public meeting settings and can still out-perform a computer graphics system when group interaction is desired. A playful model is more effective than waiting for a computer to redraw.

Massing Relationship Models
When working with complex programs and site

1-60 Transparent Modeling: New York City and Astoria, Oregon. Model-making typically manipulates solid surfaces to visualize and shape space. In these cases, the
essence of these waterborne places are visualized as occurring on and along transparency; water is treated with a plane of plastic, lit from below and pierced by the
necessities of supporting building structure. The land under the water is treated as
topography covered by a continually changing water level. Although seldom seen, the
underground workings of pier structure, building foundations, and transportation
tubes are included as events that shape the character of these places.

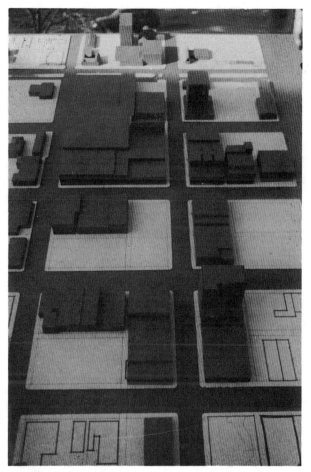

1-61 Yakima Model.

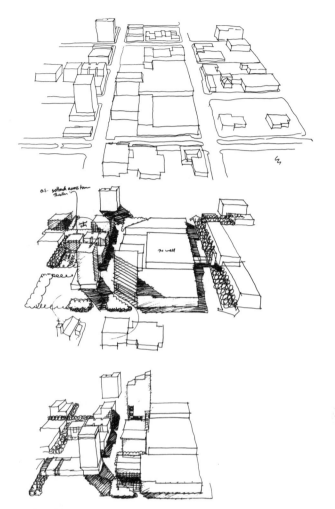

1-62 Yakima Downtown Massing Opportunities Diagrams. Pentel pen sketch studies from slide tracings of model.

conditions, relationship models can afford a view that perspectives and paralines cannot. In **TVCC Models,** eight cardboard and paper models were assembled to accompany plan and sketch diagrams for presentation and review with the client task force. The models were simply made: a print of the plan diagram was glued to a sheet of stiff poster board; building footprints were cut out of corrugated cardboard (foam core works as well), covered with a sheet of white bond paper with area quantities hand lettered; parking areas were cut out of gray chipboard in sized lots, numbered for spaces; and a red thread was used to represent a potential enclosed unheated connecting space among buildings. Each model study took approximately two hours to construct.

Circulation Model Diagrams

Circulation model diagrams are three-dimensional cut-outs using color coded illustration or poster board to represent circulation hierarchies. In **Twenty-first Century Circulation,** a portion of the east bank of the Willamette River front in central Portland, Oregon was recreated in a model that articulated for public meetings the proposed hierarchy of circulation and pedestrian spaces. The illustration board and poster board model is composed of:

- a gray chipboard base glued on to a plywood sheet for rigidity and background;
- a blue board layer for water;
- white board building footprints within the city block grid to establish a strong context scale and definition;
- red-orange sidewalks within the block grid;
- green board topography layers for proposed peninsula extensions of the shoreline;

- orange poster board strips for the relocated eastside freeway;
- red poster board strips for east-west arterial connections across the freeway and river; and
- gray strips for local streets.

The model provides a three-dimensional context view of circulation, connecting it to surrounding building form/pattern and open space—-not separating it as an unconnected or disjointed infrastructure network. The three site study models are similar in concept, focusing on critical interface areas with the riverfront, integrating buildings, public access and open space, and vehicular circulation.

Base Models for Photography
Slides of massing models can be the basis for three-dimensional sketch diagrams of complex areas. In **Yakima Model,** a 1"=50 feet scale massing model was constructed of chipboard for the central downtown area. Slides of a similar model provided a base for sketch diagram studies and the model itself was used as a tool in public meetings for community reference and orientation. Study areas could be modelled in white chipboard and inserted into the gray base model to demonstrate proposed changes. Detail on buildings was minimal and included only where a particular historic facade was prominent or critical for public information.

References

American Institute of Architects. 1992. *Designing Your Town.* Contributors: William C. Apgar, Jr., Joint Center for Housing Studies, Cambridge, Massachusetts; Ron Kasprisin, University of Washington; Alex Kreiger, Harvard University; Mary McCumber, University of Washington; Ted Peck, Joint Center for Housing Studies, Cambridge, Massachusetts; Charles Redmon, FAIA, Cambridge Seven Associates; Robert Sturgis, FAIA, Architect; James Vaseff, AIA, Georgia Power Company; Sherry Kafka Wagner.

Arnheim, Rudolph. 1969. *Visual Thinking.* Berkeley, Los Angeles, London: University of California Press.

Bettisworth, Charles and Company. 1982. *TVCC Master Plan.* Fairbanks

Ching, Francis D.K. 1990. *Drawing.* New York: Van Nostrand Reinhold.

Cullen, Gordon. 1961. *Townscape* New York: Reinhold Publishing Corporation.

Donette, James/Zuberbuhler, Douglas R. 1975. *Design Graphics Laboratory 310.* Seattle: ASUW Publishing.

Forseth, Kevin. 1980. *Graphics for Architecture.* New York: Van Nostrand Reinhold.

Gosling/Maitland. 1984. *Concepts of Urban Design.* New York: St. Martin's Press/London: Academy Editions.

Ramsey/Sleeper. 1981. *Architectural Graphic Standards, Seventh Edition.* New York: John Wiley and Sons.

Webb, Frank. 1990. *Webb on Watercolor.* Cincinnati: North Light Books.

2 Visualizing Place in Context

Introduction

Context: Inherent in the Definition of Place

"Context" and "place," two terms used often in the design of cities, represent complex spatial concepts of physical realities. They contain the intimacy, diversity, and reflections of human activities in spatial "settings". They represent the combined effects of the biophysical, socio-cultural, and economic-political aspects of human settlements and the relationship of those settlements to the underlying environment. The terms are used by professionals to describe the quality of built spaces as well as to measure quantity. "Place" is often distinguished from context as a localized and focused space with special values in the eye of the beholder. Too often, these complex entities are given limited definitions by planners and designers, reduced to perfunctory or segregated quantitative or whimsical qualitative "analysis." Context and place stimulate the designer and become the foundation for planning and design directions and solutions. Consequently, depicting place in context can help the designer by expanding the boundaries of place to include a larger context of connected places or places within places.

The planning and design process can benefit from an expansion of the definitions of context and place, their complexities—the understanding of their parts or components as time-relative statements of spatial-cultural organizations, where context and place have a constant dynamic between them.

The explorations in this book view place as the basic building unit of context and context as both a collective-place and a source of ingredients for the make-up of place. This chapter discusses ways of using graphic visualizations to recapture as a process of design the richness and diversity found in the connected places of human settlements, both as an internal act of design and as an external act of design-communication.

Context as Place

Context

Context is often referred to in planning and design as "setting" or "background"—words synonymous with the stage, props that carry stylized bits of information in support of the live actions on stage. It can often be portrayed as static information to be taken in consideration as the planning and design activities occur, almost as outside or external options. When context is separated from the observation and definition of place, place loses much of its definition.

Context is dynamic; it is reality as defined by the "natural and cultural history" of a place (Hough, 1990). And because nature and history are always being reshaped by present actions, the context is always changing or emerging in its representations of those actions. Context also means to weave together, the parts that surround a (place) and determine its meaning. Determining its meaning ". . . is inherent in the definition of place," as Arnheim (1969) describes it. Everything in this world, Arnheim points out, presents itself in context and is modulated by that context.

Context is an umbrella term used by planning and design professions to represent the larger scale and its components. It provides the professions with a larger framework for observation with which to more accurately understand the formation of human settlements in the landscape. It is also used as an analytical vehicle for the study of the smaller, more focused, and special realities of context, referred to as places. Context and place are synonymous by definition; they are both spatial entities of special identity and value, made that way by the very act of recognition by an observer. They are distinguished for purposes of differentiation and analysis as being a connection of places (and connections among places) on one hand and the place itself (and its adjacency relationships).

The underlying formative processes of both context and place include metabolic-like processes resulting from the actions of people, other animals, insects, and plants in the real world (i.e., build-up of settlements and their reduction to waste or release as energy through socio-cultural, health, economic-political, and functional processes). Context as planners and designers use it is a spatial representation of these metabolic processes in motion in space and time. It becomes a four-dimensional construct composed of culture-based organizational and structural relationships. Planning and designing can become insulated or isolated actions if these underlying processes are not understood as a part of the design process.

"Seeing" Context As Design Opportunity

For planners and designers, to "see" an object in space is to see it in context, where "see" means to see in relationship. (Arnheim, 1969). The appearance (definition) of a building, landscape, or other artifact in the visual field has been shown to depend on its place and function in the total structure and "to be modified fundamentally by that influence" (Arnheim, 1969). Context is the total framework within which objects (shapes and patterns) are seen. Without it they lose meaning or relevance. This leads to the basic premise that the perception of shapes and patterns as context, or place(s) in context, is the beginning of concept formation, the beginning of the act of design.

Shapes are concepts

Communicating perceived relationships in shapes and patterns is greatly facilitated by a graphic or visual language that integrates parts, organization, and structure.

Visualizing Context

Portraying Context with Visual Thinking

The graphic language is an appropriate and fitting way to describe the spatial integrity of context.

"A perceiver and thinker whose concepts are limited to the kind foreseen by traditional logic is in danger of performing in a world of paralyzed constructs." (Arnheim, 1969)

Visualization can be a cognitive act that captures the sense or insight of place, an act of discovery, furthering an understanding of a given and changing reality and providing ongoing clues for the design process. Gordon Cullen was a master at graphically depicting context, place, and the qualitative dimensions he so artfully identified. (Townscape, 1961). His drawings are pictorial in that they provide the layperson with reference and orientation material that is familiar and real, and are enriched by a semi-abstraction that combines pictorial with diagram to emphasize structure, order, texture, massing, and so on, without unnecessary information. These type drawings have a power or strength the conventional doodle or bubble diagram does not have. They have contextual foundations. They are connected to place using graphic images.

This chapter explores ways to visualize, as a cognitive process, the analysis of the parts of place within the framework of a larger context. Examples express conventional data in two- and three-dimensions: two-dimensional when quantification and horizontal or vertical relationships are the focus and three-dimensional when multi-axis views provide better data integration (relationships). In both cases, the drawing act defines and describes relationships for both the planner/designer and the public (client) participant. Visualization is a basis for translating data into provocative, spatial, connected differentiations that gives the designer freedom to explore more connections or ideas.

Lastly, visualizations are art as constructed with tools and techniques, rather than arbitrary decoration or renderings; interpretations and translations using the elements and principles of art as integral parts of the design process. Line quality and value bring out certain relationships that themselves become part of the organizing principles of a design. Recurring themes in many of the examples emphasize edge conditions, the border or meeting place that defines how different places relate as expanded context. Other examples expand the overall view of a project or city sector's larger place. The example drawing types are varied, from conventional slide-traced pictorial perspectives to diagrams that explore organization, structure, and parts relationships.

Basic Principles of Context Visualization

Drawing can use art's principles and elements to capture the structural and organizational influences of context on place. The act of defining context's limits and characteristics in graphics initiates the design process.

Principle One
Visualize context as places within places; focus on the manner in which one place is joined, interlocked, in confrontation with other places to form a contextual portrait.

Drawing can articulate a settlement composed of shapes and patterns. It can highlight the network shape (i.e., a river or valley) by its edges and connections to adjacent shapes and patterns and an urban block to other urban blocks through massing, style, and ground network connections.

Principle Two
Visualize context in relationship to boundaries that are sufficient or adequate to tell enough of the larger story.

Thinking about an object can begin with the way the object or study area is perceived to be bounded. The act of drawing an adequate context requires the planner/designer to observe and make decisions regarding the extent of adequacy, thereby engaging the issues and relationships. Sketching out

what the adequate context can entail is a cognitive process that builds upon itself, moving away from mental abstraction and entering a form-generative process at the outset. Constructing a simple two-dimensional map that locates a town in an eco-region is an act of recognition of the eco-region and its general physical characteristics that can play a part in assessing the nature and opportunities of the town under study. A panorama or aerial oblique can visually identify the extent and adequacy of context for the layperson's perspective and the designer's field of opportunity.

Principle Three
Visualize context in relationship to the underlying bio-physical features and systems of the environment. Watersheds, geology, habitats, and other systems in the landscape are the underlying containers for human culture and impact and relate to all other aspects of context.

Principle Four
Visualize context according to overall composition of spatial organization, spatial structure, and key parts.

Principle Five
Visualize context as changing patterns over time. Visualizing context over time can uncover pattern changes, bio-physical to cultural relationships, and design opportunity in historic patterns.

Examples and Applications

Visualizing Context as Larger Patterns

Range of Examples
The following section presents examples of graphic visualizations of context for both quantitative and qualitative analysis. The section is organized according to context expressed in land forms and features, land forms and settlement patterns, and bio-physical, socio-cultural, and economic-political characteristics. In some examples, the bridge between large scale land form context and human settlement pattern is constructed to demonstrate the importance of making that connection, at least in scale.

Juneau

Gulf of Alaska

Anchorage

Fairbanks

Aleutian Islands

Nome

ALASKA
The View from Russia

2-1 Alaska.

Large Scale Landform Visualizations

Land form provides a basis for describing the characteristics of place within a larger physical and spatial context. It is the underlying surficial condition determining the spatial array of settlements. Graphically visualizing land form allows the planner/designer to investigate natural systems such as surface drainage, habitats, and vegetation as interacting functions of the landscape rather than isolated elements. The following examples portray different means and methods of visualization useful in resource management planning and all fields of urban design.

Alaska

Large scale, multiple region, three-dimensional diagrams are effective in dealing with natural resource issues, large scale transportation issues, and settlement impacts. **Alaska** is an aerial oblique ink sketch prepared on quality tracing paper with a Pentel Sign pen. The model for the sketch is a slide that was photographed from a USGS Topographical Relief map and projected to the desired size. The map provides the basis for numerous studies of the Alaskan regions and is a valuable resource tool for future studies.

Alaskan Interior

Regional scales of large land areas such as the northeast quadrant of Alaska are difficult to use as a basis for data due to the complexity of surface features and natural systems. At this scale, it is useful to limit the types of base reference data. In **Alaskan Interior,** a USGS map was used as a base for region-wide data such as transportation systems, village locations, and generalized habitat and wildlife information depicted later as **Yukon Crossing.**

Lynn Canal is an aerial oblique perspective depicting the surrounding land form for the City of Haines in southeast Alaska. Haines is a city of over 1,100 people located in the northern portion of the state's southeast panhandle, 75 air miles northwest of Juneau, and 16 air miles south of Skagway (more than 300 miles by road). The drama of the place is created by the Coast Mountains of the Pacific Mountain System, called the Chilkat Range, characterized by glaciers, inlets, and fjords. That drama must become indigenous to the planning and design process. The planner/designer must commit the time and effort necessary to portray the area's wonder in ink drawings.

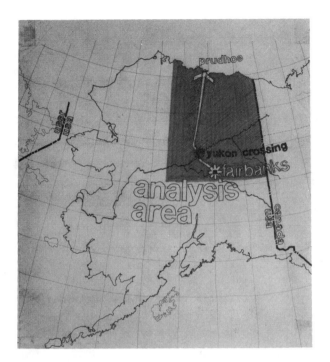

2-2 Alaska Interior.

The visualization is a graphic pictorial or real-life interpretation, with a perspective obtained from an aerial oblique slide photographed from an airplane. The community's place in the land is an integral part of its culture, politics, economy, geography, and history, reflected in its spatial arrangement. The Tlingit people are the earliest known inhabitants of this area and had established profitable trading outlets with the Athabascan Indians of the Yukon by the mid 1800s. Haines is the doorway from the southeast coastal region to the higher and colder interior regions of the mainland via the "grease-trail," formerly the Dalton Trail during the gold strikes, and now the Haines Highway. John Muir, environmentalist and naturalist, travelled to the area in 1879 with S. Hall Young and selected the location of the future city of Haines for a National Presbyterian Mission with school and health clinic serving the Tlingit villages in the area. The land selected was a saddle used as a portage by native peoples.

The drawing techniques used to prepare the sketch include hatching and scribbling with a fine point technical pen on tracing paper. The looping technique used for tree cover is an example of repeated shapes varied in size and consistency to create visual interest. The closer loop forms were filled in with a loose and fast diagonal hatching motion. Distance was created by diminishing the size of tree shapes until they merged into a textured carpet on the mountain shapes in the midground. Trees were individually articulated in the foreground to provide a graphic image for distant textured shapes. The graphic visualization serves its purpose of setting the conditions of land

haines area

2-3,4 Lynn Canal.

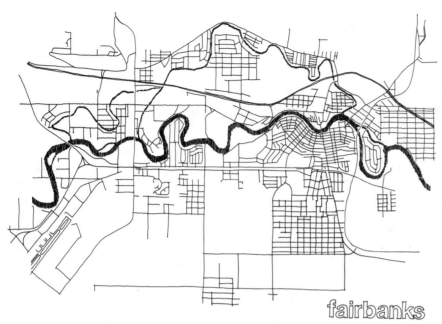

2-5 Fairbanks Plan.

Michigan, specifically the lake edge morraine. In the pursuit of clues in a limited and intense time frame, natural landscape responses to the lake action, primarily sandy dunes and secondary dunes, were visualized in exploratory diagrams. The morraine land form historically influenced early settlement patterns and was re-introduced metaphorically into the downtown lakefront, serving as an ordering device for human activities and built patterns.

The **Milwaukee Diagrams** summarize the integration of context investigation and opportunity identification, locating clues at the ecoregion level and carrying that information down in scale until the clues become the framework for detailed site development proposals.

form and location for the local residents and the planning team. It "freezes" the context in a viewable frame.

Land Form and Settlement

Fairbanks Plan depicts a basic street pattern map for two-dimensional quantitative relationship studies. It is useful for network data such as traffic and transportation demographics, and for land use. Such maps can be simple, providing reference and orientation but saving detail for more focused studies.

Lake Edge Morraine: Land Form as Opportunity

Milwaukee Lakefront is an aerial oblique diagram that was part of a winning entry in an international design competition for the design of the downtown Milwaukee, Wisconsin, lakefront.[1] The search for a physical element to spatially organize the redeveloped waterfront led the designers to a review of historic geology patterns along the shores of Lake

Putting Settlement in its Place

Bethel Circle

Plan diagrams are a basic tool in describing context and providing scale reference and orientation. In visioning, they can help exaggerate the obvious; they can highlight in one graphic what it may take pages of statistics to dramatize.

The Bethel Area plan diagram is a fifty-mile-radius circle around the City of Bethel on the western coastal plain of Alaska, with peak elevations above sea level of 12 feet. The drama of the seasonal changes to the land form is represented by the inclusion of all lakes and ponds within that radius. These highlight the results of an ecosystem that is characterized by spring flooding of the Kuskokwim River and the freshwater lakes that are left as the flood recedes, trapping many species of fish and providing a rich waterfowl habitat. This staff drawing is a symbol of that ecosystem and sets the stage for commu-

---

[1] This design concept was one of several honorable mention design approaches, published in the Final Report by the International Competition for the Redesign of the Milwaukee, Wisconsin Lakefront: *Planning and Design Competition*, 1980.

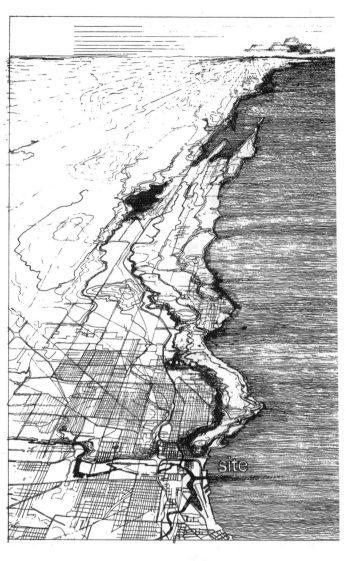

2-6 Regional Forces. The aerial perspective places the study site in its regional setting and identifies the moraine as an organization principal that is further diagrammed at the study site scale.

The glacial landscape of tall grass prarie, forest, river and lake is Milwaukee's origin and structures its urban form and culture. Natural and human systems converge at this site and can find integration in a lake edge moraine land form which will help shape the evolving culture and physical growth of the city.

The new moraine form reflects the origin of the regional landscape.

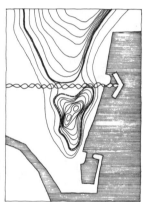

The **moraine** mediates highway scale from regional to local, and . creates a portal to the city.

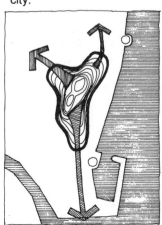

The moraine molds cultural subdistricts within the city.

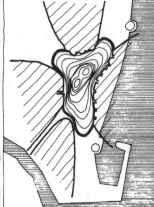

The moraine extends the forested green belt into the city.

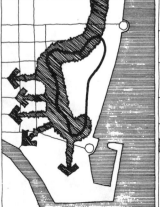

The moraine directs and organizes transportation while buffering recreation.

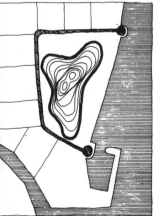

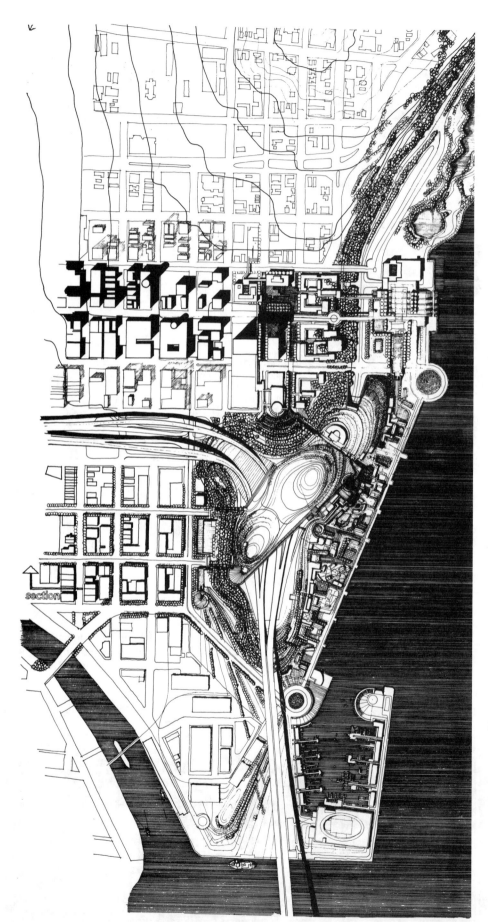

2-7 Milwaukee Lakefront Design. Drawing value in the final site rendering reiterates the organizational principle identified by previous site diagrams. The focus of the drawing is the moraine as it shapes new city precincts, resolves an unfinished freeway inte-section, and carries a park amenity into the city.

2-8 Lakefront City Section. The perspective through the site references the design proposal to the existing cityscape and freeway structure.

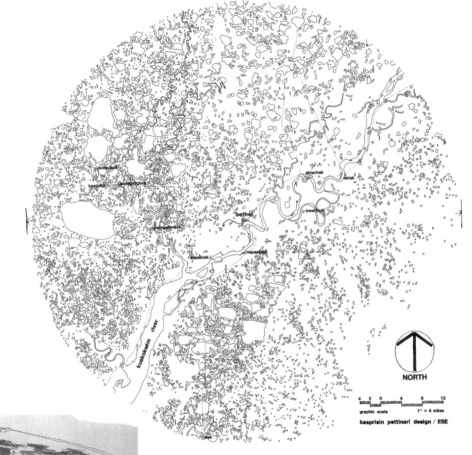

2-9 Bethel Circle.

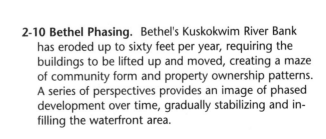

2-10 Bethel Phasing. Bethel's Kuskokwim River Bank has eroded up to sixty feet per year, requiring the buildings to be lifted up and moved, creating a maze of community form and property ownership patterns. A series of perspectives provides an image of phased development over time, gradually stabilizing and in-filling the waterfront area.

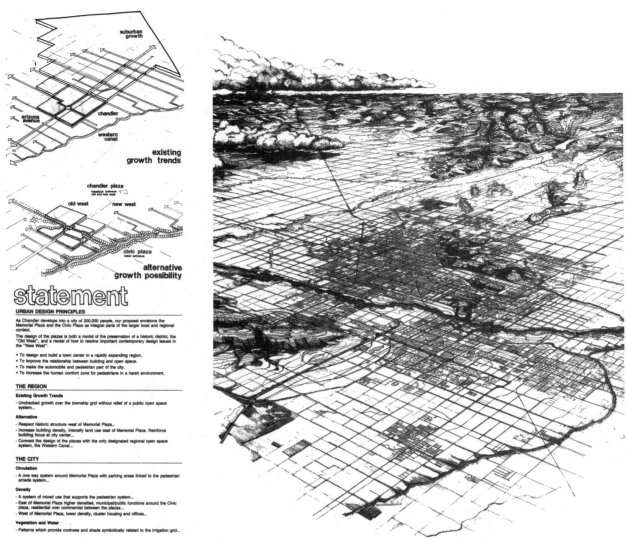

2-11 Chandler Town Center Design. The aerial perspective places the study site in its regional setting to identify an organizational principal at the study site scale.

nity planning efforts. The drawing is in india ink on tracing paper, crafted with a fine point technical pen. Additional diagrams for Bethel represent phasing issues portrayed in three-dimension.

Chandler Region is a perspective that uses the built pattern at the eco-region scale to demonstrate opportunity and its carry-over to the building scale. Part of a national design competition for a town center in Chandler, Arizona, the drawing was used to visualize Chandler as a small speck on an agricultural plain gridded and nourished by an irrigation canal system originating at the Arizona River. A piece of the same aerial view is enlarged in the vicinity of Chandler in **Chandler Grid,** illustrating the city as a flat block attached to the grid growing toward the

nearby Phoenix metropolitan area. A second diagram using the same context framework visualizes alternative growth possibilities, using the canal as an open space and the water element as an ordering principle. Finally, opportunity is carried in more detail to the city scale, using **Chandler Town Center,** another aerial oblique, to illustrate site concepts. A series of plan diagrams, **Chandler Opportunity Diagrams,** highlights circulation water systems, green space systems, and building density. Opportunity emerges from context discovered through visualizations as internal/external communications. Details of the finalized proposal happen within the framework identified at the town and regional scales.

The Port Gamble Townsite is a company-owned sawmill town 25 miles northwest of Seattle on the

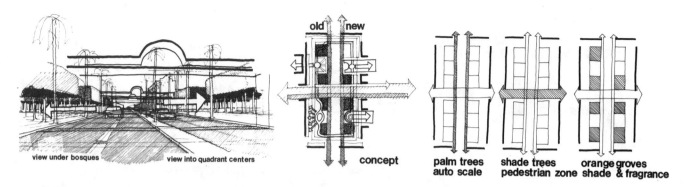

view under bosques — view into quadrant centers

old / new

concept

palm trees
auto scale

shade trees
pedestrian zone

orange groves
shade & fragrance

2-12 Chandler Town Center Organizational Diagrams. Using plan diagrams to break the study site into connected parts.

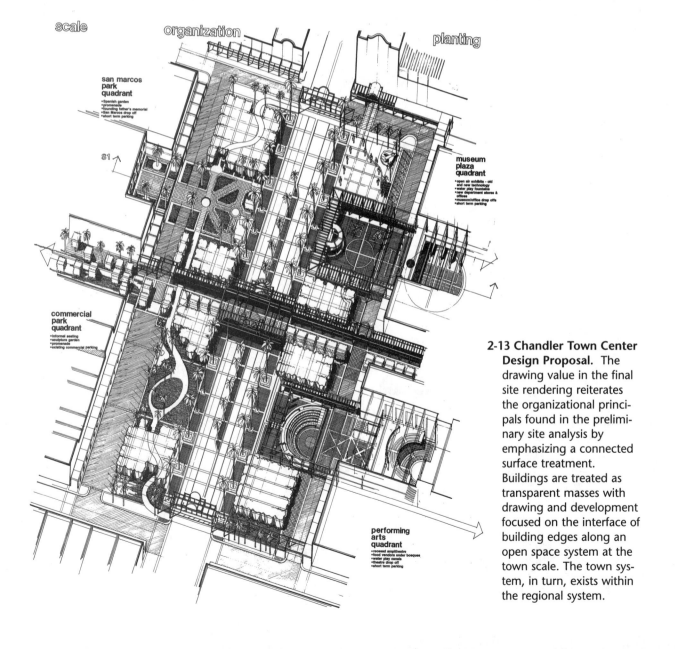

scale — organization — planting

san marcos
park
quadrant
•Spanish garden
•promenade
•founding father's memorial
•San Marcos drop off
•short term parking

museum
plaza
quadrant
•open air exhibits - old and new technology
•water play fountains
•new department stores & offices
•museum/office drop offs
•short term parking

commercial
park
quadrant
•informal seating
•sculpture garden
•promenade
•existing commercial parking

performing
arts
quadrant
•recessed amphitheatre
•food vendors under bosques
•water play canals
•theatre drop off
•short term parking

2-13 Chandler Town Center Design Proposal. The drawing value in the final site rendering reiterates the organizational principals found in the preliminary site analysis by emphasizing a connected surface treatment. Buildings are treated as transparent masses with drawing and development focused on the interface of building edges along an open space system at the town scale. The town system, in turn, exists within the regional system.

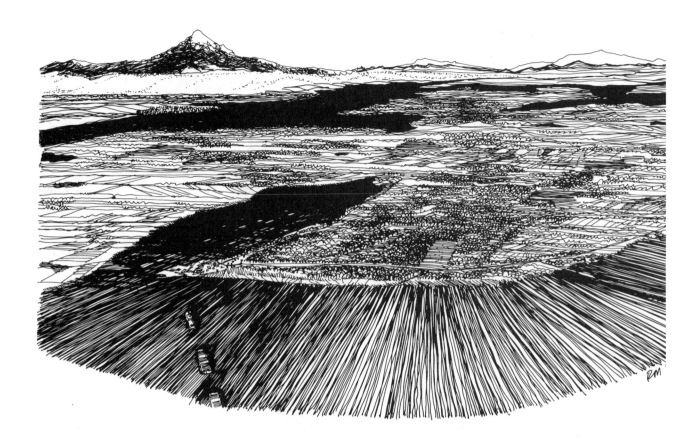

2-14 Puget Sound and North Kitsap Peninsula.

2-15 Townsite Aerial Views. These aerial oblique sketches have enough detail to clearly communicate the physical landscape of this historic working town, from a vantage point taking in the entire town and zooming in on the town center.

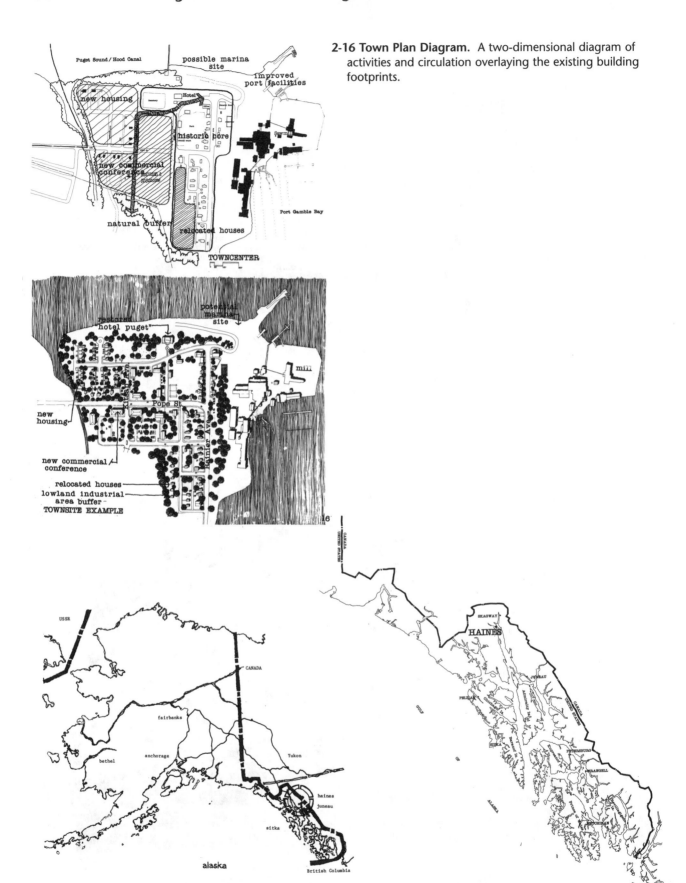

2-16 Town Plan Diagram. A two-dimensional diagram of activities and circulation overlaying the existing building footprints.

2-17A,B Haines Context Map and Sketch Diagrams. This sequence of drawings characterizes for the public the various physical conditions, components, and relationships of Haines, Fort Seward, and their terrain.

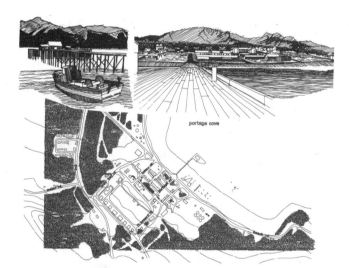

2-18 A,B,C Fort Seward/Portage Cove. This sketch series combines semi-abstract graphic characters (loops for trees) with value patterns (varying densities of loops) to dramatize the incredible location of Fort William H. Seward.

Kitsap Peninsula in western Washington. The townsite, the mill, the barge landings, and the adjacent timber resources are all intertwined in a classic Northwest resource-dependent settlement pattern. The connections among the regional and local contexts required a variety of scales in the visualizations: from the Puget Sound area to the townsite to the town center. **North Kitsap Peninsula, Townsite,** and **Town Center** are linked aerial oblique perspectives that together describe the context and relationship among the various districts comprising the townsite. A plan diagram such as **Townsite Plan** is useful to complete the reference and orientation base. The drawings were all prepared in a sequence of descending scales, using technical pens and Graphos nib pen on mylar or tracing paper.

Fort Seward/Portage Cove is an example of a human settlement place connected to a land form (a natural saddle of land between two bodies of water), connected to a fjord, connected to its mountainous walls and neighboring icefields. Pictorial perspectives portray a settlement form in the context of a series of progressively larger land forms. Historic Fort William H. Seward, constructed between 1903 and 1910, is located on the side of another saddle of land between Portage Cove in Lynn Canal and Chilkat Inlet at the mouth of the Chilkat River. Fort Seward is among many forts in the United States designed in Washington DC and referred to as "fort anywhere" because the same building design was used throughout the country. Place this "fort anywhere" on a saddle of land with the Cathedral Peaks of the Chilkat Range as a backdrop, visualize its placement for participants in the process, and the drama of the place soon becomes apparent—a great way to begin a series of meetings on town planning.

Settlement patterns are a part of the land form, for better or for worse. Recognizing the connection of settlement to land form increases the realization that context is a part of the definition of place. In **Upper Main Street Series,** eye-level sketches are used to make the connection between land form and settlement, using darker values in the land form shapes to dramatize the strength and influence of the larger place-context on the town form. This living room window view is a place-context connection and sets the stage for design opportunity.

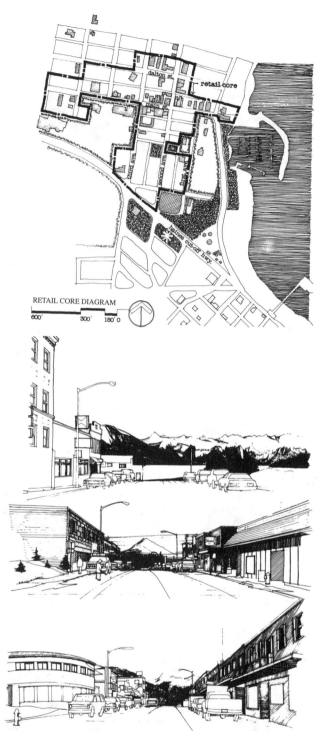

RETAIL CORE DIAGRAM

600'   300'   180' 0

2-19A,B Upper Main Street. Treating the downtown as an outdoor room, these views look "outside" to emphasize the influence and power of the surrounding fjord and its relationship to the town form and site energy.

Islands

An island is a special event in the landform, formed by fragments of larger adjacent land masses or exotic migratory masses from other locations. The clarity of a land mass in a water setting is a memorable image

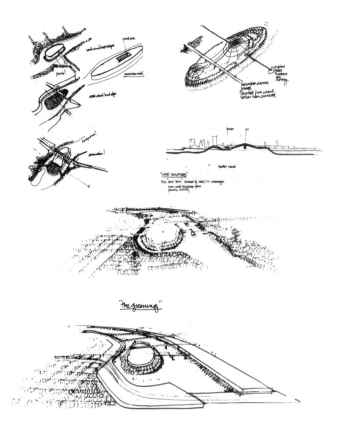

"the greening"

2-20 Island Form Explorations. These visualizations focus on the nature of islands by manipulating drawing value along the interface of land and water. Various crossings of built systems are diagrammed as to their impact on island clarity.

reminiscent of a large vessel at sea, with distinct profiles and water-land edge tensions. Few cities have islands. Their occurrence can make special places within the complexity of urban settlements. The island of Manhattan and the left bank of Paris are islands absorbed in that complexity but still having an ordering force on its parts.

Nicollet Island and **Hayden Island** diagram various development scenarios on islands within changing metropolitan areas. Both examples are excerpts

from public discussions regarding future development on these strategic sites.[2] Despite its strategic location in downtown Minneapolis, Nicollet Island is not perceived as an island even by its closest neighbors due to the "cementing" of the Mississippi river corridor with industrial facilities and the closeness of the island mass to the city, especially on the north. Hayden Island, in the Columbia River, is part of the border crossing between Portland, Oregon and Vancouver, Washington. Both islands were used as stepping stones, first by railroads, then highways, electric transmission lines, and freeways, to cross their respective rivers. The crossing artifacts do not discriminate between island and mainland. Building development in and around the islands is scattered, with no coherent pattern relating to the island's form, especially their edges. The bridge crossings by which the islands most experienced do not distinguish it as a separate land mass, rather a simple extension of the adjacent city, obscuring important clues to the islands' past significance as historic gateways.

Visualization techniques were used to focus on the island as an ordering entity for development. The island itself presents a unique design opportunity and a scarce resource in urban areas. The diagrams, part of the visualization process for both the designer and the public, explore potential landscape and building forms in several combinations that clarify island edges and contrast the island crossing event.

Manhattan

An international design competition[3] for the lower west side of Manhattan in New York City generated a series of drawings dealing with island river edges, exploring the role of proposed building form to clarify and link vacant water edge to the city. To communicate the design proposal, plan diagrams present the riverfront design concept, a pattern of alternating points of built and open districts woven together

[2] The Nicollet Island drawings are part of an environmental study, "Images of the River," conducted by the Walker Art Center in Minneapolis, Minnesota. Published: *Design Quarterly*, 1977. The Hayden Island drawings are part of a study to locate the latest island crossing element, a light rail line between Portland, Oregon and Vancouver, Washington. This work was conducted by the public outreach program of the Regional Rail Program of the City of Portland, Oregon.

[3] This work was recognized among several entries in the International Design Competition for the Lower Westside Waterfront, New York City, sponsored by the Municipal Art Society of New York and the National Endowment for the Arts. Published: *Arredo Urbano*, October 1988.

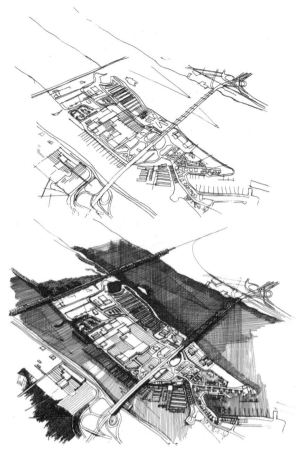

2-21 Hayden Island. Visualization of existing conditions developed from a line drawing of an aerial photo. Drawing value emphasizes the island edge.

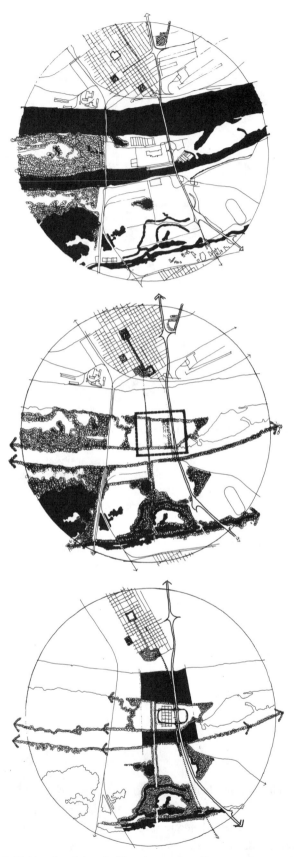

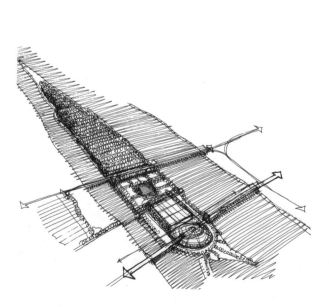

2-23 Hayden Island Crossing Exploration. The aerial perspective explores potential island crossing events created by the interstate freeway, proposed light rail line, and existing railroad.

2-22 Hayden Island. The three plan diagrams focus on different aspects of the island's structure: water, vegetation, and built crossing systems (freeway, proposed light rail, and railroad).

principles

•parallel to river
extension of riverside park into site creating a continuous promenade between riverside park and battery park

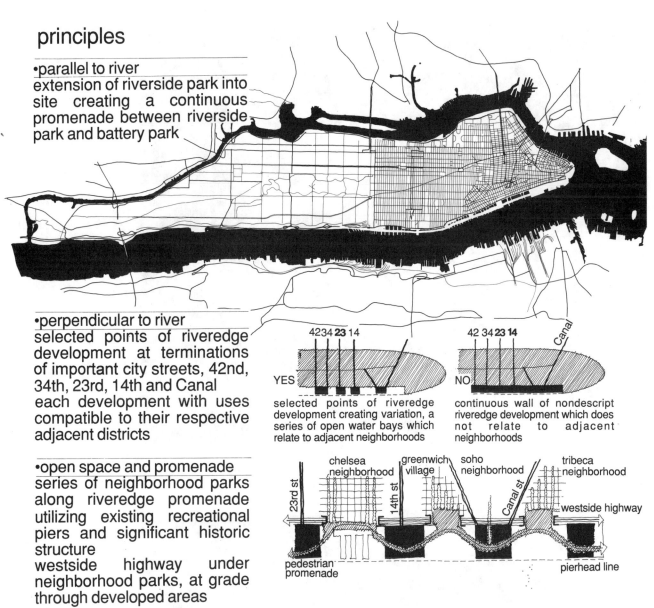

•perpendicular to river
selected points of riveredge development at terminations of important city streets, 42nd, 34th, 23rd, 14th and Canal each development with uses compatible to their respective adjacent districts

YES
selected points of riveredge development creating variation, a series of open water bays which relate to adjacent neighborhoods

NO
continuous wall of nondescript riveredge development which does not relate to adjacent neighborhoods

•open space and promenade
series of neighborhood parks along riveredge promenade utilizing existing recreational piers and significant historic structure
westside highway under neighborhood parks, at grade through developed areas

2-24 Manhattan Lower West Side Edge Proposal. The diagrams outline an approach that extends the key streets to the water's edge.

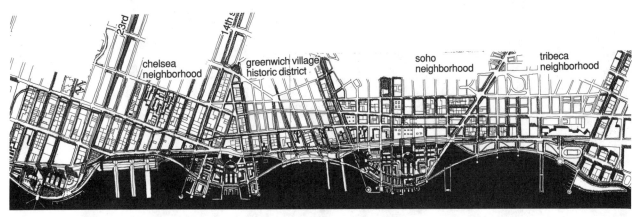

2-25 Manhattan Lower West Side Edge. The rendered site plan reiterates the connections outlined in the conceptual diagram.

2-26 Island Edge Proposal, Lower West Side Manhattan.

2-27 Port Townsend View. Interface between the natural and built edge of Port Townsend, Washington.

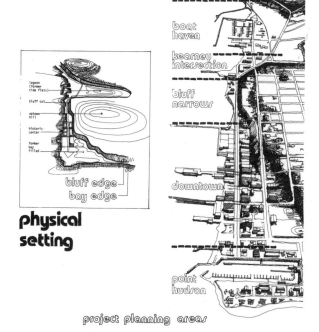

2-28 Port Townsend Aerial Diagram.

with a continuous promenade along the water edge, alongside the antithesis of that idea, a continuous solid wall of building development. The design approach was developed into a site plan and a model detailing building massing at the foot of important streets such as 14th, 23rd, 34th, and 42nd.

Port Townsend

Many settlements impose their patterns on the natural landform rather than following a natural fit. The charming character of Port Townsend, Washington was generated by severe manipulation of the natural shoreline in the late 1800s. Using the up-to-date technology of the 1890s, namely high pressure water hoses used for mining gold, the base or shelf for the downtown was made by literally washing clay and silt

away from the adjacent 70-foot high bluff.

The perspective panorama of Port Townsend, **Port Townsend View**, drawn from sketches and slides taken on a boat off shore, celebrates the meeting of water and townscape. The predominant message in shapes is composed of the water surface texture and the historic buildings clustered along the shore and on top of the bluff. In contrast, the **Port Townsend Aerial Oblique Perspective** relates the positioning of Port Townsend in its larger peninsula context within Puget Sound and the Olympic Mountain Range. The cut and fill along the bluff are clearly visualized. This assists the local residents in understanding the contrived nature of the town's construction; to understand the relationship between the museum-quality historic architectural artifacts of the lower town and their instability and fragility based on the unconsolidated earthquake prone fill upon which they sit.

Port Townsend Aerial Oblique became the base for multiple color marker overlays that were used to represent "big-picture" visions at community meetings. The drawing was reproduced on blackline diazo prints and colored marker diagrams were added representing everything from ecological systems to ferry terminal site options. It consists of india ink on mylar drawn with a fine point technical pen.

The Port Townsend Aerial Diagram takes this imposed-settlement issue a step further by visually emphasizing the original water edge before settlement. The diagram is a simple line drawing that semi-abstracts land forms and features, selectively screening out features that are less of a determinate at this scale and level of understanding for the viewer.

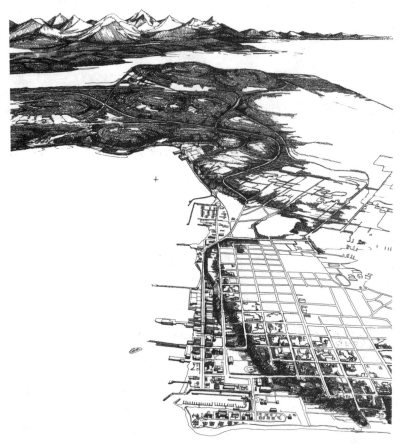

2-29 Port Townsend Aerial Oblique. Drawing composition is chosen to reference the settlement to the mountain and bay context of the Puget Sound region.

2-30,31 Yukon Crossing. This series of drawings was made with a Graphos nib pen on photocopies of an original mylar base.

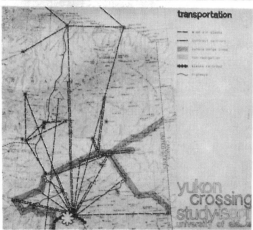

The diagram states what it needs to state and not any more: a decision of interpretation by the designer based on an analysis of detailed geologic and topographic information.

Differentiating Context's Parts Through Visualization

Bio-Physical, Cultural, and Jurisdictional Parts

At some point in the planning/design process, the parts of the whole need to be differentiated and assessed, then placed back in relationship to the whole. Terms commonly used to represent the categories of parts include: bio-physical, cultural, and jurisdictional. They include aspects of the environment ranging from geology to tenancy patterns of buildings.

Bio-physical Parts

Bio-physical information represents the physical patterns of biologic relationships present in a given place. These form the basis for normative analysis of existing conditions in all planning and design fields, from resource management to architecture.

Conventional parts of bio-physical information are:

- geology—hazards, minerals, seismicity, volcanism, mass wasting, sediment transport, etc;
- flood and ice hazards;
- topography and surface features;
- watersheds and drainage basins;
- soils and slopes;
- water resources—surface and ground water;
- vegetation cover;
- wildlife—terrestrial and marine and aquatic species;

- coastal and inland habitats (wetlands and tide-flats, vegetated bluffs, off-shore and estuarine areas, rivers, streams and lakes, upland habitats); and
- air and climate conditions (precipitation, temperature, wind, fog, incidents of inversions).

A principle to remember when collecting and analyzing information is that it does not exist as a real separate entity. It represents relationships and patterns isolated and condensed into measurable quantities for observation and use by humans. Information is given real value when placed in relationship or context.

Bio-physical information is effective if put into a reference/orientation base so that relationships can be determined among elements. Topography is the minimum reference element that is used for bio-physical information. Present Geographic Information Systems (GIS) may be technology-dependent and inaccurate, not available in small towns and some rural areas, or slow regarding data input and turn-around. An effective manual alternative is the pin-bar overlay system for scaleable two-dimensional diagrams. Each level of biophysical information is drawn on a mylar sheet with attachable pinholes that line up a series of sheets over a topographical base. These overlay sheets can then be compared for commonalities, conflicts, and relationships among information elements. Ian McHarg popularized an overlay/conflict identification method in *Design with Nature*; see "Composite Physiographic Obstructions" map (McHarg 1971).

Yukon Crossing

Generalized relationships and specific information can be depicted for very large regions. One example is the northeast quadrant of the State of Alaska, an area encampassing the size of a number of midwestern states placed together. The information is generalized using graphic symbols so that its core implications are visualized as patterns. A Graphos nib pen set with india ink was used on photocopy paper (opaque) with an imprinted base map of the quadrant.[4]

---

[4] These diagrams were drawn on-site in Fairbanks and north where, at the time of the work, access to drawing supplies was limited. Reproduction quality was important and a high black and white value was used for information shapes and patterns.

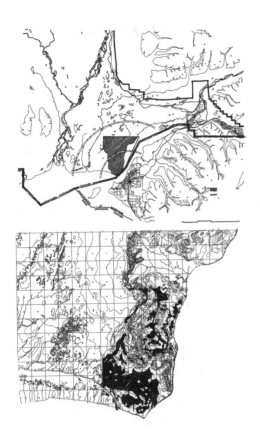

2-32,33 Point MacKenzie Series. These maps are resource visualization diagrams prepared by staff that locate, reference, and specify the spatial implications of data or information in context. The graphics are pen and ink on mylar using both Graphos nib pens and fine point technical pens. These are handmade Graphic Information System (GIS) visualizations with more flexibility and character than standard GIS graphics.

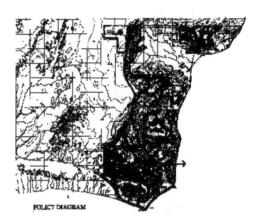

POLICY DIAGRAM

2-34,35,36 Pelican Resource Map Series. The Pelican resource maps visualize biophysical boundaries, coastal habitats, terrestrial mammals, geophysical hazards, and subsistence fishing information as examples of quantifiable data that benefits from being spatially referenced and oriented. Staff drawings.

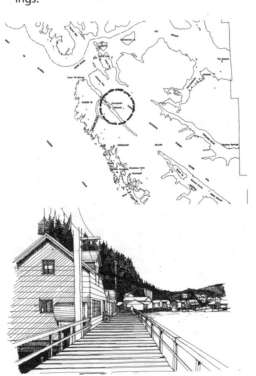

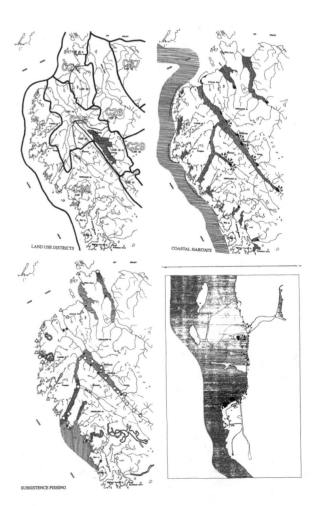

LAND USE DISTRICTS

COASTAL HABITATS

SUBSISTENCE FISHING

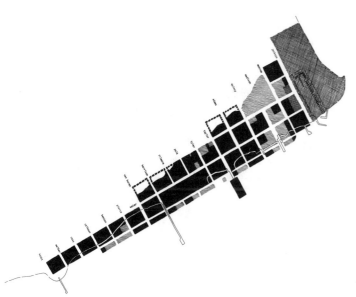

2-37 Port Townsend Ownership Map. Black represents private; hatch is town; cross hatch is semi-public.

In the **Point MacKenzie Series**, examples of biophysical information were produced with india ink on mylar to map critical information relative to wildlife and land form characteristics. Pin-bar alignment devices were used to permit overlay analysis of information, and the printing of selected overlay combinations. Black and white reproduction requirements, plus multi-agency review procedures, necessitated the use of graphic techniques that can withstand large quantity printing. Two-dimensional diagrams are preferred in this case to allow a reference scale that is measurable and consistent for all layers of information. Policy diagrams are shown in the series to demonstrate the use of base information as a foundation for recommendations. Policy is general yet spatially referenced, located, and oriented for the reader. GIS maps were available, but of limited use due to their less effective visualization principles.

Pelican Resource Map Series illustrates an information sequence diminishing in scale from an eco-region to a community scale, expanding the level of information from the semi-abstract and filtered state-wide scale to the more detailed and site-specific community scale. Each map staff assembled represents a differentiated part of a complex natural environment necessary to understand prior to the development of planning policy. All maps are on mylar or tracing paper, drawn in india ink with technical pens and Graphos nib pens. Providing a frame of reference

for the lay viewer is critical. The reference and orientation diagrams begin with the state and scale down the ladder to the community. The visualizations were a part of a State of Alaska Coastal Management Community and Regional Affairs funded study of the community of Pelican and its surrounding coastal context.

Jurisdictional and Ownership Characteristics

Jurisdiction information refers to the authoritative or administrative control of public or semi-public agencies. Stating that a state agency controls a certain parcel of land is not sufficient. Coastal management, fish and wildlife, forestry, health, and others all have separate policies, regulations, and permit requirements and the extent of the land that they control requires identification within a project area and surrounding region.

Jurisdictional and ownership information is critical to getting plans and designs accomplished. They are the hidden agendas and control factors. Visualizing this information requires more than creating lists of names or writing them on a parcel map; it means looking for spatial patterns through graphic techniques that often produce a basis for implementation strategies or encourage or discourage certain design directions. **Port Townsend Ownership** illustrates public and private jurisdictions. In addition, it displays the pattern of local and non-local private ownership for individuals who own at least 50 percent or more of a given city block, for example. In public meetings and strategy sessions with local officials, the visualization communicated key information in pattern form on a city sector reference map. India ink on mylar with technical pen was used to create simple strong patterns and values.

Transportation, Circulation, and Infrastructure

Transportation and infrastructure information can be made more relevant to the community by depicting it in a more detailed context, using base drawings with repeated consistency of reference and orientation information such as building footprints, adjacent activities, etc. Data maps can be barriers to public understanding if considered out of context and modelled only as isolated linear and unconnected data pieces. In these examples, circulation and transporta-

2-38,39,40,41,42,43 Shelton Series. Data visualizations drawn in pen and ink and colored marker.

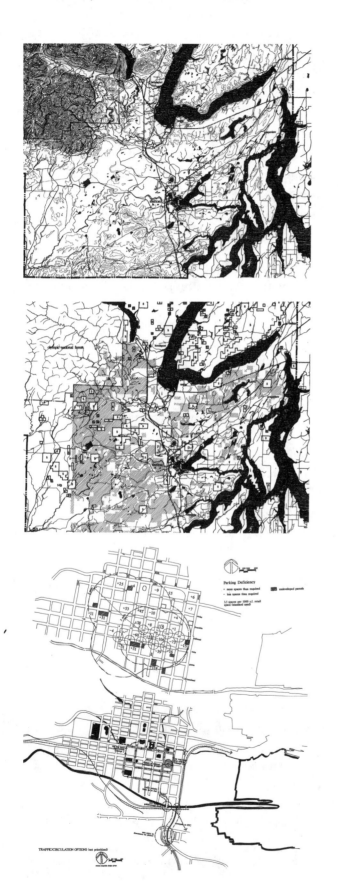

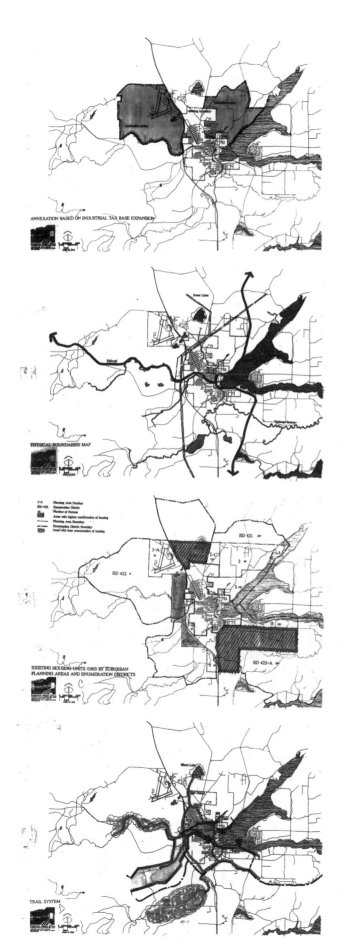

ANNEXATION BASED ON INDUSTRIAL TAX BASE EXPANSION

PHYSICAL BOUNDARIES MAP

EXISTING HOUSING UNITS (1985) BY SUBURBAN PLANNING AREAS AND ENUMERATION DISTRICTS

TRAIL SYSTEM

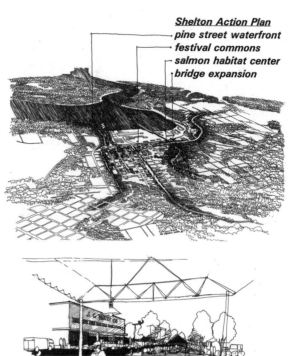

Shelton Action Plan
- pine street waterfront
- festival commons
- salmon habitat center
- bridge expansion

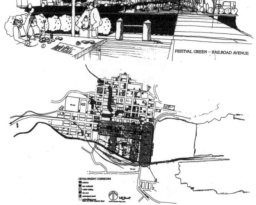

FESTIVAL GREEN – RAILROAD AVENUE

tion information is added to the fine point technical pen and india ink base with colored markers to dramatize the contrast between the new information and the base drawing. The **Shelton Series** illustrates a range of information visualization diagrams ranging in scale from the metropolitan to the city district.

Issues, Concerns, and Opportunities

It is common practice for planners to list issues, concerns, and opportunities and prepare matrices of issues. This is an outgrowth of a more quantitative context analysis—patterns emerge from the combination of graphic thinking and analysis, helping the designer/planner recognize form-generative opportunities. These diagrams can become too "boiled down" and are helped by supporting diagrams and context information.

Additional clarification and improvement to the concerns within a project area can be provided by a spatial/temporal display of conditions, problems,

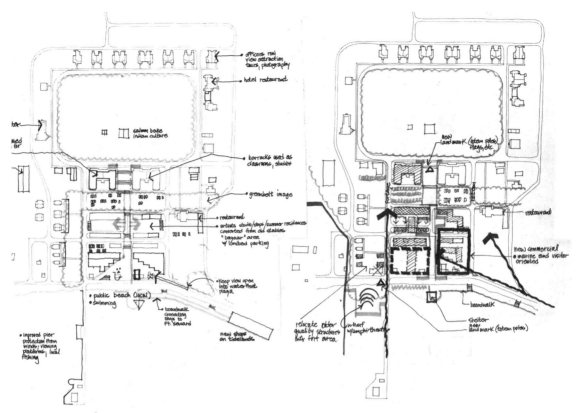

2-44 Fort Seward Opportunity Diagrams. Drawings are colored felt tip pens and technical pen on tracing paper.

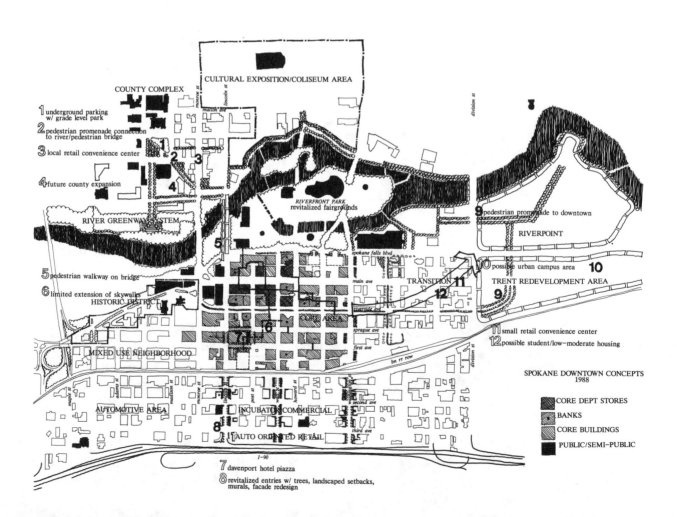

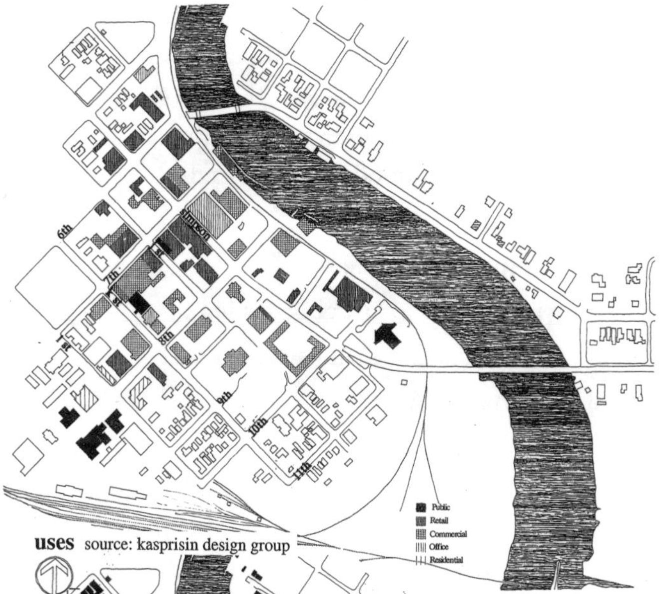
6th
7th
8th
9th
10th
11th
Public
Retail
Commercial
Office
Residential
uses source: kasprisin design group

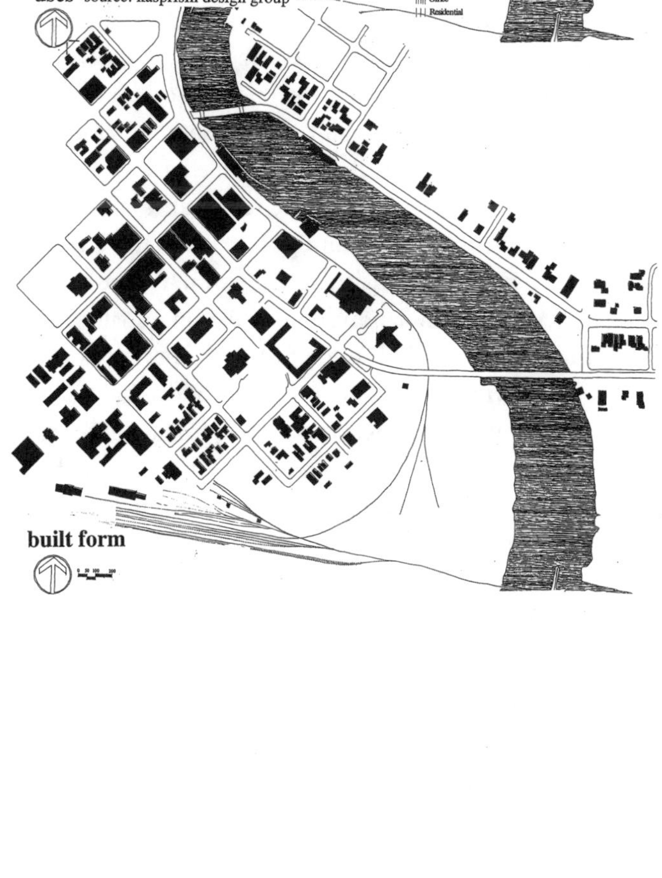
built form

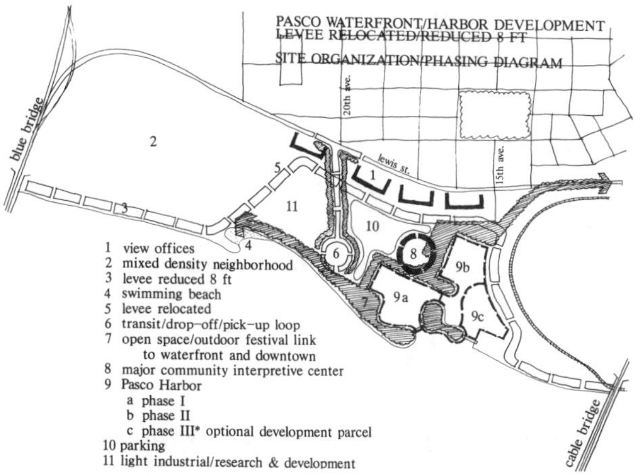
PASCO WATERFRONT/HARBOR DEVELOPMENT
LEVEE RELOCATED/REDUCED 8 FT
SITE ORGANIZATION/PHASING DIAGRAM
blue bridge
20th ave.
15th ave.
lewis st.
cable bridge
1 view offices
2 mixed density neighborhood
3 levee reduced 8 ft
4 swimming beach
5 levee relocated
6 transit/drop-off/pick-up loop
7 open space/outdoor festival link
to waterfront and downtown
8 major community interpretive center
9 Pasco Harbor
a phase I
b phase II
c phase III* optional development parcel
10 parking
11 light industrial/research & development

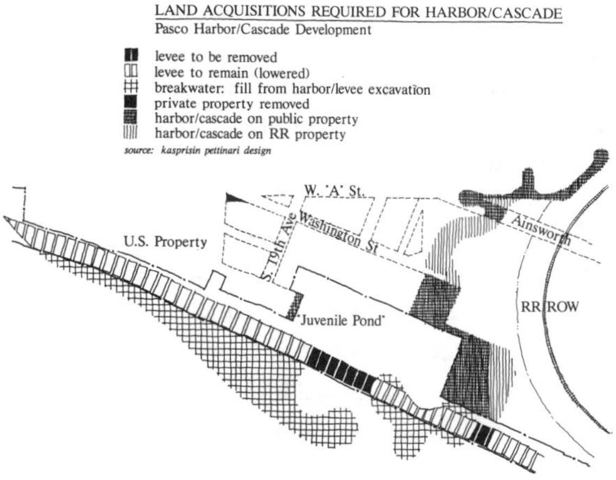
LAND ACQUISITIONS REQUIRED FOR HARBOR/CASCADE
Pasco Harbor/Cascade Development
levee to be removed
levee to remain (lowered)
breakwater: fill from harbor/levee excavation
private property removed
harbor/cascade on public property
harbor/cascade on RR property
source: kasprisin pettinari design
W. 'A' St.
Washington St
S. 19th Ave
Ainsworth
U.S. Property
'Juvenile Pond'
RR ROW

2-45,46,47 Activity Patterns and Relationships Diagrams. A variety of techniques from technical pen to colored markers all provide effective means of informing the public regarding the spatial implications of "data" or "information."

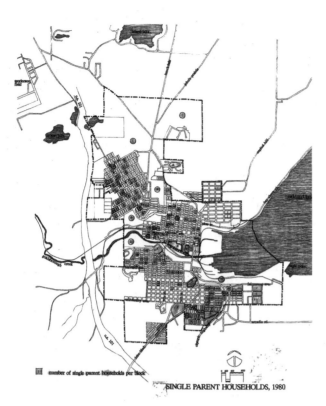

number of single parent households per block

SINGLE PARENT HOUSEHOLDS, 1980

2-48 Socio-economic Characteristics. Colored marker on sepia paper with a base map; fast and visual pattern-making for public involvement. Quantitative information can have little meaning to the general public unless it is spatially referenced and oriented.

trends, etc. on base maps, aerial photography prints, and three-dimensional diagrams. Colored marker is effective on line drawings when screened during printing. Care is needed in visualizing issues, concerns, and opportunities so that the analysis does not oversimplify and isolate items not fully connected to a larger context.

Fort Seward Opportunity Diagrams

Two-dimensional diagrams are useful for depicting opportunities on a generalized yet measurable or to-scale base for public review and discussion. At this stage, a broad conceptual approach with a definite spatial reference system is preferred to a non-referenced "doodle" common to many early studies.

Activity Patterns and Relationships

Activity patterns usually refer to human activities and include everything from conventional land use to pedestrian behaviour patterns. Land use information often needs to be quantified for comparative purposes and is depicted in two-dimensional maps and diagrams as well as paraline three-dimensional diagrams.

Activity patterns may include, but not be limited to, the following:

- open space—impervious surface auto-related, parks and recreation, habitat and natural systems (floodways, floodplains, wetlands);
- housing;
- commercial/retail;
- public and semi-public facilities;
- industrial and manufacturing; and
- cultural.

Visualization of these uses takes many forms. When a personal saturation with the information and relationships is critical, the graphic method can be in black and white and/or color. The following examples are cost-effective black and white format providing ease of printing for budget-conscious clients such as small cities and towns and neighborhood groups. Color can always be added to a black and white base drawing. Line techniques often used include hatching, screening, and outlining. The value structure of the diagram is critical to providing a hierarchy to the land use information, usually assigning a strong or dark value to higher intensity or density activities such as commercial and industrial uses (more intense impact on the land) and a lighter value for lower intensity or density activities such as housing and parks and recreation. The outline characteristics of certain techniques add to the communication of uses: An organic or non-linear outline technique for open space assists in saying vegetated open space. Make the line work represent the intent of the underlying message.

Social-Cultural Patterns and Relationships

Planners and designers can miss important spatial clues in the process by skipping a spatial analysis of social and cultural context elements. The effort to spatially delineate and relate all aspects of human settlement context provides design starts or at a minimum identifies spatial relationships of human behavior patterns. For example, if a project information search identifies a sector of a community as having a high percentage of single-parent households, and another percentage of those households to be in a lower income range, the analysis will have lost substantial meaning to planning and design strategies if it remains in numerical tabulations and not placed in spatial relationships. Using block and census data, it is possible in many communities to prepare a spatial diagram locating the numerical percentages by block within the community's neighborhoods. This can be used to explore the spatial distribution of those social characteristics. By supplementing the information with field surveys of those blocks, the designer/planner can record physical conditions of structures, support facilities within the neighborhood, and other spatial features to articulate a more complete picture of context.

Political Patterns and Relationships

Politics is the affairs of people regarding the positions, needs, demands, and requirements of differing individuals and groups within a common or community environment. It is more than participation in government, and is a critical ingredient in the context of human settlements. Political patterns are also lost in the physical analysis of place and context, because planners and designers are unaware of the spatial implications of political positions and agendas. A planning commission that is composed of a homemaker, a merchant, a realtor, a design professional, and a builder has an array of spatial agendas that can be identified in varying degrees of detail. The homemaker may represent a constituency in favor of more neighborhood parks or safer and slower streets. The realtor and builder may support less design guidelines and more density allocations for certain parcels of land. The merchant may want more parking for downtown and no signage control, or at least fewer trees in the sidewalk to block the store signs. All of their agendas have spatial implications and can be spatially diagrammed as parts of the larger picture.

More subtle are the hidden or masked agendas of advocacy groups, elected officials, community councils, or neighborhood activists. A group of residents may be opposed to a park plan as being too costly when in fact they may be using a public street end as their own park and do not want it made public, taking it out of their control and domain. Agendas are not always obvious and identifiable, yet many can be identified and at least noted spatially for an in-house assessment of decision-making strategies and alliances that relates directly to the implementation success of a project.

Context and Opportunities

Built patterns are expressed in two-dimensional semi-abstract visualizations such as solid-void diagrams, detailed footprint plan diagrams including roof ground details, two-dimensional semi-abstract diagrams that generalize reference and orientation forms and highlight key or critical forms and relationships, and three-dimensional eye-level and aerial oblique drawings. A key word is *patterns*: the recurring or pronounced relationship between or among forms as shapes. The built pattern is both a record of achieved and emerging spatial realities and of pre-emergent and changing reality tendencies, essentially occuring at the same time. The built pattern has a number of key dimensions that contribute to its contextual qualities:

- environmentally reactive—its material components react to the conditions of temperature, humidity, wind, etc. and change in accordance with the level of reaction;

- time determinate—time is the dimension that controls the period of change;

- culturally sensitive—it is manipulated by occupying cultures in different ways, changing its characteristics and overall pattern; and

- duality of message—it is a construct that represents the outcome of a historic process of decisions and crafting, and it is a real physical condition that is part of an on-going definition of context and alters that definition as it continues to change according to the other factors of built pattern.

Solid-void diagrams provide a fundamental beginning for built pattern analysis as a measure of land coverage and intensity. It is the beginning of the process, not the end product. They set the reference of scale, settlement configuration, and density/intensity of building footprints in a horizontal plane. Combined with natural systems diagrams and three-dimensional drawings, they delineate the spatial conditions of settlement, suitable as a base for the additional overlays of time, culture, and environment as modifying elements to built pattern.

Shelton Base is a detailed footprint outline diagram that records the built pattern and serves as the base for overlay information. **Shelton Built Form** dra-

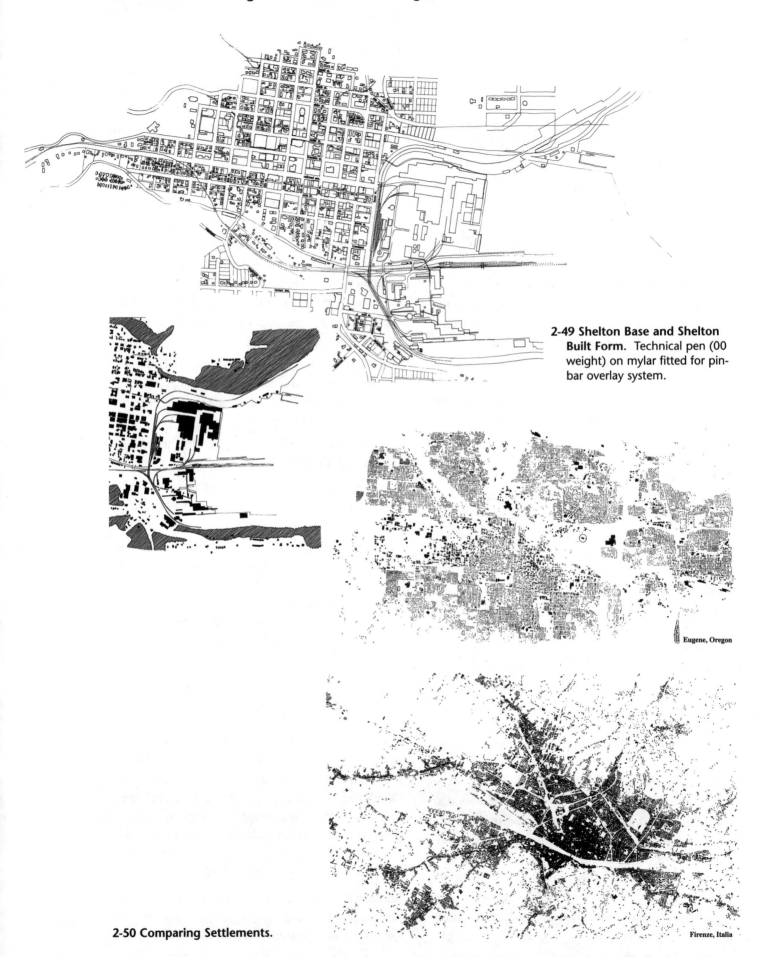

2-49 Shelton Base and Shelton Built Form. Technical pen (00 weight) on mylar fitted for pin-bar overlay system.

Eugene, Oregon

2-50 Comparing Settlements.

Firenze, Italia

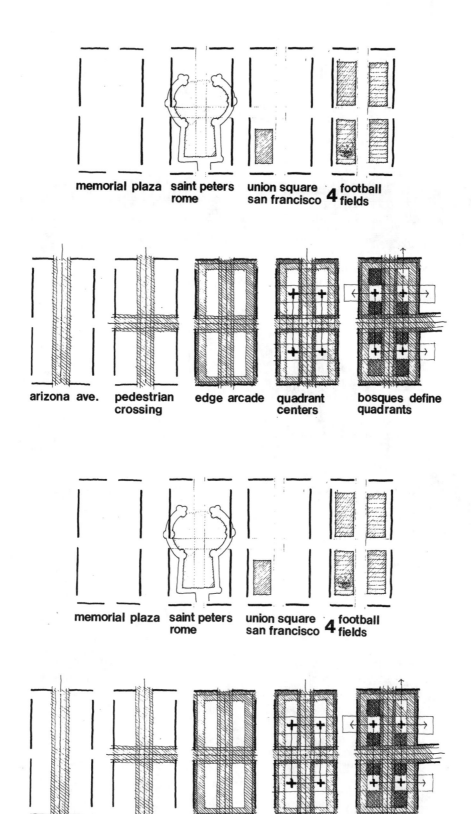

2-51 Understanding Study Site Size. The scale and size of large study sites are often misunderstood or difficult to comprehend. The diagrams compare Memorial Plaza, a proposed town center in Chandler, Arizona, to known urban public spaces and to four football fields. Plan diagrams sequentially break down the size of the site into its more understandable parts.

2-52 City Entry Sequence. The sequence of drawings describes the entry experience into the city: passing across open marsh land, along a bluff cut enclosure, and into the historic city itself.

2-53 Historical Mainstreet Building Enclosure.

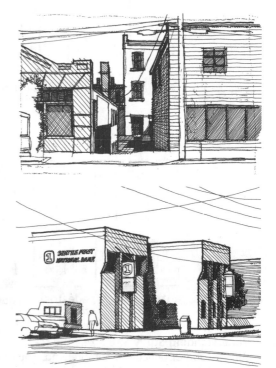

2-54 Historical Building Characteristics and Contemporary Interventions.

2-55 Historical View Characteristics.

matizes the intensity of the built pattern and communicates the structure and organization of the downtown and waterfront mill without any text backup, a semi-abstract expression of human manipulation to the environment.

Comparative Settlement Visualizations

Comparing settlements from different times and places at the same scale puts their sizes and densities in a new light. In this example, two river valley cities from different times and places; Eugene, Oregon and Florence, Italy, occupy approximately the same amount of land. The visual comparison of their built patterns at the same 1:100,000 scale gives a startling contrast of density that numbers would fail to do. Perspective sketches provide a pedestrian's eye view of the three-dimensional characteristics of buildings and the spaces between, as in **City Entry Sequence** and **Main St. Historic Enclosure.** Due to the his-

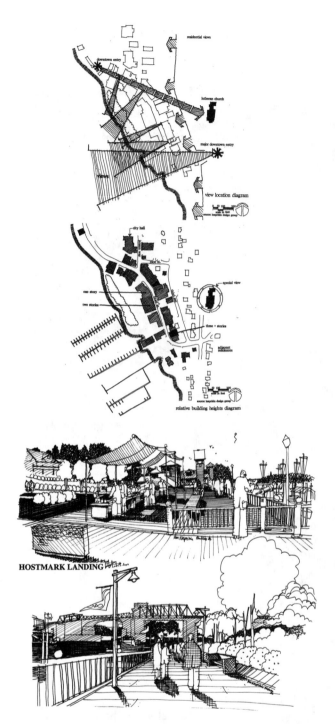

HOSTMARK LANDING

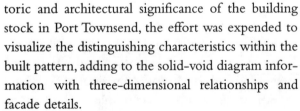

VIEW EAST OF RIVERWALK I

2-56,57,58 Waterfront Viewpoints.

toric and architectural significance of the building stock in Port Townsend, the effort was expended to visualize the distinguishing characteristics within the built pattern, adding to the solid-void diagram information with three-dimensional relationships and facade details.

Aerial axonometric sketches constructed from two-dimensional base maps visualize block patterns with enough architectural detail to articulate design character and historical significance. These drawings are used again in visualizing opportunities and impacts for public review, providing a reference and orientation for the viewer with existing built pattern in three dimensions.

Other examples of built pattern details are shown in **Historical Building Characteristics,** where architectural style, scale, setbacks, and historic precedents can add to the context description. In all of these drawings, edge contrast using darker values with the technical pens, and hatching for window areas provides a contrast designed to highlight detail within the building facades.

Scenic and Visual Characteristics

Scenic and visual characteristics are a part of built pattern, but are also an expression of the relationship between built pattern and the surrounding context. Built pattern can sometimes be a part of the scenic

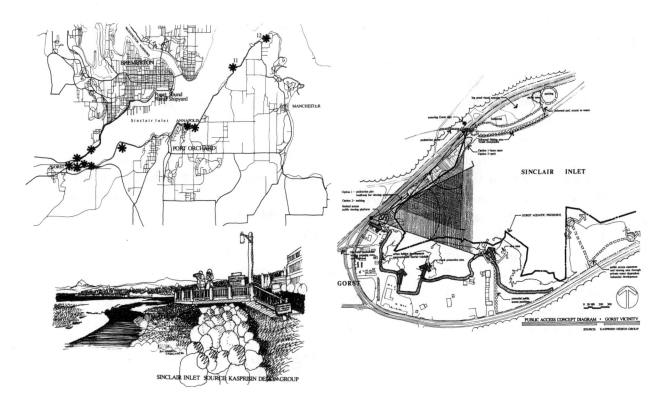

2-59 Gorst Policy Diagram. Policy is both tested and communicated when visually articulated. Policies can be semi-abstracted within a spatial setting, distinguishing them from "design" schemes where form is a necessary component. Policy, as action statements, may mean more to the general public when people can visualize where, to what extent, and by whom an action is to take place.

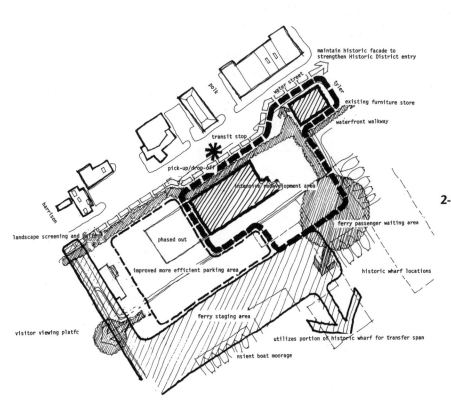

2-60 Port Townsend Ferry. The design of this site was the responsibility of private owners; however, community policy as it related to transit access, bike access, ferry dock configurations, and waterfront access all are possible to designate in a policy visualization without offending private owners with illustrative site plans. A policy diagram states intent in a less intimidating manner than design drawings.

character, viewed as a frame for scenic character, as in **Waterfront Viewpoints.** Views such as **View Characteristics** are connections that represent important windows for a settlement to the larger context. Such important relationships are worth protecting. Visualizing historic building architectural patterns is also a way to communicate the physical attributes felt positively by the public, but difficult for them to put into words. These drawings can be used to develop and support written design guidelines.

City entries are often the subject for improvement in downtown redevelopment projects. Key landmark buildings or built form/patterns can become centerpieces in redesign efforts, based on an understanding of the characteristics of the built pattern. In **Waterfront Viewpoints**, the three sketches define the view out in relationship to the point of view, the vantage access areas.

Policy Visualization

Opportunity can become an action statement of officially adopted policy. Lay people who may have difficulty imagining policy statements can be assisted by a complementary drawing that references and orients the text to spatial framework. In **Gorst and Port Townsend Ferry,** drawings locate, place, specify, and highlight accepted actions.

This is a valuable tool for physical planners who do not have design backgrounds. By working through a two-dimensional diagram of land use, transportation, or regulatory policy and guidelines,

the planner can *test* the spatial implications of policy *before* it is adopted, and communicate it in a more accessible manner for the public and private sectors.

Policy visualizations locate and specify activities and *their physical forms* as well as identify the relationships of intensity, density, fit, impact, and others.

The drawing language used in these diagrams is within the capability of most non-design planners. The language is composed of geometric symbols such as circles, triangles, asterisks made from circles, wide and narrow and solid and void lines, radii, arrows (also made from circles), and value—the light to dark relationship among shapes that structures their importance within the communication. It is important to underscore their uses: *testing* and *sharing* (*internal* and *external* communications).

References

Arnheim, Rudolph. 1969. *Visual Thinking.* Berkeley, Los Angeles, London: University of California Press.

Cullen, Gordon. 1961. *Townscape.* New York: Reinhold Publishing Corporation.

Hough, Michael. 1990. *Out of Place.* New Haven & London: Yale University Press.

McHarg, Ian L. 1971. *Design with Nature.* Garden City: Doubleday & Company, Inc.

3 Visualizing Place and Scale: The Scale Ladder

Introduction

Is it feasible to graphically investigate the significant scales for every project? Realistically not, but a reminder that an upward and outward connection is fitting on occasion. In using a scale ladder, the visual focusing from planet scale to room scale reminds the designer/planner that networks of information exist at each scale. This information carries over from scale to scale, and the designer/planner needs to decide what the form implications are of the next added level of information. The scale sequence visualizes the following increments: a continent within a planet, a bio-region within a continent, eco-regions within a bio-region, settlement within an eco-region, a district within settlement, buildings within a district, and finally, a room within a building. The

bio-region to local context drawings establish reference and orientation, the range and extent of information. During the design process, each step along the scale ladder contributes information that must be edited and incorporated into the next step.

The Scale Ladder

The Bio-region Map; Eco-regions Within the Bio-region

A workable starting point for understanding the larger context is the bio-regional scale. Bio-regions comprised of numerous eco-regions have been identified for the North American continent and are

3-1 Scale Ladder.

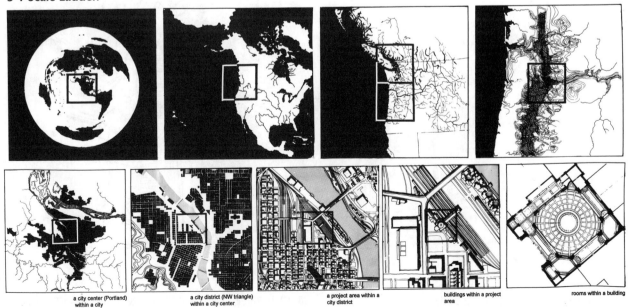

a city center (Portland) within a city   a city district (NW triangle) within a city center   a project area within a city district   buildings within a project area   rooms within a building

87

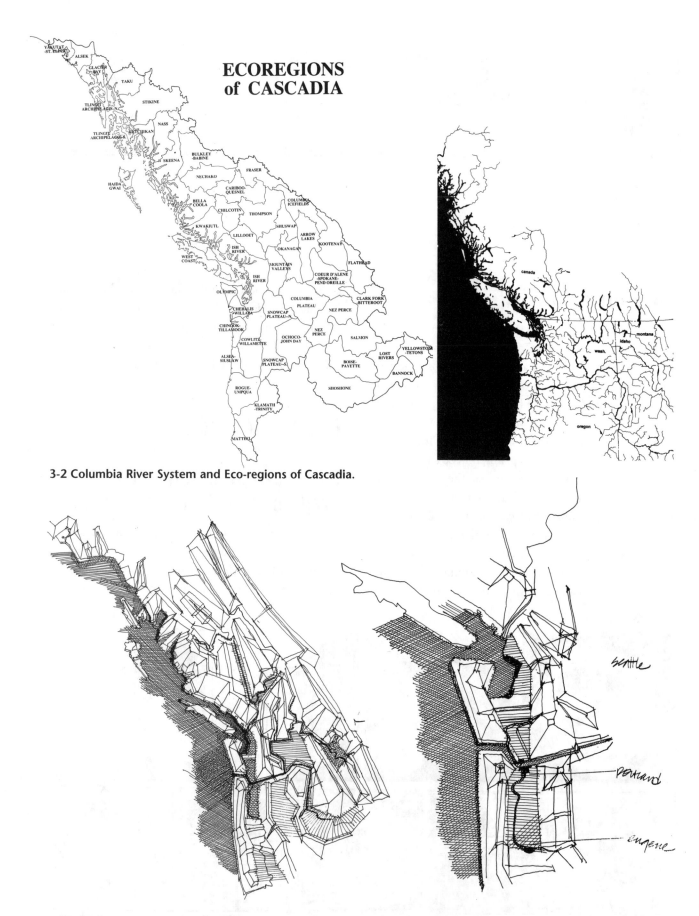

ECOREGIONS of CASCADIA

3-2 Columbia River System and Eco-regions of Cascadia.

3-3 "Eco-region Rooms" of Cascadia.

3-4 Ish River/Cowlitz-Willamette Eco-region Rooms.

available in the geography sections of most libraries. The bio-region called Cascadia[1] extends from northern California to central Alaska and is bordered on the east by the Rocky Mountains and the west by the Pacific Ocean. Eco-regions represent "spatial places" that act as containers for geological forces, organic systems, and human settlement patterns. The isometric sketches of Cascadia "architecturalize" the complex plan topography of the bio-region into its basic spatial form. Individual eco-regions are organized as watersheds, each with a primary river system that drains into the Pacific Ocean. The plan emphasizes the Columbia River and its network of tributaries as organizing most of the settlement in the southern half of Cascadia and the isometric diagram takes this organization a step further by visualizing eco-regions as a series of immense outdoor rooms drained and connected by the Columbia system. By virtue of their different locations within Cascadia, each eco-region has a unique structure and character that must be recognized and brought down the scale ladder to the project site. The Ish River and Cowlitz-Willamette eco-regions, the scene for most growth and settlement, are more closely examined in the same isometric view.

The Eco-region Perspective Diagram: The Willamette Valley

Putting the eco-region into perspective with a bit of artistic license creates a dynamic visual tool for comprehending its spatial energy and sense of place. The aerial perspective visualizes the south chamber of the Cowlitz-Willamette eco-region as one of the many "rooms" that is physically defined by the topography of the larger bio-region called Cascadia. The drawing places highest value on those edges defining the eco-region room: the walls of the Coastal and Cascade mountain ranges and the floor of the Willamette Valley. The next emphasis is given to the natural and built networks: watercourses, roads, and railroads that crisscross the valley floor. The eco-region, essentially

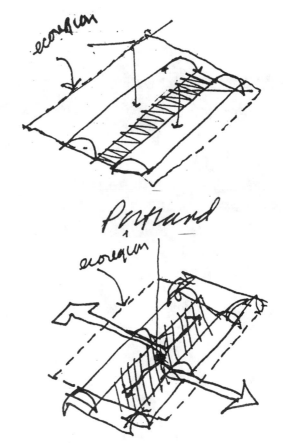

3-5 Eco-region Boundaries.

a watershed drained by the Willamette River as it passes through its center, sets the scene for a network of settlements, each of which can be understood as a unique place within the network. The settlement of Eugene, Oregon, in the foreground of the drawing, is seen in detail. Other settlements far off in the perspective view are drawn as generalized shapes.

Technique/Approach

Looking down the scale ladder, the eco-region can be seen as a large place containing many smaller places. Looking up the scale ladder, the structure of any single settlement can be visualized as extending into the eco-region. The latter approach was taken in this drawing. The perspective structure of the entire Willamette eco-region was built up from a single settlement grid. From a perspective structure of the city grid of Eugene, Oregon, a much larger perspective grid at the eco-region scale was established and information was added:

---

[1] The Cascadia Bio-region designations were developed in part by David McCloskey at Seattle University, founder and director of the Cascadia Institute

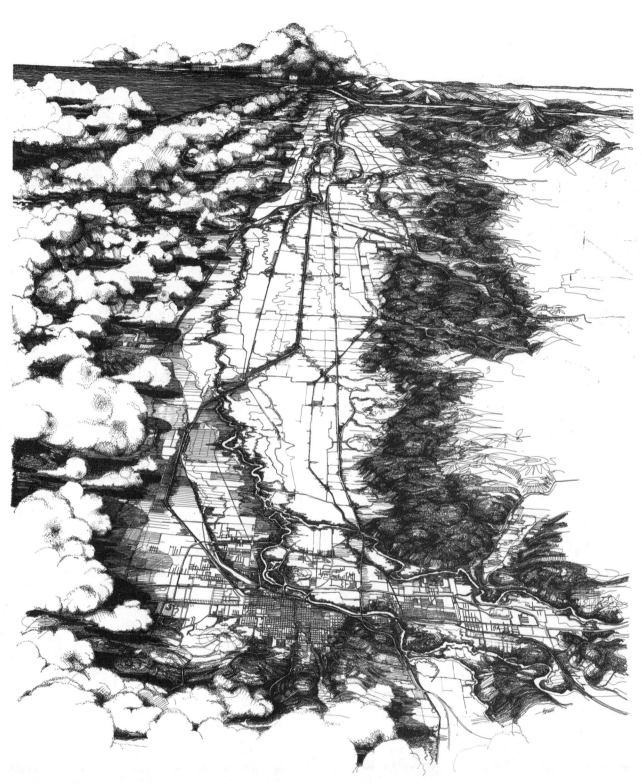

3-6 Willamette Valley, Cowlitz-Willamette Eco-region. The aerial view looks due north up the south chamber of the Cowlitz-Willamette eco-region, one of the many immense "rooms" that sets the scene for historic settlement and new growth. The visualization highlights those aspects of the landscape that define the topographic boundary of the room: the parallel Coastal and Cascade Mountains ranges forming the east and west edges; the valley floor; the boundary of the Columbia River along the background's horizon line; and the foreground's south foothills of Eugene, Oregon. The weather is characterized by the prevailing wind that blows off the Pacific Ocean and piles up against the lower slopes of the mountain ranges.

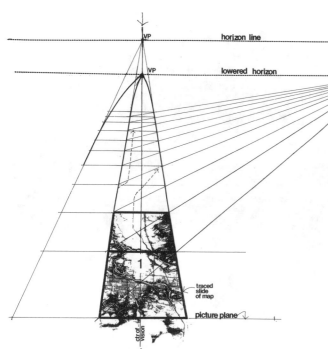

3-7 Perspective Structure of the Eco-region. The Earth's surface is gridded out with two vanishing points found from a photographic slide of a single USGS map.

3-8 Map Quadrant From Photographic Slide.

- The settlement pattern of Eugene, lying along the south edge of the eco-region room, was traced from a slide of an USGS map in a square format;

- From the square in perspective, two vanishing points were found to create the entire perspective framework of squares vanishing toward the horizon line. One of these points was found by extending the parallel vertical edges of the square until they met at the horizon line. The other vanishing point was found by connecting the opposite corners of the square traced in perspective and extending that 45-degree line until it also met the same horizon line; and

- The horizon line was lowered in the upper quarter of the drawing to control the size of the drawing and to accurately focus on the settlement pattern in the foreground. The two vanishing points, located along the new horizon line, were used to create a progression of squares vanishing into infinity. The upper squares of the perspective are distorted where the horizon line is lowered and the surface of the earth's curvature is exaggerated. Information within all diminishing squares in perspective was approximated from USGS plans of the eco-region. The farther away the square, the less detailed the information.

Settlement Within the Eco-region: Eugene, Oregon

The understanding of a settlement pattern as an integral piece of the eco-region can be a clue in carrying information from the bio-region and eco-region scales down through the settlement and study site scales. What does this mean for the designer? In this example, the larger forces that have the settlement form—the river and the topographic container—are both a constraint and an asset. The original settlers explicitly laid out the city's main axis, Willamette Street, north—south between major landmarks that referenced the settlement to its site. These landmarks are a butte in the foothills forming the edge of the eco-region and another butte along the river's edge at the first point of settlement. The sequence of perspective drawings build up value along the resulting city grid composition within the landscape. The edges and interfaces of natural and built systems, rivers, roads, railroads, streets, and topographic boundaries receive the darkest shades. The defining edges of Main street connecting the two buttes receive the strongest value, arterial streets connecting

3-9 Settlement Within the Eco-region: Eugene, Oregon.

other parts of the city receive the next, and local streets the last. The surface areas created by the edges—city blocks and landscaped areas—receive little to no value.

A Line of Settlement Within An Eco-region: Willamette Pass

The drawing of Willamette Pass describes one of the entrances into the Cowlitz-Willamette eco-region room. Here, a place is created by passage through a topographic edge of the eco-region. The overall form of passage is determined by the mountain topography constraints, and the resulting drawing composition reflects their interaction with the transportation lines that weave themselves into the great topographic barrier they must cross. The energy of the passage connecting the high desert plateau on the east side to the lower Willamette Valley on the west side of the mountain creates a place at the eco-region scale and orders a line of sparse settlement at the town scale.

Technique

The aerial perspective was created in two steps with the help of a slide of a USGS map. The first was a diagrammatic tracing that reduced complex photographic information into a few essential lines. This

drawing served as a plan for a more finished rendering of the same view:

- The diagrammatic drawing represents information edited from the slide of the Willamette Pass area map. Several slides were taken of the map lying on the ground from different angles and heights. This view was chosen to best represent the settlement line passing through the mountain topography;

- General topographic features in the photograph were traced, not every peak, mountain, and tree. Key shadowed surfaces and the main mountain peaks were cross hatched. The most important element in the tracing is the lines of Highway 58 and the Southern Pacific Railroad;

- The structure of the mountains themselves is not the focus of the drawing, but rather the continual edge that is created by the parallel lines of road and railroad cutting through the thick forest and dramatic topography. This linear system becomes the rendering spine of the drawing with greatest value along the edges of the system gradually dissipating up the mountain slopes. The transportation spine organizes a series of settlements along its length, each with a common and unique relationship to the lines;

- The second drawing, a more detailed rendering, was developed over the first. Rough topograph-

3-10 A,B,C Settlement Pattern Value. The series of the same view sequentially builds up a hierarchy of drawing value along the city of Eugene's settlement network.

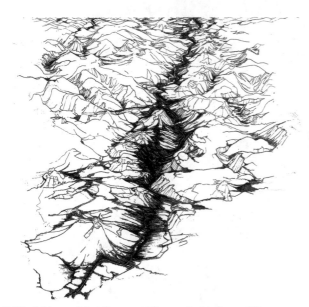

3-11 A Line of Settlement Through An Eco-region Edge.

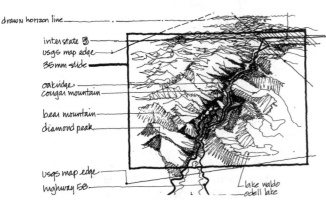

3-12 Perspective Sketch Layout from Map Photography.

ic edges are turned into treed edges and shadowed areas are given a dark value. Large treed surfaces are done with a continuous scribbling stroke, individual trees are not drawn. The heaviest line weight, a thick solid dark edge, is placed along the passage of the road and railroad lines.

Small Town Settlements Within the Eco-region: Introduction

Along the scale ladder, it is possible to visualize the size of the small town as an entire structure within the landscape. Such drawings reveal constraints, connections, and opportunities. The aerial views of towns within Cascadia are composed to understand fundamental relationships between the built and natural patterns. These drawings focus on the juxtaposition of the settlement patterns with the natural forces that are responsible for emphasizing form and a unique sense of place. When visualized in this spirit, even the smallest project within a town can be a catalyst that connects and influences future events.

Coquille, Oregon

In this aerial perspective of the small town of Coquille, Oregon near the Oregon coast, city form is clearly seen in relation to a set of surrounding natural forces. The town lies on the edge of the Rogue-Umpqua eco-region within Cascadia, a place defined

3-13 Small Town Settlement Within the Eco-region. It is possible to visually comprehend a small town settlement structure as a whole within its landscape. The aerial perspective was conceived as a built pattern that developed along a natural network. One diagram isolates the built pattern; the other, the existing natural pattern. The final drawing puts the two together by using line weight to focus on the important boundaries and edges that knit the two systems together. The axonometric drawing explores a river edge parkway proposal along the city/water interface. Drawing value emphasizes the energy of the water edge and its penetration into the historic city center via proposed park blocks.

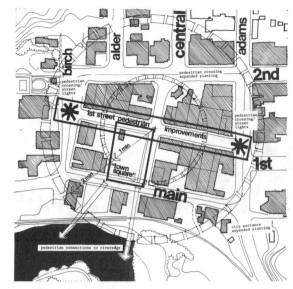

3-14 Downtown Walking Times.

by the coastal range on the east and opening into a vast wetland plain stretching to the Pacific Ocean. The Coquille River, a watercourse originating in the higher elevations of the interior coastal mountains, organizes the town's form as it winds through the flood plain on its way to the Pacific Ocean.

Visual Connections/Process

The diagrams overlay the formal city grid structure over the natural course of the river, flood plain, and forest edge. The interplay of natural and man-made events begins to identify opportunities regarding the city and river. These opportunities are expanded upon in another axonometric diagram that focuses on the city center where the community touches an important bend in the river. Value is given to the river's surface, its edge, and a proposed pedestrian park connecting the city to the river. Time/Distance relationships are portrayed in the plan diagram by overlaying a two- and a one-minute walk radius over the downtown. Within the diagram, improvement

areas are blocked out to address the repair of First Street and the void left by the city's main hotel. Other perspective views compare improvements to existing views at the key entrance and downtown street locations. These smaller and seemingly isolated improvements take on meaning when viewed as part of a larger downtown place with clear boundaries, entrances, and a relationship to its natural setting.

Caldwell, Idaho

Stepping back to visualize the whole can profoundly reshape an approach to the more immediate problem. The aerial perspective, done during an AIA R/UDAT[2] visit to Caldwell, Idaho, composes the city within the built and natural networks that have connected the city over time to its region. Some citizens of Caldwell, assembled to discuss various downtown improvements, were shocked when they first saw the downtown from above. The aerial diagram visualizes the downtown as a large void filled with scattered remnants of historic building structure. The visualization emphasizes the void by placing value on the treed neighborhood edge that completely surrounds the city's historic center. Seen in this light, the importance of rebuilding and reestablishing the downtown as a place becomes more urgent, and smaller, individual improvements become connected.

Visualizing Project Sites Within the Settlement

Smaller, project improvements occurring over time take on greater meaning when seen as part of a larger network. This diagram abstracts the same aerial view of Caldwell into an urban design framework for city improvements that include: protection of historic building groups in the downtown, a potential role for an existing canal watercourse through the city center, and a program of street trees to mark boulevards and pedestrian connections between the downtown and its adjacent neighborhoods. The drawing gives the darkest values to the important arterial streets, city entrances, and the hidden river-

2 Caldwell Renaissance, National AIA R/UDAT, Caldwell, Idaho, 1992.

3-15 City Entrance Improvements.

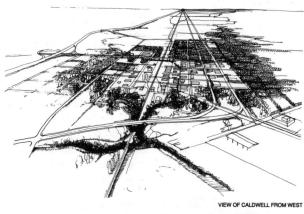

VIEW OF CALDWELL FROM WEST

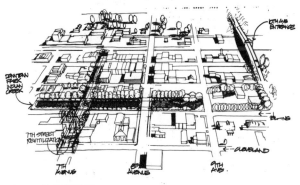

3-16 Town Networks: Caldwell, Idaho. The more literal perspective of treed residential and downtown areas is turned into a diagram highlighting town networks.

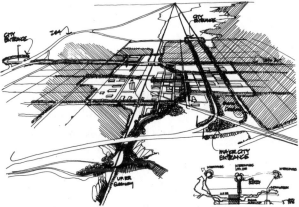

POTENTIAL DOWNTOWN PROJECTS

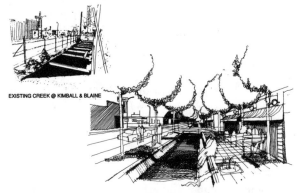

EXISTING CREEK @ KIMBALL & BLAINE

3-17 Downtown Improvements Within City Network.

course. This visualization is an outline, a brushstroke describing basic relationships formed by Caldwell and the specific geography it occupies. The small perspectives describe potential improvements at key points within the outline.

Metro Settlements and Their Districts Within an Eco-region

Contemporary metropolitan areas are made up of several co-existing settlement types. An historical city center is surrounded by older neighborhoods and suburbs. New suburban development in peripheral areas is related to an expanded freeway system and rings of smaller towns that have become part of the metro region. It is more difficult to visualize a metro area as a unit than it is, for example, a small town. Yet the metro area is the scene of most of the action, and visualizing the implications of growth and the use of land must be carried down the scale ladder into any specific project site.

Seattle

The visualization of the Seattle metro area focuses on the imposition of an ordered grid over an irregular and complex natural form. The aerial perspective of the Seattle/Tacoma metro area looks over the city of Seattle, due south down the length of the Ish ecoregion. This metro area is cradled within the narrow east/west boundaries of the ecoregion; the Puget Sound on the west and the Cascade Mountain range on the east. The drawing places value on the grid system and the edges of the irregular land/water boundary that divides the city network into a series of discernible places at the district scale. A magnification of a part of the metro aerial reveals the restructuring of a city district.

Districts Within Settlement, Introduction

As settlement grows out of eco-region networks, districts within settlements—be they special areas within small towns or larger districts within cities—grow out of their corresponding settlement networks. Districts perceived as places have recognizable characteristics that are different from their surrounding

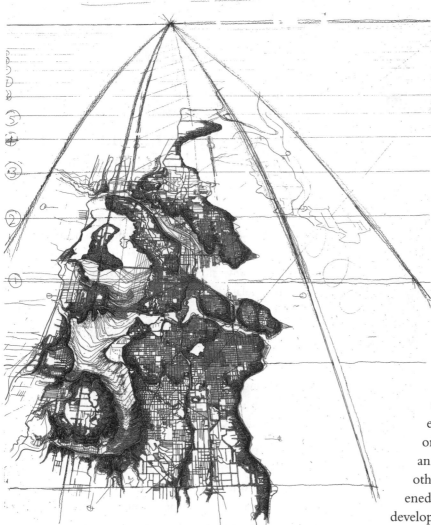

3-18 Metro Settlement Within An Eco-region, Seattle. The aerial perspective over Seattle looks due south down the length of Puget Sound. The metro area is cradled within the narrow east/west boundaries of the eco-region; the Puget Sound on the west and the Cascade Mountains on the east. The drawing places value on the grid pattern and its interplay with the irregular land/water boundary.

vary. Inter-city districts exhibit more density and complexity developed over time, while suburban districts are less dense and have an identity tied more to the landscape than the cityscape. In some examples, district identity is unclear or has been lost over time, affording an opportunity for rebuilding. In other cases, district identity is threatened or can be enhanced by large scale development proposals. In the last example, new building opportunity at the project site scale is connected to the making of an emerging city district.

The Seattle Commons is a light industrial/general commercial area north of downtown Seattle between it and Lake Union, a fresh water lake connecting Lake Washington to Puget Sound. Proposals for a 90-plus acre "Central Park West"[3] have focused attention on the area for redevelopment as a new urban village structured by a green connection between downtown and the lake. Numerous studies both pro and con have been generated that seek to define the change and pressure surrounding the existing Cascade neighborhood. Aerial oblique drawings can relate overall concepts of built form

neighbors. The boundaries can be clearly physical, like the edge of a road or river, or they can take on more subtle forms, like a change in use or the age of an area. When drawings isolate study sites from their district networks, project sites become an end unto themselves, cut off from the very information that can make a project unique. When study sites are visualized as specialized parts of a larger system, the nature of their role or potential role within that system become more clear and built form possibilities are increased rather than reduced. The visualizations of the following district examples focus on the carryover of information at the district scale into the project site scale. Each project site is visualized as a catalyst, but only within a larger system. The districts

---

[3] The *Seattle Commons* and *Pier 91* projects were one week design projects, a part of an annual spring charrette sponsored by the University of Washington Department of Architecture in association with public and private sponsors and endorsements, providing the larger community with a focused and energetic exploration of vital issues.

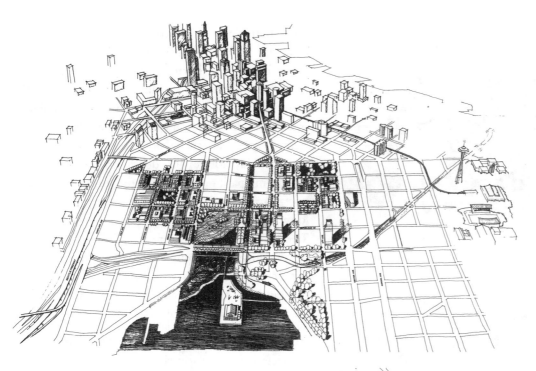

3-19,20 Seattle Commons New City District/Neighborhood. The Seattle Commons is a privately financed effort to redevelop a district of Seattle between the northern edge of the downtown business district and the southern edge of Lake Union. It is a problem of scales within scales, where the initial private proposal contained a 90-acre-plus urban park designed to be the backbone of new neighborhoods within the district. Opposition groups and alternative schemes of less grandeur such as the one depicted here suggested smaller scale "hamlet" parks and open space for direct use and access of sub-neighborhood areas, avoiding the large scale city-beautiful approach. Analysis of this proposal requires a constant changing of scale-perspective in order to avoid over-scaling and de-humanizing the area with monumental projects.

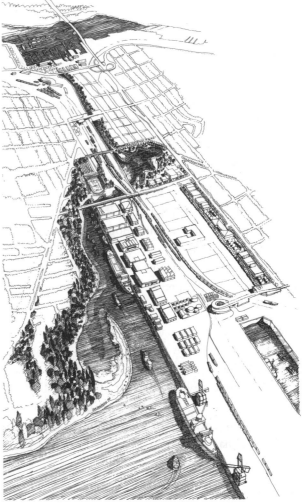

3-21 Pier 91. The Interbay area of Seattle, an industrial-port area on a former wetland between two Seattle neighborhoods.

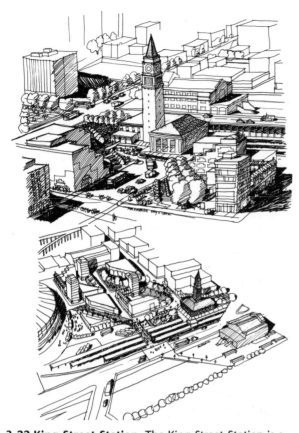

3-22 King Street Station. The King Street Station is a sub-district of the historic Pioneer Square located between the KingDome Stadium and the Amtrak rail station. The sketches are fast and loose representations of concepts previously developed for a high-density new neighborhood. The sketches were drawn with a Pentel Sign pen, copied and colored with pencil for meetings.

without the block by block detail. This example counters the large contiguous park proposal with a more defensible and neighborhood oriented clustering of smaller parks.

The drawing highlights the small parks and their pedestrian oriented greenstreet connections, leaving other details to larger scale drawings.

Pier 91 is an aerial oblique that focuses on a valley between two Seattle neighborhoods. Redevelopment of the port facilities at the waterfront was placed in context with a drawing of the Interbay district. This drawing illustrates the industrial valley, restored spit and wetlands within expanded port facilities all flanked by two established Seattle neighborhoods.

The King Street Station moves another notch down the scale ladder to a project area scale: the area around the southern edge of the Kingdome (Seahawks, Mariners Stadium) between it and the former King Street railroad station, now being developed as a transportation center. Aerial obliques were again used to articulate previously stated concepts and policies for in-fill development within the Kingdome parking lot and relating to the new transportation center. The drawings needed to be fast and loose, drawn with a Pentel Sign pen on tracing paper. The base perspectives were traced from slides. After the drawings were completed and mounted on foam core, color pencil was added for a final public presentation. Multiple views were drawn quickly to provide a variety of viewpoints.

Portland Eastside Industrial District

Districts at the historic city center contain the most layers of built development with the least apparent traces of the original natural site. The diagrams trace the development of the Central Eastside District in Portland, Oregon over the century; first as an independent city across from Portland proper, served by the Willamette River, then as a growing industrial center served by the railroad, and finally as a contemporary industrial district served by the freeway. Historically, the inter-city industrial district was a vital part of American cities, a center of production supporting adjacent working neighborhoods. Many industrial districts have been abandoned, some driven out of the cities, destroying a work/life relationship formerly typical of urban life. In this case, by virtue of its strategic riverfront position and adjacency to the downtown, the district has been the subject of several efforts to remove or modify the river edge freeway through the district and dedicate these lands to public use and development. This particular effort, funded by a grant from the National Endowment for the Arts to a coalition of east side neighborhoods, visualizes a scenario called the "21st Century Urban Production District."[4] In this scenario, alternative designs of the district were built in model form to test the possibility of developing the river front as a

[4] Produced by the Department of Architecture, University of Oregon, through a grant from the National Endowment for the Arts to the Southeast. Uplift Neighborhood Program of Portland, Oregon, 1989. Published: The Art of City Design, Notable Projects funded by the NEA, 1990

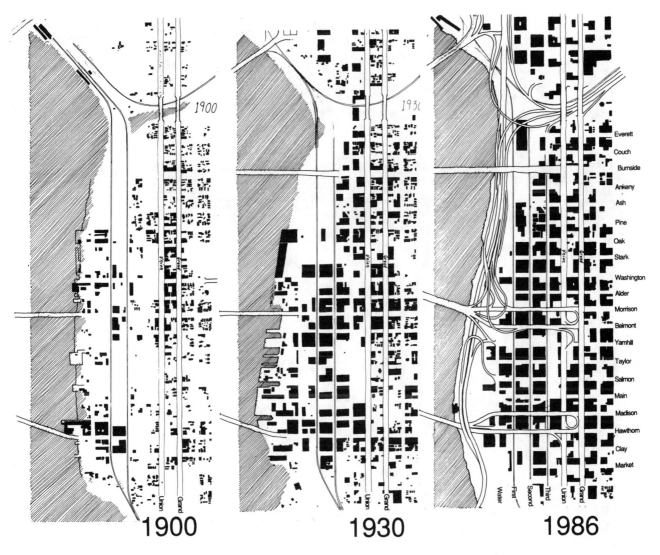

1900   1930   1986

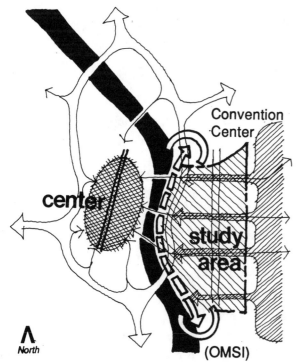

North

3-23 City District Study Area: Portland. The diagram reduces to its basic terms the location of the study district in relation to the city center, the river, east-side neighborhoods, and two major development proposals.

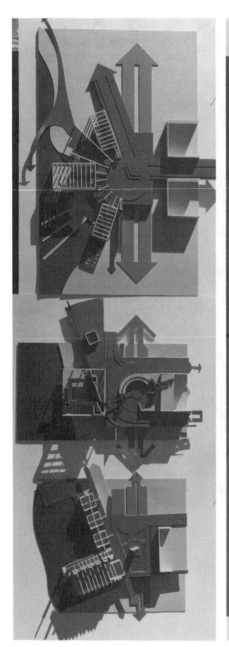

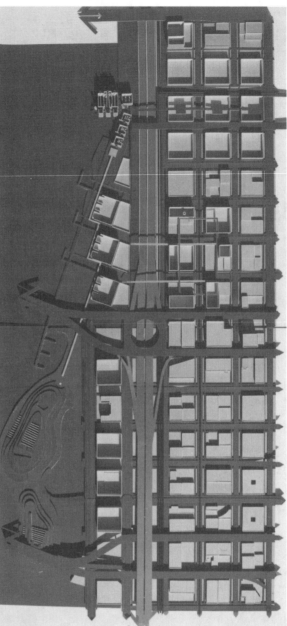

3-24 City District Reorganization Modeling. In this proposed model network, a public river way is visualized as a separate, yet connected system of the working district. Key points of potential development are modeled at a larger scale. Three versions of these models share the same organizational networks of the particular location. Individual students have interpreted the same building program within those networks very differently.

new public amenity with uses that would support the changing role and nature of industry in the 21st Century.

Process/Connection

During the citizen participation process both drawings and models were used to communicate the outcomes of alternative design strategies. Visualizing change through models was chosen because of the complex movement systems, varying uses, pockets of historic buildings, and major building proposals that would reshape the district. Three-dimensional diagrams were more understandable to the layperson and became the focus of public discussions during a

series of citizen workshops and steering committee reviews that culminated in a presentation for a city council vote.

The plan diagram references the study area to the city center and the river and describes a generalized armature of linkages within the district. The shaded area defines the boundary of the study district sandwiched between the river and the adjacent neighborhoods to the east. Arrows through the district describe possible neighborhood accesses through the study site to the river edge. The heavy dotted line along the river's edge denotes an emerging pedestrian path between two major institutions

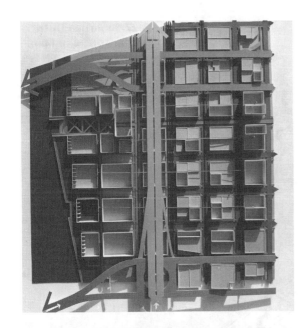

3-25,26 Central Eastside Industrial District, Portland. These model networks explore new block configurations that interface public open space with the workings of distribution and industry. Alternative organizations compose public/pedestrian streets and service and delivery streets in a coordinated way.

that will relocate on the east side, the City's Convention Center and the State Museum of Science and Industry.

The first study model visualizes the organization of the district. First, the existing city grids were cut out of red card stock and placed on a base with the existing river course along the districts' west edge. Second, proposed pedestrian and open space networks were cut out of orange cardstock. As a way of understanding the many freeway relocation schemes, proposals are overlaid over this grid. The color key established in the district base model is carried into subsequent models down the scale ladder.

The last set of models repeats a similar process

along the river edge. Here a proposed public way is visualized as a separate yet connected system of the working district. Key points of potential development in the proposed network are modeled at a larger scale. Three versions of these models share the same framework of connections, but articulate three-dimensional building and open space formations differently.

The last set of models, at the district block scale, explore new block configurations at the interfaces of public open space ways and the workings of distribution and industry. These models begin to develop new internal building/block organizations that are coordinated with both the functions of public pedestrian streets and industries need for service and delivery streets.

Other Districts Within Settlements

Peripheral districts within the metropolitan area are less built-up and many times ambiguous as to their spatial definition and sense of place. The aerial drawing of **Gresham,** Oregon, a suburban district on the

3-28A Suburban District Network: Gresham, Oregon.
The aerial diagram focuses on the existing patterns of large parking areas and scattered building/open patterns.

3-28B Reorganized Suburban District. The second diagram reorganizes the same network with a proposed open system defined as a series of connected places between a light rail station and a shopping center. Drawing value focuses on the surfaces of the open space system and their connections.

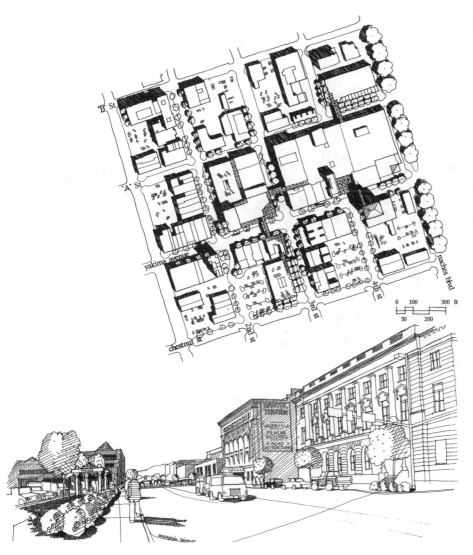

3-29 Yakima Downtown.
Sub-districts and block scales, quickly portrayed with a Pentel Sign pen for public meetings and presentations, are also suitable for final printing.

east edge of Portland, Oregon reveals a structure common to most suburbs: sparse ground settlement, little public open space, and scattered commercial development linked only to large parking areas served by freeways. Remnants of the original landscape, forest lands and watercourses marked by trees, remain here and there. The diagrammatic perspectives of the same aerial reorganize new development and open space in a conscious move to define a clear sense of place connected to the site's original amenities. Proposed development occurs along an open space system connected to a light rail station. The surface and edges of the reorganized open space network is rendered to emphasize linkages between the public open space and new development along its edges.

Yakima Place is a drawing (plan) of the larger business district of the Yakima, Washington downtown area. The building footprint map is a solid-void diagram with potential spatial envelope identified and drawn by felt tip pen illustrative technique. It provides a base for more detailed block design efforts in a quantitative and presentable (public) format.

Buildings Within Districts: Ketchikan Civic Center[5]

New building proposals can either help or hinder district identity as a place. Unless there is a continual reminder of the larger district context during the visualization process, the development of building proposals within the district takes place within a vac-

---

[5] Ketchikan Convention Center, associated with Steve Peters Architects, Ketchikan, Alaska.

3-30 New District Within a City: Ketchikan, Alaska.

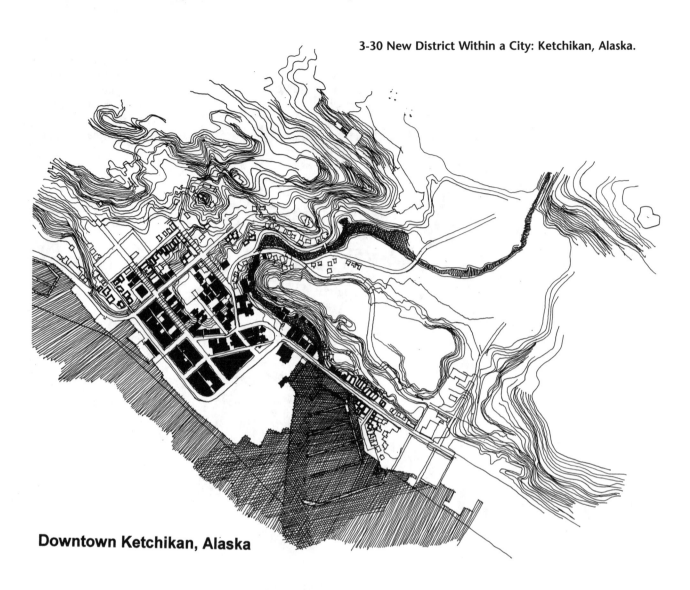

Downtown Ketchikan, Alaska

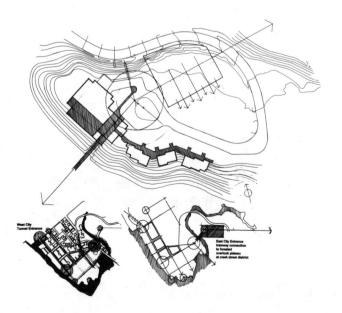

3-31 District Location Diagrams. The diagrams emphasize the connective aspects between the study site and the city. The black water of the first diagram defines the city's boundary, and the shaded circles portray the study site as one of the three key corner districts of the downtown composition. The second diagram places less value on the water and more value on the study site as a direct extension of the city street network. The site diagram begins to interpret the basic forces of the Creek Street District into the making of a building proposal. The funicular connection from the city is taken through the hotel and shifted in a common entrance circle to another site vector oriented to Deer Mountain.

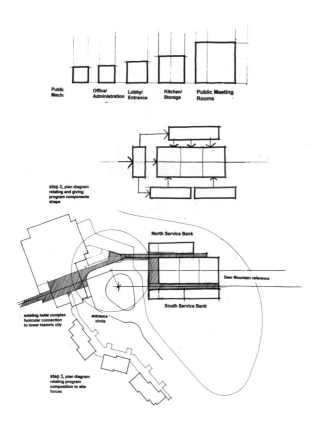

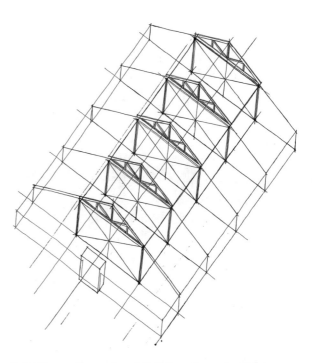

3-32A Building Program "Parts" As Comparative Sizes.

3-32B Plan Diagram Relating and Giving Program "Parts" Shape.

3-32C Preliminary Building Organization Connected to Site Forces.

3-34 Three-dimensional Building Organization: Ketchikan Civic Center. In the context of a local building culture, an axonometric view transforms traditional wood, post, and beam systems into a more complex, but repetitive structural organization; pitched triangles are incorporated into the truss system connecting each interior room with the Deer Mountain reference.

3-33 Finalized Plan Organization.

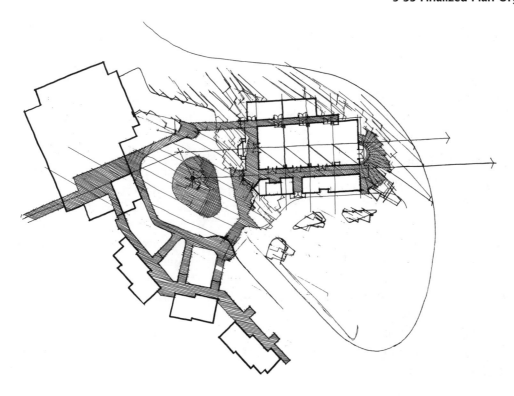

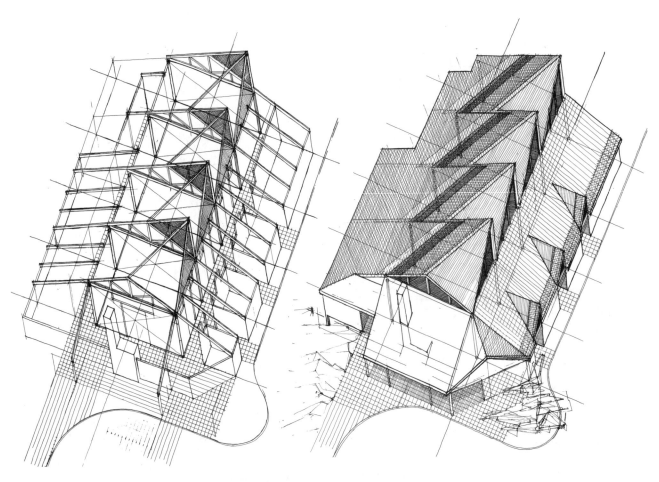

3-35 Three-dimensional Building Covering, Ketchikan Convention Center. The decorative skin of the building is connected to its structure and reflects the interior space pattern. The vast roof structure, sheltering lower interior rooms, reflects a similar response by native building to local weather and climate.

uum. District identity may be firmly or partially established, or it may not exist at all. In this example in Ketchikan, Alaska a convention center is proposed in a woodland plateau overlooking the city. A recently constructed hotel complex, with a pedestrian funicular connecting it to the lower city level, is the first building in the area.

Composing a Building Program in Three-dimensional Space

The typical design process is severely skewed because of our inabilities to quickly visualize space in three dimensions. It is convenient to deal with design concepts two-dimensionally throughout the design process, sometimes in great detail, without a clue as to a proposal's three-dimensional organization. Typically, the three-dimensional reality of space is only engaged as a last step, sometimes never at all. Visually concentrating on two-dimensional relationships during the design process severely limits the designer,

and forces him or her to depend solely upon the manipulation of a two-dimensional plan, sometimes creating awkward and arbitrary shapes that do not respond to building program. Early in the design process, visualizing building programs can be shaped into preliminary three-dimensional concepts connected to the site forces of a particular place.

In the first step, the programmatic components of the Convention Center, a multi-use meeting space, lobby/entrance, kitchen storage and rest rooms/mechanical are described in typical plan diagrams that quantify two-dimensional programmatic requirements, isolated from external site forces.

In a second step, the plan diagrams relate programmatic components, giving the entire composition a preliminary shape and direction related to a site force.

In a third step, the composition is integrated with organizational principles identified in previous diagrams as the city scale: the connection to the city

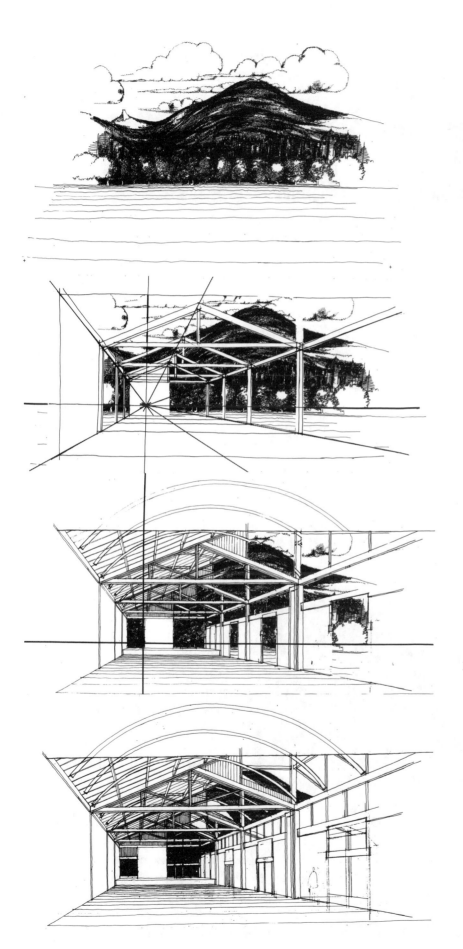

3-36A,B,C Visualizing A Room By Subtracting the Exterior Context. The one-point perspective portrays interior room design along the Deer Mountain axis. Deer Mountain is a reference for not only the city, but the district, the building, and the rooms within the building. The perspective composition is not only a way to look at the room, but also to explore its design. The mountain's presence is slowly subtracted until it is substantially, but never completely, replaced by the needs of shelter and building cover.

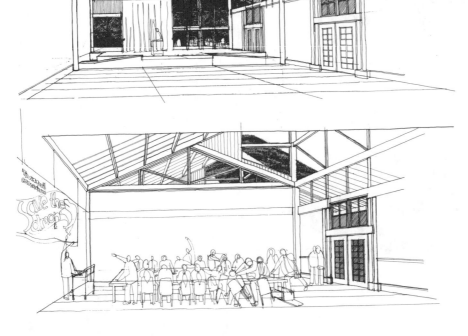

3-38 Civic Center Exterior Building Form.

spatial sequence along the axis of Deer Mountain. Implied in the three-dimensional diagram is a structural organization. The final three dimensional organization is a series of pitched forms, reflecting each public room, open to the south, referenced to the view of Deer Mountain, and connected along a pedestrian access to the city.

Rooms Within Building Form

The making of a room at the bottom—or "top," depending on how you view it—of the scale ladder, is the most immediate act of place-making. Visualizing rooms in two-dimensional plan views limits the understanding of their potential character and connection to other parts of the building and site. A room in one place may be very different than the same room in another place.

via the hotel tramway and the axis aligned with Deer Mountain. Drawing value emphasizes network connections with heavy shade and line weight outlining the programmatic blocks within that network.

In the final fourth step, the axonometric composes the programmatic parts, meeting rooms served by adjacent service spaces, into a three-dimensional

4 Place and Time, Place in Time

Introduction

Time is the vehicle of measurement for change in formative processes. In assessing human settlements, change can be viewed as a constant, occurring in periods or rhythms differentiated as distinct and emerging realities (Johnston, 1989) that, when perceived, are already changing into other and different realities. Planners and designers can miss opportunity and information if they view "place" as a finished product, without the dimension of time as a measure (and determinant) of change. Place can become an isolated piece of the built pattern, an artifact out of context and disconnected from the other realities of human settlement patterns if time is not recognized as a patterning force, something that represents the changes in a specific rhythm resulting from climatic forces, human impacts and use, and/or material characteristics. This chapter discusses and demonstrates visual assessment methods for exploring the measure of change in spatial patterns, in human settlements and their environmental settings.

Conduct an experiment on the emerging but never static status of place: select a location in a city with a normal amount of human activity, your local coffee house and surrounding shops, including support services and vehicles; from the same location and point of observation, photograph the "place" every other day or once per week for a period of a month; paste the photographs up next to one another and observe the subtle but real changes to that place that occurred over the month. Buildings settle, paint peels, roof lines bend, trees grow or shed, signs

are added or removed, graffiti appears, a fence is constructed around a front yard, a tree is cut, one is planted, an addition appears, an outdoor deck is added to a favorite restaurant. Such constant change can be taken for granted and ignored in the design process. The "place" is the same and different.

Time is the link or connection, the bridge, between differentiated periods of activity in human settlements. It is helpful to designers if viewed as a window on reality that can be constructively shaped and altered. Once made, places inevitably change, with varying degrees of stability relative to human observation and participation.

In conventional planning and design processes, historical and/or architecturally significant buildings and artifacts are a common category for time analysis relative to a given urban design issue, whether regarding a city sector or a building site. What has happened in the past and what remains from past actions are important ingredients in making development decisions which are often overlooked or deemed non-critical to the project's function and cost effectiveness. Recognizing the importance of historical features and actions is, however, only a beginning, a recognition of artifact representing a period or event, something to be incorporated into the form of new designs. If the historic artifact is viewed as a frame in an ongoing and sequential series of emerging realities, it can relate more information than its artifact status implies. Historic information and conditions must be viewed as time-relative statements of relationship (Johnston, 1986).

Time Patterning

Conventional methods used to recognize and assess historic patterns include:

- locating and identifying historic and/or architecturally significant artifacts, buildings, or event places;

- authenticating and registering for purposes of preservation specific historic and/or architectural artifacts and/or sites;

- comparing through juxtaposition the changes in historic building patterns;

- identifying, categorizing, and adapting specific architectural styles and components for incorporation into contemporary designs; and

- using the artifacts and patterns as the foundation for an organizing structure for revitalization.

Identifying historic patterns is not an end in itself but a beginning. It is a connection to a specific period— a length of settlement pattern and a reflection of a complexity of parts that emerged into reality during that period. There may be information in that complexity that has more bearing on a contemporary issue than the artifact the period left behind. *Time patterning* is a process of connecting or linking periods to add dimension to place as a changing chameleon, relatively the same in size and dimension but changing according to the dictates of context. Planners and designers can use time patterning as a learning process, researching historic patterns and the formative processes that created them, and translating and interpreting these patterns through graphic diagramming techniques as a key part of the design process. Some basic principles of time patterning are summarized as follows:

- as in conventional approaches, artifacts and historic locales have *local* value, intrinsic to the artifact and the locale and characterized by its basic elements (dimension, color, style, material, historic function, etc.);

- the value of a historic pattern is dependent on the relationship of one time period to another period, preferably in a three time-period set— value is defined as the precise worth or quality of information represented in the pattern and useable by the designer;

- historic and or architecturally significant buildings, groups of buildings, or event locales are frozen images of past realities now a part of a present reality and possessing a new definition based on their passage from the past to the present; their role in future realities is further altered by the changing definition affected by time by relating the present to its path through time;

- time patterning can assist in determining the "formative dynamic present in a system" (Johnston, 1986) at a given point in time by relating the present to its path through time; and

- time patterns have cultural rythmns within their boundaries, sources of design opportunity and context definition.

Time Patterning as a Function of Place Definition

The following example applications portray a range of techniques from the simple to the complex, and from the abstract image to the real. Their use and value depend on the situation and the level of information desired from the time patterning analysis. They are offered as a beginning exploration into the extensive use of visualization in time patterning, not a final list of techniques.

Semi-abstract Comparative Footprints

A conventional and simple diagram used by many professionals to show time-impact relationships of settlement patterns is the *solid-void footprint*. In **Port Orchard 1914–1982,** same-scale building patterns are represented in blackened building footprints as a comparison of changing building intensity. Two historic images often are insufficient to relay degrees of change and critical periods; three images provide an additional increment of comparison.

In Port Townsend Historic Diagrams, three solid-void footprint images are used to portray time

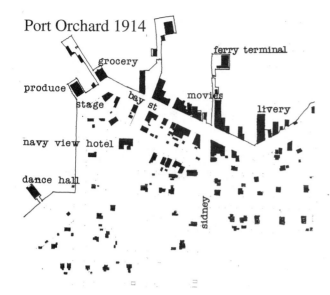

Port Orchard 1914

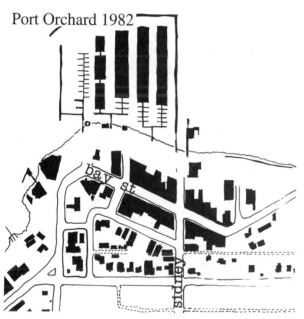

Port Orchard 1982

4-1 Port Orchard 1914–1982.

periods of 1860, 1890, and 1980. Wateredge and other topographical features are included where appropriate (as edges, barriers, etc.). This three-image set illustrates significant changes among the time periods (i.e., the higher building intensity in 1890 compared to 1980).

Juxtapositioning

Port Townsend 1890/1980 is an additional step in time period assessment; the two historic develop-

ment patterns are juxtapositioned to highlight historic elements that were compatible with the contemporary setting. Additionally, the diagram had a political purpose: One faction within the community had proposed a new boardwalk shopping street to be located along and parallel to the downtown shoreline out over the water based on "historic pattern" (a paper street right of way). The juxtapositioned diagram was constructed from research of historic photographs, fire insurance maps, and other historic records. The result demonstrated that in fact no development or street had ever occurred along the waterfront, but did occur as perpendicular wharves that contained housing, hotels, brothels, canneries, and boat repair facilities. These wharves became the focus of additional studies for a proposed ferry terminal site and new waterfront development according to the real historic pattern rather than incomplete information. The diagram was indeed worth a thousand words in a sensitive political climate.

Three-Dimensional Diagrams

Techniques of time-patterning with additional dimensions of information can aid the planner/designer in assembling a detailed assessment of past community actions and their impacts on community form. One method of adding a fourth *dimension* to information is the three-dimensional aerial drawing in a time-sequence format. This approach has value for the planner/designer and the community residents as an awareness building technique, demonstrating graphically the results of direct and indirect public and private actions.

Two graphic techniques of aerial diagrams are the *aerial oblique perspective* and the *aerial axonometric* or *paraline drawing*. The use of one over the other depends in part on the kinds of information available and the preferred degree of realism. For public meetings and awareness, realistic images are often more acceptable than semi-abstract or non-vanishing point type drawings such as axonometrics. Axonometrics are easier to work with when information is limited; they enable the planner/designer to construct a paraline drawing from an appropriately scaled plan with building footprints, aided by photographs (aerial, oblique, or ground level).

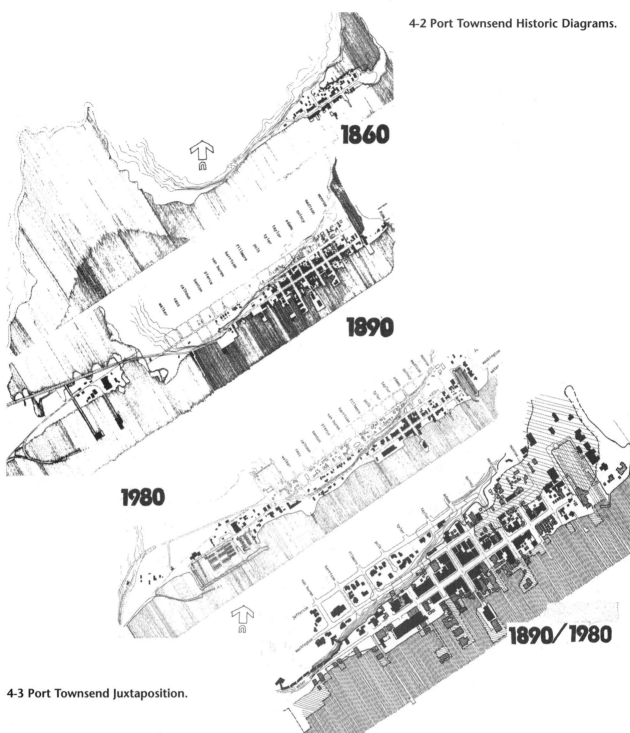

4-2 Port Townsend Historic Diagrams.

1860

1890

1980

1890/1980

4-3 Port Townsend Juxtaposition.

The Wilsonville Story: A Visualized History

The American Institute of Architects published a primer on design for smaller cities and towns entitled *Designing Your Town* (AIA, 1992). The primer's objective is to help local residents and officials get more from the planning and design processes and to assist them in gaining more control over their own design process. A device used to portray local planning deci-

sions and their impacts was a story: "A Tall Tale of Wilsonville," composed by the AIA committee charged with the project (AIA, 1992), and highlighted by a series of historical three-dimensional aerial oblique perspectives that represented development patterns in 1852, 1894, 1910, 1932, and 1992. The story and each of these time-constructs portrayed the larger context of the river valley with its vegetation and land forms incrementally altered by development patterns that occurred in an evolu-

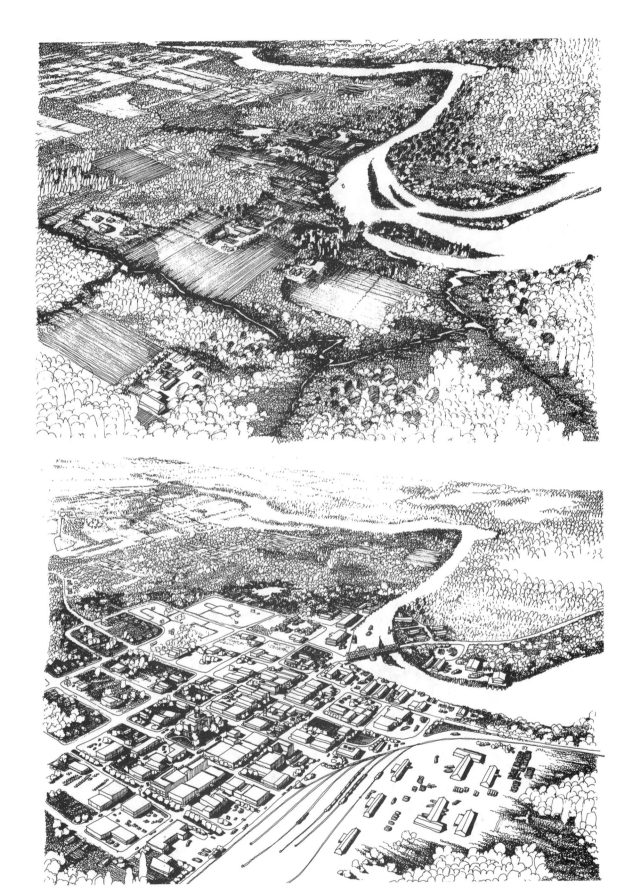

4-4,5,6,7,8,9 Wilsonville Visualized History. An imaginary community created to underscore the changes in development pattern over time based on everyday local decisions. Technical pen and ink on tracing paper.

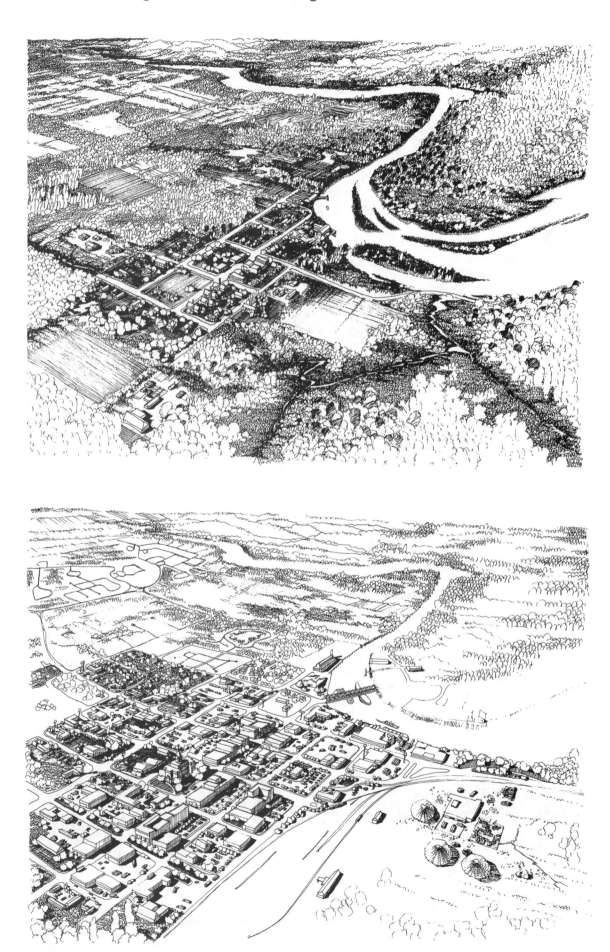

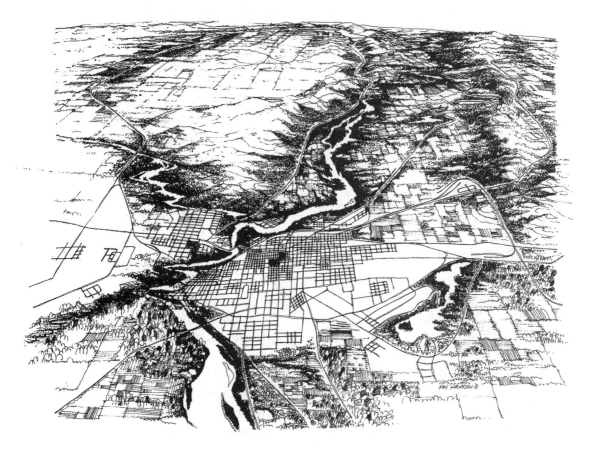

tionary and incremental manner, expanding the early grid system (changing it to subdivision cul-de-sacs), filling wetlands, and dispersing a traditional compact core area with increased off-street parking surfaces.

Each drawing portrays decision impacts in a connected manner, demonstrating the results of action and inaction, and the changes that occur to the entire system rather than one single site: patterns rather than pieces.

The 18 x 24-inch drawings were constructed from aerial oblique photography and, with the perspective grid established from the photography, expanded by using reference photographs and base maps to develop the historical sequences. The 1992 contemporary drawing was drawn first, followed by the 1852 drawing. The others added or subtracted from the first two.

These historic time patterning drawings can serve the following functions:

- they expand the public's understanding of design, beyond design as attractiveness and closer to structure, pattern, and fit;

- they increase the public's awareness of the physical implications of incremental developments on the whole settlement or district pattern—expansion, dispersal, filling or loss of natural features, and so on; and

- they assist the public in recognizing what can be altered regarding public decisions in order to affect different and more integral development results—local empowerment through a local awareness of local actions, portrayed in locally referenced and understandable graphics.

Port Townsend Street Vignettes

Contemporary scenes can articulate time patterns of historic and present-day artifacts placed in context. In **Port Townsend Streetscape One,** the same-time juxtapositioning of historic and/or architecturally significant buildings and groups of buildings with contemporary buildings and support services underscores resultant development increments coinciding at a particular time in history. This has educational values for the community as it contemplates

day-to-day development decisions (or chooses not to make them).

These drawings were constructed from slides taken on a field trip through the study area. The designers were searching for interfaces between the historic core of the community and the contemporary *edge* where change over time was directly evident in the development pattern.

Other Time–Place Dimensions

Other aspects of time that can be explored graphically and influence design decisions include: time–distance relationships, previous proposals assessment, and phasing projections.

Time–Distance Relationships

Time–distance relationships are a function of place in that they measure or indicate boundaries and limits to the movement of people and/or goods over distance within a given time. Pedestrian time–distance relationships have been used in planning for decades, as in the quarter-mile walking radius used most often in conventional master planning. With the radius comes a walking time assumption for an unencumbered adult of three miles per hour or five minutes for one quarter mile. This assumes level ground and a lack of barriers. An added sophistication is achieved by calculating the actual linear walking distance by means of established pedestrian routes rather than "as the crow flies" radii.

Past Proposals Assessment

Planning, architectural, and/or other development proposals, public and private, that have become public knowledge for a given area or district can provide clues on market and economic conditions of a given period; political and public affairs and agendas; design styles and period building material typologies; and development restraints or barriers that may have contributed to their non-implementation. Diagramming the core ideas found in past proposals can be a valuable existing conditions exercise, a form of time-patterning.

4-10 Port Townsend Streetscape One.

4-11 Port Orchard Past Proposals Diagram. A plan diagram of past proposals located in space and time can provide useful perspective to a planning process. Diagram is a felt-tip pen graphic.

Phasing Projections

Final design recommendations are dynamic, not static, and assured of changing even after final construction drawings are completed and bid upon. In urban design and planning, multiple agendas, property owners, citizen groups, and advocates often make illustrative site plans obsolete before the ink dries due to the natural complexity of diverse participants. Testing the spatial implications of proposed ideas, policies, and guidelines is critical to their effective critique and implementation. Assuming that change is constant, and that the complexities of human agendas can alter the best intentions, it is worth experimenting with *future time–place* as a means of questioning decisions and anticipating previously unforeseen influences on implementation.

Phasing is a means of staging, organizing, and managing the implementation of a project. Planners, designers, and the community can benefit from the projected phasing of a project; the process can reveal

Historic Activities in Contemporary Design

Design opportunities arise out of historic research and provide the basis for a proactive use of historic activities (as opposed to artifact preservation) in contemporary applications. Visualiza-tions can be used to represent urban design concepts for new park designs based on an event or group, such as *women's history in urban patterns* (Dubrouw, 1994). The Pentel Sign pen sketches provided a conceptual visualization of historic markers, conceived as urban art in the Boston townscape, located where the historic events occurred: examples of culture-based historic patterning leading to design opportunity.

Building Remnants as an Organization Principle: Astoria Pier

The passage of time is often obliterated by new development that removes all traces of past settlement, acting as if nothing had ever transpired in time. The design study on the Astoria, Oregon waterfront, sponsored in part by the National Endowment for the Arts, is an alternative to typical "formula-built" waterfront developments that sweep areas clean. Many times, these waterfront projects over-commercialize and gentrify working waterfronts exclusively into tourist areas. These new waterfront environments can be uninspiring places; few reflect the rich evolutionary nature of the waterfront.

The time-patterning diagrams visualize a chronology of the birth and evolution of Astoria,[1] Oregon in three increments over 100 years. In the 1860s, the first settlement developed over a filled inlet of the Columbia River. By the turn of the century, Astoria was a world center of the salmon cannery and fur trading industries and took its name from fur baron John Jacob Astor. In the 1930s, the town was

4-12 Incorporating History into Contemporary Design. Research into historic urban events can be dynamic opportunities for new design elements within in a city. These sketches represent urban parks commemorating the role of women in urban history (Dubrouw), reintroducing historic time and events into a contemporary reality. The drawings required a fast and loose approach due to budget and time constraints. A Pentel Sign pen made the task easier by limiting line weights to one and value patterns to hatching techniques.

questions that are unanswerable in present time that need to be asked in the future; it can identify long-term barriers or opportunities; and it can outline future political agendas.

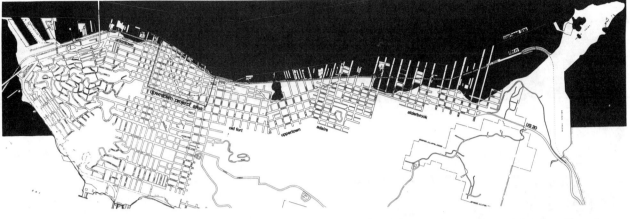

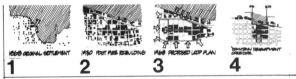

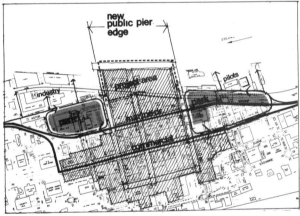

4-13 Time Patterning: Astoria Public Pier. The plan diagrams trace the development of this historical river front at critical times in its history. Any one increment of time takes on more meaning when seen with the other increments. The fourth step, a present plan proposal, represents a reorientation toward the river front.

rebuilt with many state-of-the-art concrete structures after a major fire. In the 1960s, the town considered turning mainstreet into a pedestrian mall fed by a peripheral loop located, in part, along the riveredge. This plan, that would have severed the linear city's relationship to the Columbia River edge, was fortunately never carried out. In the 1980s Astoria, still filled with the remnants of its built past, once again turned towards its riveredge for creation of a new public pier as a catalyst for new development.

Study Site, Municipal Pier Project

The drawings, diagrams, and models trace the development of a new waterfront development proposal that is connected in time from the city to the room scale. At the city scale, a new armature of street improvements reestablishes the connections between the downtown and its waterfront. Within the historical street framework, other diagrams develop a site composition that integrates a contemporary pier facility with historical built remnants. These remnants include not only buildings but also abandoned pier structure and a working railroad pier throughout the study site. The contemporary building program includes an excursion zone for tourists and a working fishery linked to the development of a new mini-cannery developed in one of the abandoned river-front buildings to serve the needs of local fishermen.

1 This work is an excerpt from an Individual Design Grant, "The Active Waterfront Place: An Alternative Design Approach," sponsored by the National Endowment for the Arts. The grant laid the foundation for waterfront rehabilitation that combined new tourist excursion activity with the needs of the traditional fishing industry.

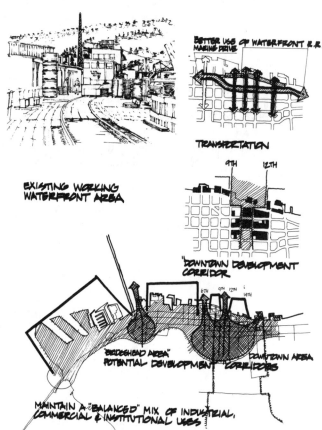

BETTER USE OF WATERFRONT R.R. MARINE DRIVE

TRANSPORTATION

9TH 12TH

EXISTING WORKING WATERFRONT AREA

"DOWNTOWN DEVELOPMENT CORRIDOR"

6TH 9TH 12TH 14TH

BRIDGEHEAD AREA" POTENTIAL DEVELOPMENT CORRIDORS DOWNTOWN AREA

MAINTAIN A "BALANCED" MIX OF INDUSTRIAL, COMMERCIAL & INSTITUTIONAL USES

4-14 Waterfront "Windows. The riverfront perspective elevation is a view seen only from far out in the water. The drawing focuses on the waterfront edge and public street "windows" that terminate and afford public access at the river edge. The diagrams at the city scale emphasize certain public corridors as opportunities to reconnect the city to the river. The two plan diagrams of the same downtown project area emphasize two different issues. The shaded diagram emphasizes a traffic/parking system, the solid/void emphasizes the definition of building blocks and public streets.

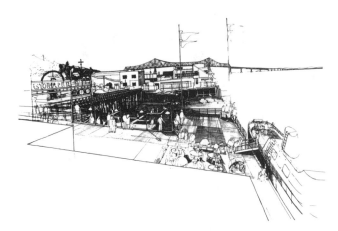

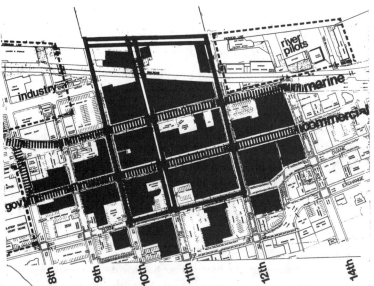

4-15 Existing Site Character. Drawing value emphasizes historical pier remnants and references them to a landmark bridge crossing of the Astoria.

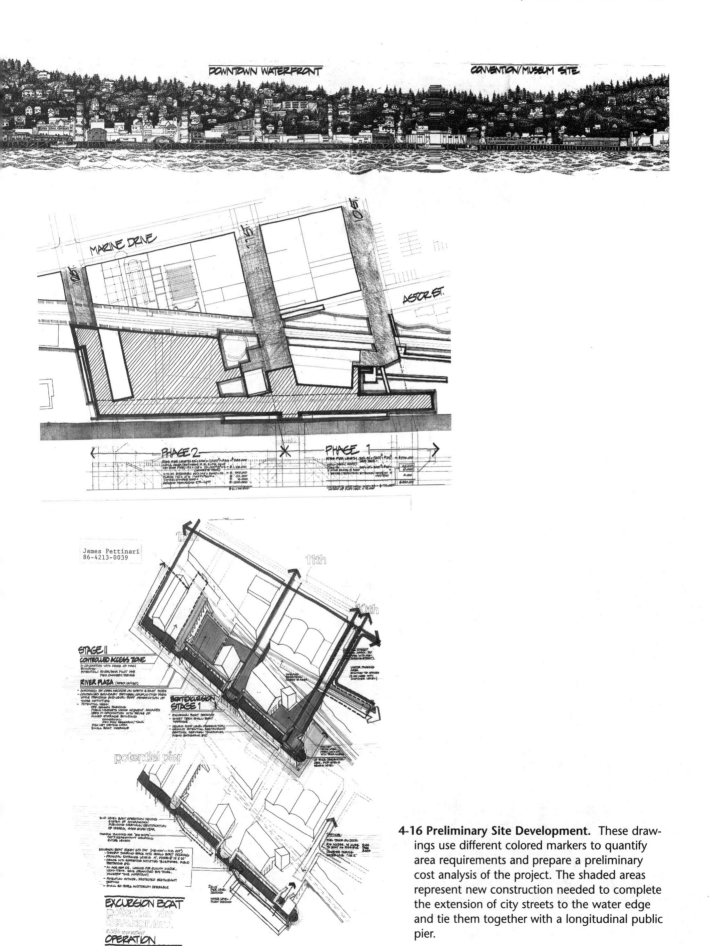

4-16 Preliminary Site Development. These drawings use different colored markers to quantify area requirements and prepare a preliminary cost analysis of the project. The shaded areas represent new construction needed to complete the extension of city streets to the water edge and tie them together with a longitudinal public pier.

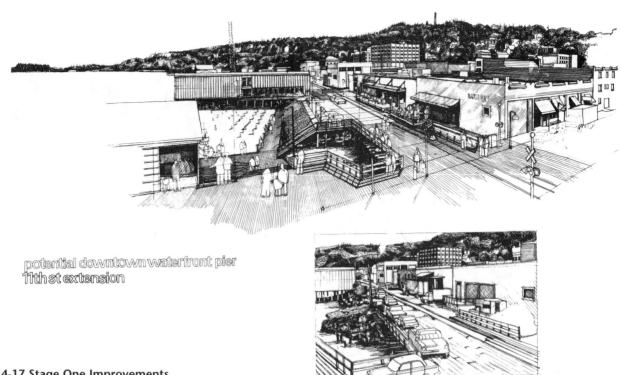

potential downtown waterfront pier
11th st extension

4-17 Stage One Improvements.

4-18 Public Pier Edge, Astoria, Oregon.

4-19 Zoning Diagrams of Pier Reorganization.
Isometrics with colored magic marker over sepia prints used to integrate exterior systems with the reuse of historical warehouse interior spaces.

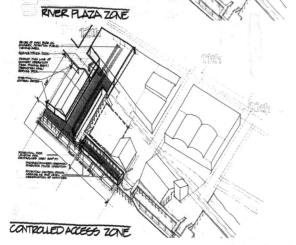

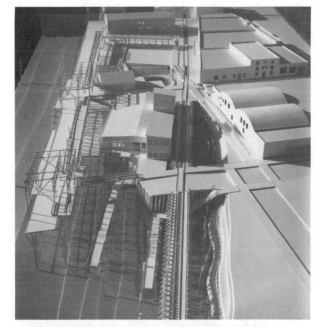

4-20 Preliminary Reorganization of Historical and Proposed Construction.

4-21 Proposed Waterfront Zones.

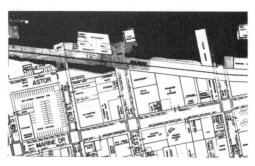

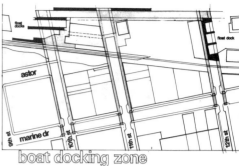

boat docking zone

4-22 Integration of Working and Tourist Zones.

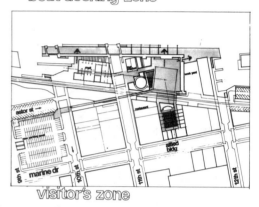

visitor's zone

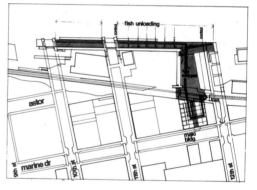

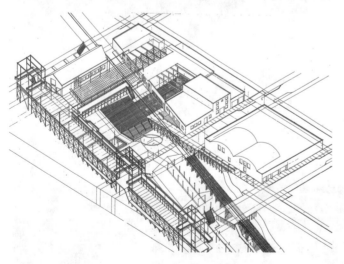

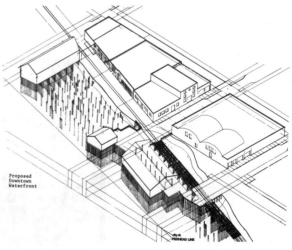

Proposed
Downtown
Waterfront

4-23 Before/After, Astoria Public Pier Proposal. The design proposal was developed over a print of the existing waterfront condition. During the process of drawing, the visual presence of historical artifacts responsible for the character of the site generate the design proposal. Design decisions are referenced to the fundamental site condition: a historical pier edge that contended over time with a swift, deep, moving river. The design proposal is continually seen as a three-demensional structure that sits "in" and not "on" the river.

4-24 Workings Made Visible, Astoria Public Pier. The model portrays the three-dimensional interplay between historic built elements: buildings, piers, railroad lines, and newly proposed building systems to accommodate, connect, and at times separate the conflicting uses of the tourist and working cannery operations.

Visualizing Lost Time

Layers of past time are often buried under the present. An aerial perspective visualizes a fascinating historic object that has been buried in time—a grand canal, a street wide and a city block long, running along a street in Minneapolis's downtown milling district. The canal functioned on the only waterfall along the Mississippi River, taking water from an upper pool along the downtown waterfront and dropping it through a series of vertical shafts that drove the turbines of adjacent mill buildings. This was the headquarters of General Mills until the facility was abandoned, the canal filled with sand, and its presence lost in time. The drawing sets the scene for a proposal that incorporates past building remnants and ruins as integral elements in the redesign of the area. The sectional elevation is cut through the mill, revealing its structure and turbine works in section with an historical composition of bridges, buildings and ruins scaled in true elevation as a backdrop. The potential interior character of the mill's rehabilitation is explored in a perspective that is structured around the view of the Minneapolis cityscape. Room character is limited to minimal drawing of the building's structural grid of columns, beams, and interior silo structures. The focus of the interior perspective is the mill's relationship to its urban location, rather than details of the room itself. Opening the building to the city and sky is the paramount value in the drawing composition and value.

The site diagram locates and describes the historic built remnants in the district and is accompanied by a phasing diagram outlining the timing of their proposed transformation.

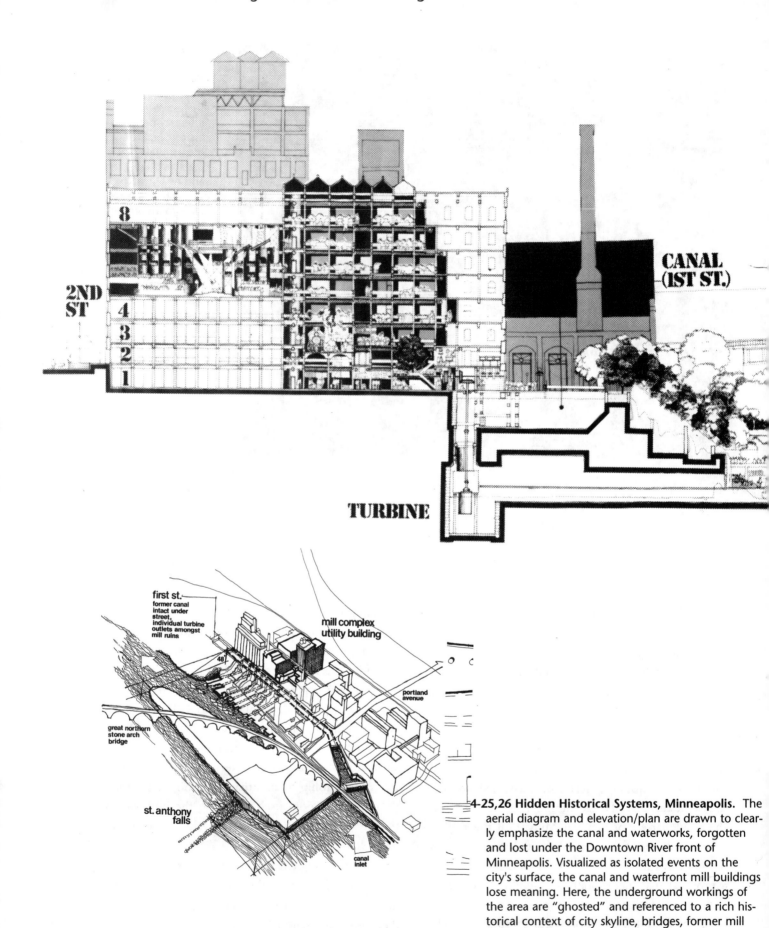

4-25,26 Hidden Historical Systems, Minneapolis. The aerial diagram and elevation/plan are drawn to clearly emphasize the canal and waterworks, forgotten and lost under the Downtown River front of Minneapolis. Visualized as isolated events on the city's surface, the canal and waterfront mill buildings lose meaning. Here, the underground workings of the area are "ghosted" and referenced to a rich historical context of city skyline, bridges, former mill foundation ruins, etc.

References

American Institute of Architects. 1992. *Designing Your Town*. Printed by Georgia Power Company, Atlanta.

DeChiarra/Koppelman. 1969. *Planning Design Criteria*. New York: Van Nostrand Reinhold Company.

Dubrouw, Gail. 1993. Unpublished Г "Claiming Public Space for Wome Boston: A Proposal for Preservation, Pu. and Public Historic Interpretation." Frontieı. *Journal of Women's Studies*, Vol. XIII, No. 1, p. 111, University Press of Colorado, Niwot, CO.

Johnston, Charles M. 1984/1986. *The Creative Imperative*. Berkeley: Celestial Arts.

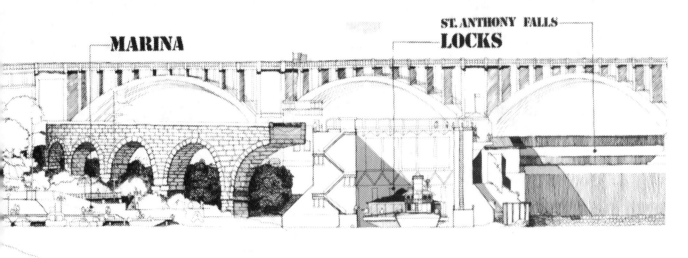

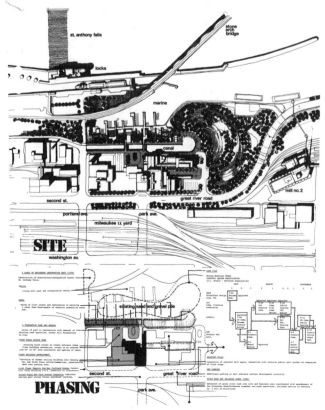

4-27 Site Proposal. The drawing places value only on those elements that surround and give definition to the canal reclamation.

4-28 Phasing Diagram. Building artifacts come and go. The plan diagram outlines the phased abandonment of railroad and individual facilities over time as an opportunity to create a site composition that preserves and incorporates historical built pieces with new development.

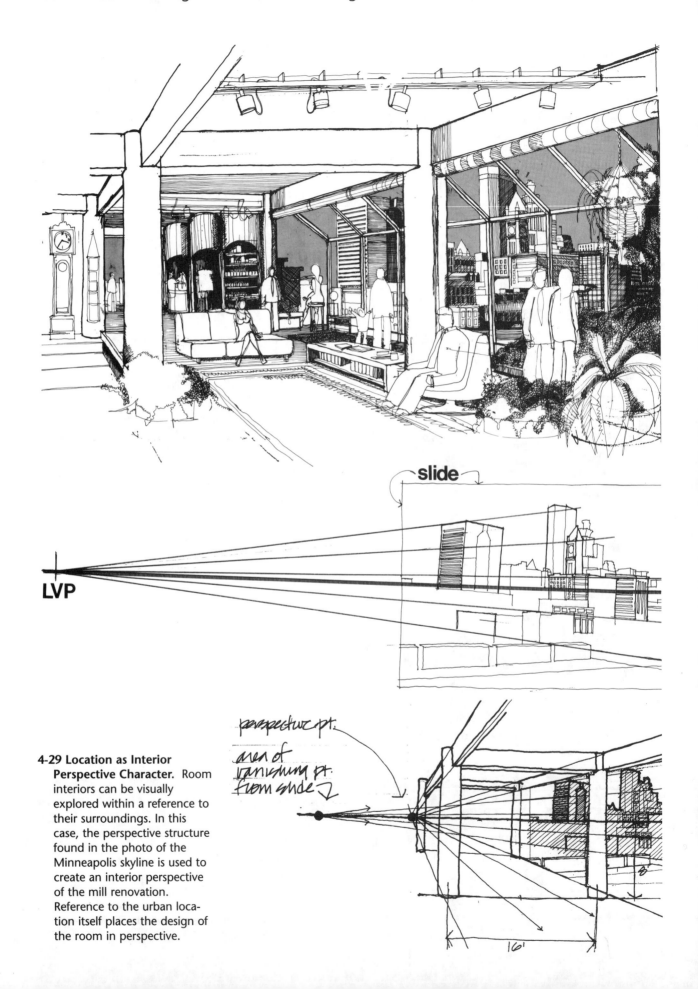

slide

LVP

perspective pt.

area of vanishing pt. from slide

16'

4-29 Location as Interior Perspective Character. Room interiors can be visually explored within a reference to their surroundings. In this case, the perspective structure found in the photo of the Minneapolis skyline is used to create an interior perspective of the mill renovation. Reference to the urban location itself places the design of the room in perspective.

5 Involving The Public In The Design of Place

Introduction

The general public, the layperson in small cities and towns, neighborhoods and office complexes define design and place very differently than designers and planners. Laypeople are often hesitant regarding design because they have little foundation or familiarity with the rules, principles, and boundaries of the process as practiced by designers and planners, and they are not familiar with the language of design both spoken and visualized.

Increasingly, however, these same people want a say-so in what happens on their turf. They want to understand the process so they can have more ownership of the decisions arising from that process that affects their daily lives. To achieve this, a language that can be used by the designer and by the layperson is needed so that concepts and implications can be communicated and understood. The challenge lies with the planner/designer to provide formats and a language that can integrate all participants into the process. This translates to communication in real and spatial terms.

For the planner/designer, design communication is inherent in the act of design, both as internal communication in the thinking process, and as an external communication with the user/client. Outside experts, no matter how experienced and knowledgeable, can not change the internal quality and structure of settlements in integral ways. The people within a given context are the agents of change, aided by a communication process that speaks to the form generative cultural aspects of that complexity. The better the communication process, the higher level of public awareness, the better the internal decisions of change.

Design Communication In Public Participation

General Rules of Conduct

Design communication fits into a larger process of public involvement. As a prelude to *design communication*, remember a few guides related to *human communication*, to both reduce the stress of being the communicator and as a means of improving the quality of communication.

Involving the people who live and work in an area to be planned or designed requires no less than a comprehensive communication process by planners and designers. The public is in reality the people who are directly impacted by planning and design decisions traditionally made by experts; it is the group of people who are asked to support, financially or politically, a change in the physical form of an area. The public is the substantive or real users of human settlements and the underlying or displaced eco-systems. Public involvement, rather than being avoided as many designers are inclined to do, can provide the required ingredient to spatially test ideas, options, and policies, enhancing the quality of design.

What does this bode for the professional planner, urban designer, and architect or landscape architect as they pursue the design of place where the inhabitants want co-participation? More responsibility in the planning/design process, not less. *Design* is *communication* in the sense that there is a cognitive process of constructing images for translation or interpretation of form-based concepts. Design is based on an internal/external transformance of data, elements, shapes,

131

patterns, and mental concepts into real images. In the complexities of contemporary settlement patterns, particularly on the American continent where only the first layer of settlement pattern has been laid (as compared to multiple European layers), people are demanding more of a role in the act of design and planning due to direct impacts on them, less space for them, and increased environmental damage and losses due to their actions. The professional can gain by this increasing demand by becoming more a part of the process—more of a translator, interpreter, instigator, integrator, and negotiator than the conventional sole decision-maker of form and pattern. This does not mean design by committee; it requires a close relationship and communication with the public as partners in a complex dance—a dance that redefines physical planning and design. Some evolving rules of conduct that can improve the designer's effectiveness in the changing nature of public participation include:

1. There is no goal as outcome but that of maintaining the integrity of a dynamic creative process (Johnston, 1989); the real goal is to engage the process, creatively, beyond the known or formulated boundaries of the situation, without a predetermination of results; this makes us better listeners as well.

2. There is no star of the process—the designer/planner is at most an equal but not greater participant in the process.

3. Respect the experience and integrity of citizens, regardless of differing views.

4. Listen.

5. Recognize the public's desire for ownership of ideas and directions.

6. Assume that creativity extends in equal capacity across different personalities and cultures; learn how to work with those creative differences without compromise.

7. Connect the public to the place and the place to context.

8. A sound process has only one leader at a time; a leader who is aware of the appropriate time to pass the leadership on to another in the process, and so on, affecting clarity,

structure, and shared ownership without compromise.

There are hidden agendas, overt and covert strategies, and politics in every public participation process. The more open the process, the more opportunity for the public within the process to recognize and deal with these agendas, without the designer/planner assuming responsibility for their exposure and risking criticism for advocating one side or another.

Design Communication Principles

Use the following discussion and principles of communication as a complement to the larger public involvement process, methods, and techniques. Communication is the glue between people attempting to find common points of view or new insights that incorporate the complexities and diversities of polarities present in most urban problems.

Principle One

(Urban) design communication is a highly patterned process that evolves through a "specific sequence of formative stages (or parts) of a larger whole" (Johnston, 1994). Visualizing pattern through drawing at specific stages is a way of constructing the story as it is drawn, building a larger design as process, not pre-determined outcome.

Principle Two

Drawings and other visualization types in design communication act as a bridge between mental and visual thinking, polarities of thinking that are both embodied in its act. Partial polarities of thinking that are assisted by drawing visualization as *thought* include quantitative vs. qualitative, fantasy vs. reality, and mental concepts vs. visual images, all seeking a larger whole that contains and integrates the diverse parts.

Principle Three

(Urban) design communication is a dynamic process that articulates relationships in "time- and space-specific statements" (Johnston, 1989) using differentiated parts of (community) to focus on the detail that is also connected to a larger context (i.e., place in context).

Principle Four

Context becomes the extent or limit of time and space-specific relationships for layperson understanding. Determining the *adequate context* for a given audience is a challenge to the designer and increases the audience's understanding of the larger area of influence, or their watershed.

Principle Five

Design communication visualizes *reality* in *context* as an outgoing process of creative self-organization; demonstrating that reality is constantly changing, emerging, and connected to all of the other parts (of community). We argue that communities are self-organizing and can benefit from a public process that builds on this idea, infusing a stronger sense of ownership in decisions internal to the community.

Principle Six

Visualizations in the public participation process aid in shaping information into concepts, visions, or stories, expanding the laypersons' understanding through a graphic story metaphor.

Principle Seven

Public involvement is en evolving process of awareness and empowerment; where public awareness and public empowerment are distinctly different from public education and public participation. Simply put, education often implies or involves an expert or master, passing on knowledge or recommendations to a group of citizens. Participation can be limited to attending meetings for review, approval, or disapproval of ideas generated in large part by outside experts or special committees. Awareness is understanding through individual attention to time- and space-specific relationships in a referenced and oriented context. Empowerment is the act of initiating and acting upon local decisions by local people.

Graphic Techniques in Public Involvement Communication

The role of graphics in public meetings, workshops, and other formats is determined partly by the audience, partly by the physical space of the gathering, the time available to prepare for the event, and the nature of the material to be discussed. Who are the people in the audience? What is their level of understanding of drawing conventions? What is their grasp of conventional reference and orientation exhibits (parcel maps, building footprint maps, perspectives) used in most planning and design projects? What are they comfortable with regarding the level of sophistication and information provided within the graphics? What is their role in the overall process: observer, decision-maker, voter, elected official, resident, all of the above?

If the object of a meeting is to question, understand, and discuss interventions to place, the language of the meeting needs to be clear, with integrated information in formats that do not distract in and of themselves from the basic agenda of the gathering. Charts and tables are not sufficient to describe and discuss settlement patterns in context regardless of the sophistication of the audience. People want to zoom in on issues in ways that can be quickly perceived, yet have a sense of the larger picture. Quantitative relationships and characteristics of place need to be expressed in spatial formats rather than in numbers and text alone, connecting them to qualitative characteristics by the act of shaping them. Visualization cannot be relegated to computer graphics unless the technician or professional understands the elements and principles of visual communication.

Principle One: ". . . a highly patterned process . . . of formative stages."

Two forms of design communication are effective under this principle: one, a sequencing of larger to smaller and more focused scales, connecting the participants and their place to the larger picture; and, two, an assembling of a story where for example, the geologic formation and structure of a place is portrayed as a foundation for the public's appreciation of watersheds and other natural resources, followed by the telling of the human history of a place, followed by a visual portrayal of its natural, cultural, and jurisdictional "parts" and how they fit together, and so on—building context with the participants. Photographs can give a glimpse of clothes, buildings and artifacts; visual patterns of watersheds and development patterns can portray *connections* among culture, artifact, and environment over time.

Principle Two: "Drawing . . . as a 'bridge' between mental and visual images . . ." Shapes are concepts (Arnheim, 1979)

The designer/planner can act as the translator and interpreter for community visions, concerns, and aspirations. By shaping a mental concept, the designer advances the process of public understanding another degree, providing more substance or snatches of potential reality for the public to review, critique, and respond to. It empowers them by instigating their senses and portraying a possible outcome of their thoughts. Some find safety in not doing any drawings of "what ifs" because what they perceive may upset some political sensitivity. If properly presented and qualified, particularly as visualizations in process for public critique, those concerns more often than not are neutralized or avoided altogether.

A group of laypeople trying to grasp the implications of functions, scales, styles, materials, and their associated impacts on other people can only do so effectively by viewing those implications in a spatial language that integrates the characteristics and measurements of place into a real (and changeable) vision. A key characteristic and advantage of visualization as an interpretive bridge is *filtration*. Drawing every tree in a context visualization is not necessary to relate to the public that certain varieties of trees, individually and in groups, exist. Drawing each building in a given city block is not necessary in all cases to relate information relative to the physical dimensions and characteristics of that block. Portraying information, selectively screened, in a semi-abstract or abstract form, can assist the layperson in focusing on the point of interest still within context; examples of these context diagrams are dispersed throughout the book.

Principle Three: ". . . a dynamic process that articulates relationships in 'time- and space-specific statements'. . . place in context"

The public involvement process is always changing, moving, and evolving. People form ideas and opinions, express fears, have questions answered and form other questions. Ways of improving the public's understanding of what is occurring during the complex process include depicting relationships in time- and space-specific visualizations. Three key characteristics of time- and space-specific visualizations are:

- Providing context reference: an indication of recognizable places (towns, villages), human artifacts (highways, powerlines), and natural features (water bodies, mountain ranges, and physical edges or boundaries);

- Providing context orientation: an awareness of the environment regarding time, space, objects, persons. The setting or arrangement of such things in a manner that provides an understanding of or improves the observer's attentativeness to the governing context. (The entire planet is the fundamental context for every project, but an intermediate incremental context governs the conditions of a particular area, where it is a river valley and its watershed or a neighborhood with awareness of the larger district and city); and

- Providing context data scale-relevance: selecting the level of information (in context) that is meaningful at the scale being used. Too much information can clutter and confuse; a filtration of information is required that summarizes and represents information that is appropriate for the scale of presentation.

Principle Four: "(Adequate) context becomes the extent or limit of time- and space-specific relationships for layperson understanding"

Using context as both the substance of place-reality and its container provides the designer with a way of differentiating the parts of community and place in a manner and boundary digestible for the public, given that the context is adequate in its expression of interrelationships. For example, when dealing with a rail transit station placement and design in a neighborhood, the context of the whole neighborhood or multiple neighborhoods may be the adequate extension of place, rather than one or two blocks surrounding the site, for a thorough assessment of impacts and implications related to the station.

The designer/planner is obligated to assess a project's adequate context above and beyond the contract or legal definitions of the study area. A river is the entire watershed, not merely a narrow ribbon of water coursing to the sea. What extent of that river's biophysical domain is critical and adequate to its study and understanding? Dealing with that question engages everyone in the process of design.

Principle Five: ". . . visualizing reality . . . as an on-going process of creative self-organizations . . ."

This can be especially intriguing and challenging for the designer/planner. Communities are complex entities that can be viewed as self-organizing, not ordered and planned from the top down. During the public involvement process, searching for and describing this self-organizing aspect of community can be one of the most revealing and awareness-building actions. It requires direct interaction with the community in order to reveal and define these self-organizations. Simple examples include:

- recording in diagrams the use of a specific street by youth congregating during the day-time—use of space, arrangement of props, clustering, and private interactions;

- time-sequencing of cultural changes occurring in a neighborhood over a given time period, spatially locating and articulating the changes in usage of front and rear yards, for example, by different family groupings;

- diagramming the physical changes in residential dwellings over time and relating them to cultural patterns; and

- assessing the political dynamics of non-elected community leaders, activists, and the turf they represent.

Changes occurring within an area that are not a part of an intentional public action or policy or large private master plan can be viewed as self-organizing and often act as indicators for other underlying form-generative dynamics. Sharing this with the public reveals a part of themselves that can add to a base of information for better decision-making.

Principle Six: "Visualizations . . . aid in shaping information into concepts, visions, or stories . . ."

Telling stories is a classic and effective way many cultures use to relate information in context, whether some social rule, a way of gathering food, or laws of the community. In designing and planning communities, information as abstract quantities can have little relevance for neighbors debating a rail station, a group housing proposal, or an accessory housing policy. Visualizing information in a story integrates it into a context and articulating information into a reality that can be discussed and changed in an integrated manner. The benefits of story-telling as part of the design process include:

- capturing the essence of a place in ways that can inform the public and expand the public's perception of place into place-context;

- demonstrating physical impacts of past actions with little or no words;

- portraying physical implications of proposed actions by visualizing potential outcomes;

- describing public policy in spatial terms as a testing mechanism for that policy;

- describing a larger context within which projects and issues occur for greater public awareness; and

- interpreting public wants and needs in a manner that can be reviewed and modified by the public as a building block for citizen planning.

The important distinguishing characteristic of public awareness visualizations that is different from the conventional illustrative plan or designer's doodle is the *contextual diagram* or *place-context diagram*, representing incremental environments that are connected to a larger whole.

Improving Conventional Public Involvement Formats

This section explores public involvement formats that add to conventional formats with context-oriented drawings. Some examples are serious, others are humorous with a serious message. The following list summarizes both conventional and experimental formats, each with a particular and appropriate application that is determined by the audience and the situation.

Formal Public Information and Education Formats

The Public Hearing

Public hearings provide for and record public comment on a given issue. Graphics for them include background and reference exhibits, followed by a summary of key recommendations for public comment. Meeting spaces are large-capacity rooms and are usually better served by slide and overhead presentations augmented by graphic display boards for individual viewing.

Putting the issues back in context is of particular importance in hearings where the opinions of those in attendance are in response to isolated or out-of-context issues. Aerial obliques and models that encompass a larger area than the project, or slides that point out the connections of the issues to the larger place can do this.

City Council/Planning Commission Presentations

Presentations to city councils and planning commissions are conventionally designed to inform and update, providing officials the opportunity to review progress on a project. Time periods are short, usually 15 to 30 minutes prior to a regularly scheduled meeting. Graphics are critical to a brief and succinct communication of information and ideas. Slides used sparingly put less people to sleep after their day's work. Slide presentations of graphic visualizations are best kept under ten minutes if used at all with complementary oral presentations. Given the short presentation time normally allotted for these formats, graphic visualizations of projects-in-context are better expressed as three-dimensional sketches or sketch-diagrams that strongly emphasize the critical points and deemphasize or filter out extraneous and distracting information, no matter how interesting. This process is similar to outlining a sentence, articulating the relationships among subject, verb, and object, adding adjectives and adverbs that significantly improve the communication, and dropping those that are filler or lower in priority for the time, location, purpose, and level of message. Story sheets are

an excellent technique in that they serve as both large notecards for the speaker and visual exhibits for the audience. They are effective in 24 x 36 inch sheet sizes, aided by one-inch grids for lettering. Drawings, diagrams, photographs, and notes can all be added to the sheets and referred to during the presentation. In this manner, the speaker is not the sole center of attention.

Informal Meetings, Workshops, and Brainstorming Sessions

Task Force/Steering Committee Meetings and Workshops

Task forces or steering committees are small groups of citizens, usually appointed by a mayor or council, organized to probe or explore a detailed aspect of community design and planning. This can be one of the most intensive public interaction formats with which planners and designers are involved. Task forces are usually convened for a specific topical area of investigation and resolution. Waterfronts, downtowns, neighborhoods, housing, and transportation are all topics that can be effectively focused upon with a small public group.

Task force or steering committee meetings are work meetings, where information and ideas are shared, discussed and critiqued, and agreed upon. Graphic visualizations are critical to the success of the process and its subsequent products and determined by the working informality of the format. Laypeople require reference and orientation for issues, opportunities, problems, trends, etc. that are researched by planners and designers.

Visualizations are influenced by the size of the task force, distance or travel requirements for the designer, and the extent of the project area, as well as content and issues. As laypeople, task force members appreciate the immediacy of reference and orientation for context depictions: three-dimensional scale models, three-dimensional diagrams, and three-dimensional drawings all communicate more context than two-dimensional illustrations. Drawing styles can be formal and straight-edged or loose and free-

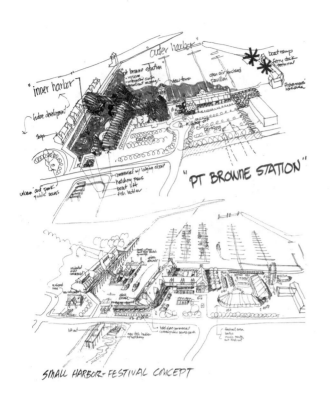

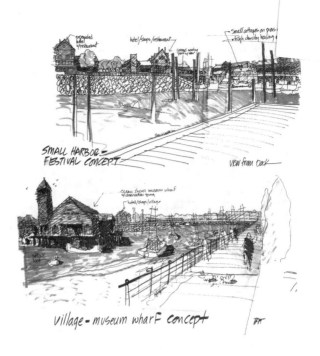

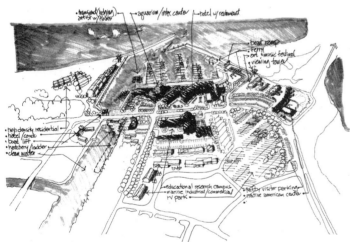

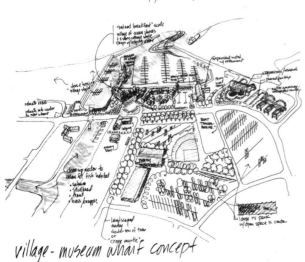

5-1 A–F Ocean Shores Series. The Ocean Shores Marina and Uplands Design Project required extensive public involvement sessions, including small group/task force meetings, large idea gathering public meetings, workshops, brainstorming sessions, and final presentation meetings. This sequence of drawings represents visualizations completed during and as inherent parts of the process. Initial diagrams were compiled to summarize existing conditions and begin a contextual base. Sketches were made on site in meetings in response to citizen enquiries. Following a day of brainstorming meetings in large and small format, the design team prepared concept sketches, *Ocean Shores Concepts*, during the next day and prior to another evening meeting, enabling the public to review and comment on ideas from the previous day, fresh in the minds of all participants.

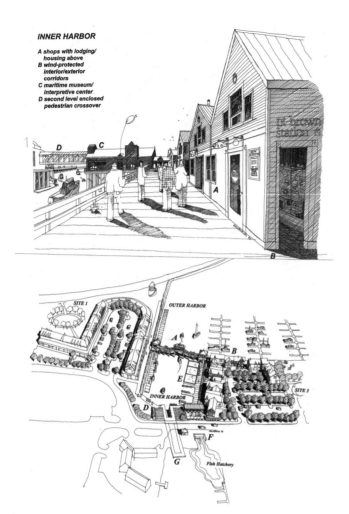

INNER HARBOR

A shops with lodging/
  housing above
B wind-protected
  interior/exterior
  corridors
C maritime museum/
  interpretive center
D second level enclosed
  pedestrian crossover

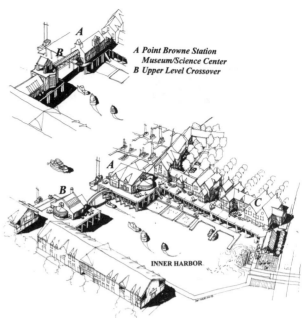

A Point Browne Station
  Museum/Science Center
B Upper Level Crossover

INNER HARBOR

5-2,3 Ocean Shores Recommendations. The final visualizations had interchangeable parts so that options could be spliced into a full perspective sketch of the final recommendations for sub-options. This permitted the city and its residents to pursue a more generalized concept with specific parts subject to additional study or funding exploration without hindering the overall process.

hand, or a combination of both. Drawings that represent ideas in progress are often friendlier than finished or formal drawings so as not to imply that final decisions have been made without the task force's participation.

Three-dimensional Models

Paper, cardboard, or foam models can be quickly constructed to demonstrate ideas-in-progress and their implications for a committee. Such models demonstrate abstracted concepts to scale and encourage people to play with ideas using removable parts. These study models serve a number of functions for the planner/designer: They enable an alternative internal communication to occur using a medium in addition to the drawn visualization, increasing understanding and awareness of form implications through the very act of building the model; and they provide a base for multiple sketch vignettes made from slides photographed from the model and its interchangeable parts. Depict multiple ideas quickly

by photographing the same base from multiple camera angles. Multiple-color materials are useful in communicating existing context and changing features in the models: a grey or brown cardboard material for existing context and a white cardboard for changing or proposed features, for example.

As a public interaction technique, prior to a workshop, at a convenient scale cut out building types from corrugated cardboard, doubling the layers where necessary to get the necessary building height approximation. Shape the cardboard based on building typologies for given uses (planners can check with local architects for the widths of single- and double-loaded corridor residential buildings or the depths of retail stores, etc.) cutting the shapes into rectangles or other geometry that closely represent the typical buildings. With a colored marker, code the top layer of cardboard for its use (red for retail, blue for public uses, orange for multiple family, etc.), usually by drawing a colored border around the top layer. It is helpful to mark the square footage or num-

5-4 Ocean Shores Model. In *Ocean Shores Model*, the design team prepared cardboard cutouts of anticipated uses and square footage, color-coding each piece for public information. On an aerial photograph, the pieces were arranged by citizens around the work table. Each scheme was photographed. This visualization process provided two important public involvement ingredients: It allowed the citizens to "play" and create in a comfortable and understandable manner, and it produced a range of sound ideas based on a crafting method. People learned from the play or crafting process about the context of the site, its potentials, and the opportunities it offered.

ber of units represented in each shape on the top layer for easy reference.

Parking lots can be cut out of flat chipboard or thin cardboard, usually in widths of 60 or 120 feet by ten foot increments in length, marked with the number of spaces represented by each piece. Recreational components, ball fields, etc. can also be cut out in the same manner.

With the game pieces shaped and marked, they can be placed onto a quality aerial photograph of the same scale as the pieces, showing existing conditions, buildings, roads, etc. so that the public, task force, or design team can brainstorm by arranging the pieces around the photo. Once an idea is developed, a simple camera slide or print can be made and the next idea can be arranged, and so on. Using this technique can be very effective in engaging a group of laypeople, usually with a little coaxing or example arrangements to reduce their intimidation.

More sophisticated base models can be pre-prepared with topography and existing buildings with the same effect. These interactive model slides can actually be projected and used as the basis for slide traced sketches.

Three-dimensional Model and Drawing Diagrams

Color-coded three-dimensional diagrams are useful tools to demonstrate complex systems or networks of activities. A diagram, remember, is a drawing that outlines the parts and their relationships, not necessarily their detail. As such, it conveys overall framework: horizontal, vertical, and perspective relationships; reference and orientation elements and relationships; and key emerging trends, patterns, shapes, and/or networks and principles. Effective and well-executed examples of three-dimensional diagrams are contained in studies with large scale complexity

5-5 Vashon Town Meeting. The more we can make visualizations understandable to the public at a meeting, the more open the meeting discussions become and the more substantive are the meeting interactions.

such as *Urban Design Manhattan* (Regional Plan Association, 1969) and "A Comprehensive Plan for Downtown Buffalo, New York" (City of Buffalo, 1971) in which movement systems are studied in model form (Regional Plan Association) and a building network and movement system are studied in drawing diagrams (Buffalo).

Methods to create loose or in-progress drawings or visualizations include multiple sketches, using the same base perspective sketch. The sketches can be taped, tacked, or overlaid on the base perspective in a meeting setting to discuss and demonstrate opportunities and elicit response and contributions from the laypeople on the committee.

Open Exhibits ("Open House")

Open exhibits are defined as informational displays for public view. They attract a large number of viewers over an extended period of time, with each viewer present for a shorter duration than in a more formalized presentation. Exhibits may be an all-day affair, offering the public the opportunity to view materials at their own convenience. Facilitated exhibits can be more productive in terms of the quality and documentation of viewer feedback, assisting in answering questions and/or completing survey forms. Options for facilitated open exhibits include:

Small group interaction exhibits. Within an extended time period (e.g., eight hours), an exhibit is staffed with people familiar with the information and

explorations presented in a graphic format; the exhibit is arranged in a sequential pass-through configuration. Staff arrange themselves so that each is near one or more displays to answer questions. Their presence greatly increases the effectiveness of displays, permitting clarification and explanation of graphic symbols and the ideas they are communicating. The staff are also in a position to encourage the completion of surveys and other tools useful in obtaining feedback in qualitative and quantitative form.

Small group interaction with scheduled presentations. Open exhibits with facilitated staff participation can be enhanced further with scheduled presentations at key points during the exhibit, as a summary or a kick-off event. Presentations are characterized by a reasonable presentation time (20 to 40 minutes) for necessary information or recommendations followed by questions and answers from the audience.

Open exhibits with side events. Exhibits can be further enhanced with side events programmed to attract and assess the public's viewpoint on various related issues. Side events can consist of staffed preference surveys using graphic and/or photographic tools, set up and configured in close proximity to the main exhibit; video presentations, up to 15 minutes long; interactive games using game boards, computers, or staff; and quiet places for people to sit and unhurriedly complete surveys and other requests for written comment and feedback.

In all of these open exhibit variations, the visualization of spatially related information and ideas is critical to the public's qualitative participation and understanding. Information ranging from demographics to cultural and economic trends eventually needs to be translated for the public into a spatial framework or language. Charts, tables, and text have limitations during a set timed event where information in-take and feed-back is critical to the progress of the project. Basic components of an open exhibit visualization package include:

Reference and orientation visualizations. These are maps and diagrams that illustrate relational locations, landforms and systems, infrastructure networks, settlement patterns, relational sizes, configurations, directions, and emerging patterns.

Instructional and interactive diagrams. A base map of a city with street names, with or without building footprints, can be used to instruct people regarding how to read the map and orient themselves by having them place a colored dot on the location of their home and another colored dot on the location of their place of employment. This activity requires them to study the map and orient themselves, increasing their familiarity with the base for other informational graphics using the same or similar base maps. It also connects them to the project by indicating their locational involvement in the project and provides a qualitative and quantitative documentation of resident/employee participants in the exhibit.

Overview graphic diagrams that integrate complex information. Aerial oblique diagrams, photographs, and models all provide an overview for land features, settlement patterns, building massing and scale, and other information relevant to the project. These diagrams are useful early in the sequence of the exhibit so that the public's review and understanding of issues and recommendations is not clouded or confused by attempts to understand basic graphic conventions and symbols rather than the substance of the communication.

Public-friendly visualizations. Information and ideas can become complex when separated from context and put on display, even for professional planners and designers. Determining who the audience is and their degree of familiarity with graphic conventions is an important step in deciding the nature and method of graphic visualization. Public-friendly visualizations consist of drawings with easily understood conventions and symbols characterized by realistic and familiar landmarks and/or built form components (tower, dormer, porch). Among the more successful realism type formats is the before and after sequence, where a portrayal of an existing condition in three dimensions (preferably) is accompanied by a subsequent drawing of the same view showing proposed changes. The public is familiarized through the reference and orientation of the original drawing to more easily comprehend the changes represented in the second drawing. Other three-dimensional diagrams that are user friendly include semi-abstract shapes mixed with realistic shapes, again strengthening the reference and orientation of the viewer.

Other suggestions for open exhibit visualizations include:

Consistent use of a scale ladder. Either descend or ascend in scale from the beginning of an exhibit sequence to its end. In other words, don't jump around from macro- to micro- to macro- to micro-scale and expect the public to follow the sequence or the rationale of the presentation.

Consistent use of conventions. If north is at the top of the sheet in one drawing, it should be there in all drawings with no exceptions. If an asterisk is used for one type of design or planning element on one drawing, it must be used on all other drawings where appropriate, and not used to represent a different element within the same presentation. Sheet sizes for story sheets, presentation boards, etc. are more appealing if they all are consistent in size and orientation (portrait vs. landscape).

Information Events

Information events can benefit from enticement formats to bring people together. These consist of dessert potlucks, dinners, auctions, etc. where exhibits can be displayed for public information. Variations on these events can be similar to those for open exhibits.

Forums

Forums are assemblies or programs for the open discussion of public matters. Successful types of community forums in planning and design include:

Panel—facilitator—audience. Panel members are selected from stakeholders within a given area or regarding a selected topic. The panel members may provide an opening statement of position followed by questioning from the moderator-facilitator. This format is dependent in large degree on an informed facilitator who can follow up on comments made by panelists, who can seed the discussion and focus on critical issues. The audience members in this format act as observers.

Audience—panel—moderator. More direct audience participation can be achieved through an audience-panel exchange with a moderator. Graphic visualizations are useful in conveying information to the audience as a part of presentations given by each panelist. Slides and pin-up or paste-up displays are effective, but visualizations that can be used during

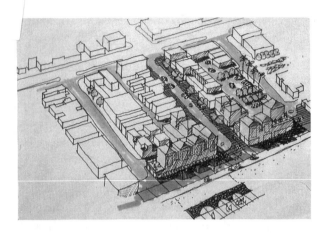

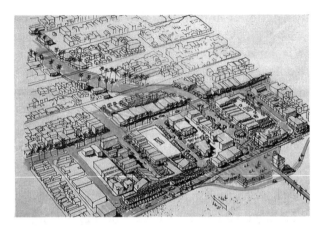

discussions between the audience and the panel are better suited to this format than slide presentations requiring dark rooms.

"Busy Corner" Display/Interview

Getting information to the general public can require on-the-street techniques to intercept and stimulate reaction. Public and semi-public pedestrian-intensive areas such as street corners, plazas, interior shopping malls, and public building lobbies are all effective display locations where graphic visualizations can play an integral communicative role. Effective visualizations in these settings must be dramatic and high-impact with either photographs or graphic drawings to focus in on relevant images. In addition to photographs, three-dimensional graphic images such as before-and-after sketches, aerial oblique sketches, and study models attract and capture the attention of passers-by. When space is limited, multi-image display boards can communicate sufficient information to encourage public participation in filling out interview or survey forms. A facilitator can record on a flip chart (a graphic and visible recording device) the comments and suggestions of passers-by. This type of format achieves three objectives: **1)** it communicates information and ideas informally in a public domain; **2)** it elicits a response from a portion of the public that might not have participated in more organized formats; and **3)** it advertises the planning/design process to the public, at a minimum informing the public of the process and its progress.

Conference

A conference format consists of a multiple-day program with an invited group of stakeholders all committed to consistent attendance and consensus build-

ing. The conference is organized around a topic such as "visioning," goal-setting, or alternatives development. The purpose of a conference format is to saturate the participating public with contextual information and issues using a variety of techniques, augmented by technical presentations and discussions, arriving at a consensus position. Conferences can be characterized by multiple sessions, evolutionary program, consensus building, and/or creative integration. An advantage of the conference format is the opportunity to build a learning curve for participants over the initial sessions, arriving at the idea sessions *after* informed saturation.

Charrette: R/UDAT, Main Street

A charrette is a short-time-period-intensive effort where the planning/design team works with a local community to arrive at a concept, or implementation strategy for a project. Two models are widely used for charrette intensives in the United States. The Regional & Urban Design Assistance Team (R/UDAT) and the Main Street Program's Resource Team approach.

R/UDAT. The Regional & Urban Design Assistance Team is an American Institute of Architects (AIA) sponsored program that began in 1967 when a group of architects visited Rapid City, South Dakota to provide outside advice on community design issues. The city benefited from the advice and other communities began requesting the assistance of similar teams from the AIA. Since 1967, AIA R/UDATs have provided assistance to more than 100 counties, cities, and towns across the United States, using a four-day format of public forums, design sessions, site visits, and public presentations to work out creative recommendations for local action.

5-6,7,8,9 Hermosa Beach R/UDAT. Diagrammatic sketches were done in a day's time along with another half-dozen drawings that articulated the R/UDAT recommendations. Every conceivable aid is used to assist in preparing the sketches: aerial photography, field sketches, photographs, and models. The sketches are on flimsy tracing paper in Pentel Sign pen with colored marker scribbled on the reverse side to add muted color.

Pictured below (top row, from left to right): David Andrews ASLA; Ron Kasprisin, Architect/Planner; John P. Clarde AIA, AICP; Kenneth H. Creveling Jr. AICP; Dennis Tate, Architect/Urban Designer; Jane Howard; Herbert W. Stevens AICP

This is a public service of the AIA with no fees paid to participating team members.

> **A R/UDAT is an "outreach effort . . . to help communities create 'vision' of their future and target realistic ideas for achieving that future vision." (R/UDAT: AIA, 1992). Its model is as follows:**

- Application, Evaluation, and Commitment: a consortium of local citizens and organizations invites the AIA to perform an R/UDAT, usually assisted by a local task force group. The community makes a formal application to the AIA, which evaluates the community's capability to participate. A team of outside experts (eight to twelve) is assembled and the process begins.

- Pre-visit Preparation: Due to the intensive and short term nature of the actual charrette, the community and the team's leaders prepare for the team's visit up to a year in advance, arranging work locations, lodging, supplies, printing, publicity and media-coverage, student participation, etc., in order for the team to complete its tasks effectively and efficiently within the four-day time frame.

- Team Visit: The visit occurs from Thursday through Monday evening, highlighted by team meetings, site tours, meetings and interviews with community leaders and stakeholders, open town meetings, detailed work sessions individually and in groups, a written and printed report, and a major presentation to the public of findings and recommendations—all in four days.

- Follow-up Activities: The team leader revisits the community within six to eighteen months of the charrette, meeting with local groups to assess the success of the process and provide additional advice short of actual implementation.

Main Street. The National Main Street Program was formed as a means of providing design, marketing, and implementation assistance to downtown areas across the United States. Participating states allocate funds for Main Street programs with local contributions for a Main Street Director. The public involvement aspect of Main Street is similar in format and organization to the AIA R/UDAT.

Resource team members, usually three including an urban designer and a retail marketing specialist, are brought in from other states. The significant differences between Main Street and R/UDAT occur in their overall approaches; Main Street focuses on urban beautification and short-term implementation strategies, (i.e., streetscape, facade redesign, retail marketing and parking), whereas R/UDAT focuses on short- and long-term design recommendations and political as well as economic implementation strategies.

Constructive Humor

Humor can overcome barriers generated by politics, cultures, and opposing agendas within the community. Drawings can serve as cartoons or humorous satire in the public involvement arena. Care must be given to the sensitivities of the various individuals and groups involved; but like many editorial cartoons, the subject matter is rich and varied and a way of encouraging people to laugh at their predicaments or their conflicts with others.

In Bellingham Cartoons, two drawings were prepared for a community visioning process that reflected issues regarding the influx of Canadian shoppers into this northern Washington community; and, the often-expressed desire for a closer connection between the Western Washington University and the downtown. Let the graphics speak for themselves.

In Port Townsend Spaceship, one of the first meetings organized for a waterfront master plan occurred one week prior to a contentious mayoral election in the community with various factions present to begin and discuss the study. The design team took a gamble, sensing a changing political climate of the community, and developed a mylar overlay of a space ship that aligned with an aerial oblique perspective of the downtown and waterfront. During the meeting, amid solemn faces, the team began a seemingly technical presentation referred to as a new way of conducting aerial photographic surveys for a new (and contentious) ferry terminal site, intentionally rambling on a bit about new Washington State Department of Transportation equipment used in the process, to the confused looks of the audience. At a key time, an upper portion of the aerial oblique per-

5-10 Maple Leaf Shopping Center.

5-11 Machine Over the Landscape. The sight of a giant machine flying over your city or neighborhood, can for a moment, give pause and break the tension of a public meeting.

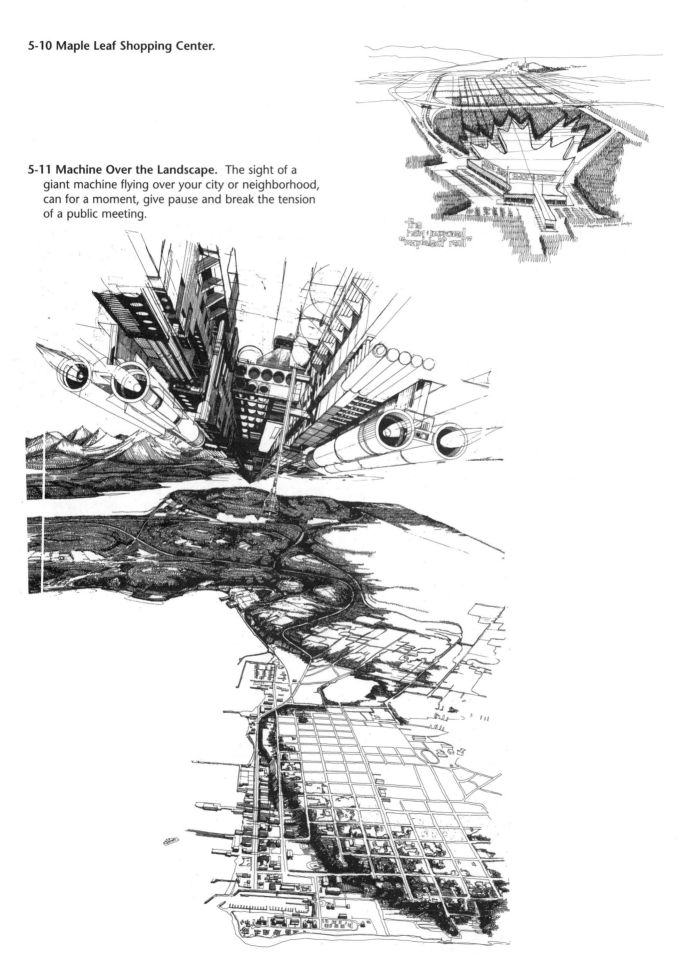

spective was quickly and flamboyantly removed by staff, revealing the spaceship in all its glory, fitting into the aerial perspective. The audience erupted in laughter and later people lined up for copies of the drawings as souvenir posters, breaking the ice and creating a more congenial atmosphere.

The authors like spaceships as metaphors and drawing vehicles that are useful in public meetings. Three science fiction creations were useful in work conducted in the Fairbanks, Alaska area during the 1980s, working with education program department heads and other university staff. There is a side aspect to these drawings that added to the excitement of drawing: Each drawing was made without any forethought of what it was to be. The drawings, *the phu surrender* and *maltese class* began with the placement of a technical pen to a sheet of mylar and any shape being initially drawn. From there, the shapes that began appearing also began to dictate direction and concept. No rough or draft drawings were made and no erasures were needed. For example, in *the phu surrender,* the first shape drawn was an oval-like shape without intent or content. It turned into the lifeboat entering the docking bay of the starcruiser *Fairbanks.* Loosen up and try it by concentrating only on the lines and shapes at hand.

Newspaper Inserts. Using drawings in local newspaper inserts can be a highly effective means of get-ting the public involved and informed. People respond to creative visualizations that reflect local context, issues, and events. Check with local newspapers, regarding the size and format that are used for inserts, how they are inserted and by whom. Newspaper print inserts are inexpensive and can double as final products for small towns and rural areas. Many small newspapers will insert the section as a public service document, for free, and in the hope of increasing circulation.

References

National Trust For Historic Preservation, *National Main Street Center Training Program: 1981.*

The American Institute of Architects, *R/UDAT, Regional & Urban Design Assistance Team.* A Guidebook for The American Institute of Architects Regional & Urban Design Assistance Team (R/UDAT) Program, 1992.

University of Washington, Department of Urban Design and Planning, *Sedro-Woolley, Community Visions;* URBDP 507 General Planning Lab report: 1993.

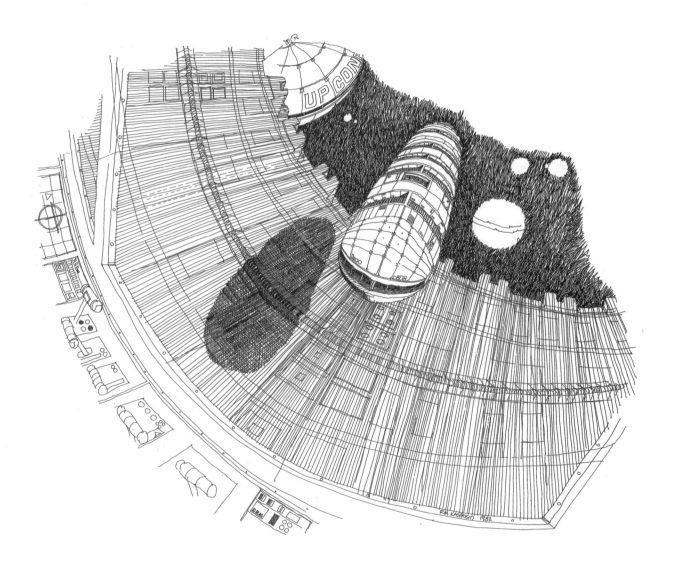

5-12 Phu Surrender. A line drawing developed without a rough sketch or initial concept. The concept evolved from the drawing effort.

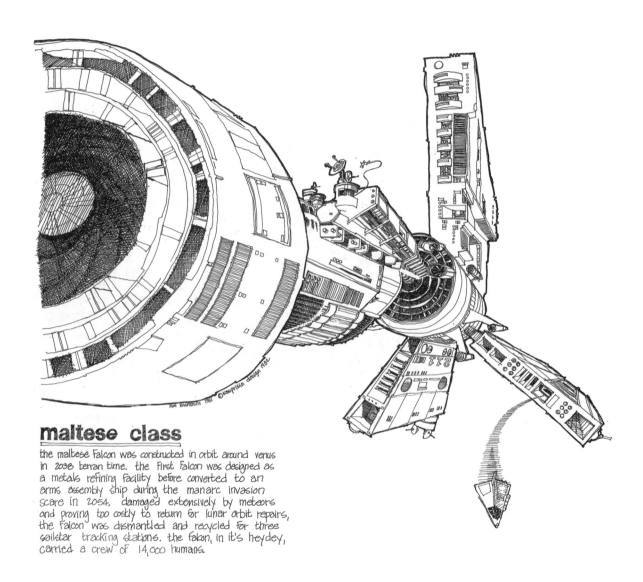

maltese class

the maltese falcon was constructed in orbit around venus
in 2038 terran time. the first falcon was designed as
a metals refining facility before converted to an
arms assembly ship during the manarc invasion
scare in 2054. damaged extensively by meteors
and proving too costly to return for lunar orbit repairs,
the falcon was dismantled and recycled for three
sailstar tracking stations. the falcon, in it's heydey,
carried a crew of 14,000 humans.

5-13 Maltese Class. A story developed from the act of drawing shape to shape, leading
to the final pattern as a cumulative process of discovery using visual thinking. These
drawings captured the excitement of public workshops as they departed from the
planning tasks and tapped into the imagination of participants.

Part Two

Case Studies of Cascadia

Introduction

Part II consists of four case studies within the Cascadia bio-region. Community planning and urban design projects are used to exemplify means of integrating the notion of bio-regional context, the scale ladders within that context, time patterning, public involvement, and graphic language. Not all were accomplished as one design effort but are the result of numerous projects extended over years' offering examples of differing scales, objectives and issues, within larger contexts and the visualization techniques used to develop designs and plans. The focus eco-regions include portions of southeast Alaska, Ish River (Northwest Washington State), the Cowlitz-Willamette in the Pacific Northwest, and Clark Fork/Bitterroot east of the Cascade Mountains. Case studies focus on existing large and small city structures, and on human settlements within the natural environment. All case studies have a public participation orientation—a public awareness agenda. The projects required work with community task forces, neighborhood groups, steering committees, leadership committees, and/or larger groups of citizens. Advancing these individuals and groups beyond participation to a better understanding of change and settlement impact stemmed from the use of an extensive visual language using hand-drawn graphics. The visual language provided a mutual communication and design method for planner/designer and resident alike.

6 The Tlingit Archipelago Case Study Background and Overview

Purpose of Study: Long Term Planning/Design Effort

The authors had an opportunity to partake in a planning and design process that spanned multiple scales, project issues, and time within a single community and its geographic region in Ketchikan Alaska. Beginning in 1974 to the present, they worked on various urban planning, urban design, and architecture studies involving a borough-wide comprehensive plan, highway impact studies, historic preservation and design, and site-specific building designs. The Ketchikan Case Study provides the opportunity to review and discuss the idea of places within places. It explores the carry-over of place definition from scale to scale and place to place, understanding that place is not only defined by the interactions of its interior elements and activities but equally by its context, a network of exterior connected places, healthy or distressed, from the bio-region to the adjacent building or natural feature.

Regional Place Connected to Local Place

Ketchikan lies in the Cascadia bio-region within the Tlingit Archipelago in southeast Alaska. These definitions were developed in part by David McCloskey of Seattle University, Founder and Director of the Cascadia Institute. Its human settlement patterns are directly related to the regional morphology and the natural bio-systems of the region, from mountain/water interface, to watersheds, to salmon and halibut habitats, to treed mountains, to the tenuous settlement footholds on precarious edges and the transportation devices used to connect them to one another and the outside world. Each community is different in its adaptation to the landscape but each directly reflects the larger context.

Water Dependent/Resource Industry Communities

The planner and designer needs as much influence from the real world as possible in arriving at responsible solutions to stated problems, not just interesting geometry isolated from that real world.

One tool is the craft of visualization, portraying in different ways the smaller within the larger, and identifying the transference of identity carry-over. Visualization weaves itself into the design process and acts as an integral part of the planning process.

Cascadia Bio-region

The City and Borough of Ketchikan, Alaska lie in the Tlingit Archipelago South eco-region of Cascadia, part of an island system separating the Alaskan/British Columbian mainland from the Pacific Ocean. This portion of Cascadia forms the panhandle of Alaska along the coast of British Columbia and is referred to as southeast by residents and most visitors.

All three plan diagrams include reference and orientation shapes for the reader's ease in spatially appreciating the relative size of Cascadia and "southeast."

6-1 Cascadia Bio-region.

6-2 State of Alaska Southeast/Tlingit Archipelago.

Ketchikan is located in an archipelago that provides a significant part of its physical definition, characterized by river and stream watersheds, 3,000-foot coastal mountain ranges, and the expansive saltwater of the Inland Passage.

Part of Ketchikan's physical drama is its island location, Revillagigedo island. It is equivalent in size to the State of Rhode Island and contains the geographic and topological characteristics of the larger eco-region, (i.e., major watersheds and spruce covered mountains). The borough-island has geologically broken away from the mainland, forming Behm Canal, and is notched along its west and south edges by inlets, some extending into the center of the island. This defined ecosystem provides habitat and sustenance for diverse life forms including humans and their activities. The communities of the Tlingit Archipelago South eco-region are dispersed along the edges of the archipelago islands, from Prince of Wales Island to Revillagigedo Island, connected by air and water transportation systems. These communities are insulated but not isolated, establishing interrelated cultural patterns defined in large degree by their physical surroundings.

Community In The Larger Context: The Ketchikan Gateway Borough Comprehensive Plan, 1976

Introduction and Background

In 1976 the Ketchikan Gateway Borough Planning Department published the *Ketchikan Comprehensive Plan Policies 1976* for the Ketchikan Gateway Borough, focusing on social, economic, and physical

6-3 State map: A basic location and reference tool for every project. Zooming in on Ketchikan, a 38-hour boat trip from Bellingham, Washington; one and one-half hours by jet to Seattle. Revillagigedo Island is the gateway to Alaska from the water, an island borough the size of the State of Rhode Island and home to over 20,000 people.

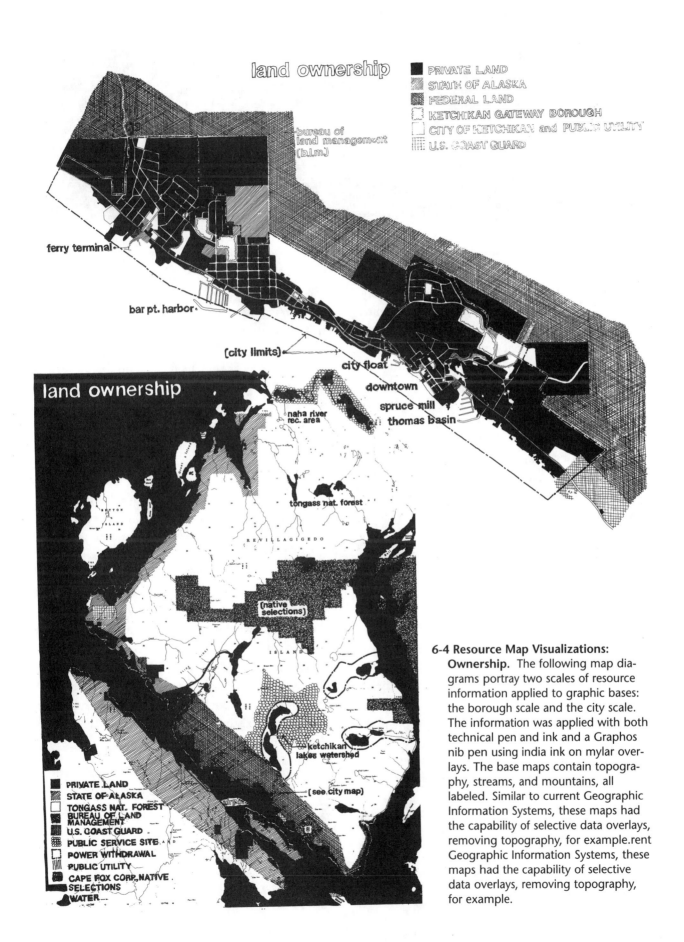

land ownership

- PRIVATE LAND
- STATE OF ALASKA
- FEDERAL LAND
- KETCHIKAN GATEWAY BOROUGH
- CITY OF KETCHIKAN and PUBLIC UTILITY
- U.S. COAST GUARD

bureau of land management (b.l.m.)

ferry terminal

bar pt. harbor

(city limits)

city float

downtown

spruce mill

thomas basin

land ownership

naha river rec. area

tongass nat. forest

REVILLAGIGEDO

ISLAND

(native selections)

ketchikan lakes watershed

(see city map)

- PRIVATE LAND
- STATE OF ALASKA
- TONGASS NAT. FOREST
- BUREAU OF LAND MANAGEMENT
- U.S. COAST GUARD
- PUBLIC SERVICE SITE
- POWER WITHDRAWAL
- PUBLIC UTILITY
- CAPE FOX CORP. NATIVE SELECTIONS
- WATER

6-4 Resource Map Visualizations: Ownership. The following map diagrams portray two scales of resource information applied to graphic bases: the borough scale and the city scale. The information was applied with both technical pen and ink and a Graphos nib pen using india ink on mylar overlays. The base maps contain topography, streams, and mountains, all labeled. Similar to current Geographic Information Systems, these maps had the capability of selective data overlays, removing topography, for example.rent Geographic Information Systems, these maps had the capability of selective data overlays, removing topography, for example.

6-5 Ketchikan From the Water. A fine point technical pen and ink drawing of the immediate Ketchikan waterfront, using simple vertical lines in varying densities to establish a distant tree texture and value pattern.

development of the City and Borough. The book's format was inspired by the San Francisco Comprehensive Plan, discussing and illustrating policies for planning. Public participation was encouraged and incorporated into the process and document, necessitating a policy visualization technique that was quite innovative in Alaska in 1976. The majority of the work was conducted in Ketchikan, Alaska over a period of three years, culminating in the publication of the document in August 1976.

Ketchikan, Alaska is a rugged landscape of large-scale water, mountains, and weather systems. It embodies the places-within-places concept from its archipelago and 3000-foot island mountains to the tenacious native and in-migrant human settlements that cling to its water edges. From the definition of large bays and inlets surrounded by immediate mountain forms to the narrow and intimate streets of downtown Ketchikan and Creek Street on Ketchikan Creek, the sense of place as defined by present and historic forces and the surrounding larger places is intoxication, fed by the smells released from the land in the rainstorms and by the whistles of the eagles high up in the spruce trees on the nearby slopes.

To do a policy document of Ketchikan as a place required more than static two-dimensional drawings and text, resulting in an effort, albeit young at the time, to portray in drawings the power of the verticality and scale of the place.

The terrain of the Tlingit Archipelago dictates linear narrow human settlement patterns occurring along the wateredge. The Ketchikan Gateway Borough represents a settlement pattern some 36 miles in length, extending from Clover Pass on the north to Carol Inlet on the south. Within this linear pattern are the City of Ketchikan, the native village of Saxman, and small borough communities such as Point Higgins and Mt. Point. Popu-lations in this area have nearly doubled from 8,500 in 1960 to 16,000 in 1990.

The status of land, its use, control or ownership, is the underlying Monopoly board. The spatial depictions of ownership and use define the stakeholders in any planning and/or design action. In this case, information mapping was done in the Ketchikan Borough offices without access to major suppliers or producers of graphic methods. The maps were constructed of Graphos pen and india ink diagrams on mylar overlays, freehand over preliminaries.

The borough scale diagrams illustrate the use of an overlay system to add information to a spatial reference system where the base has substantial data (rivers, creeks, names, land masses, and so on) that would be difficult to repeat by hand drawing. Topography is represented by hatching, with the lightest value the highest elevation and the darkest value (the water) the lowest. Population is shown in dark value letters and numbers on a white background to indicate estimated population over census population. Existing land use and future land use are shown through simple hatching techniques with a Graphos drawing pen.

Townscape Within the Regional Form

The City of Ketchikan is located at the foot and west of Deer Mountain on the western edge of

6-6 Ketchikan Vicinity Future Land Use.

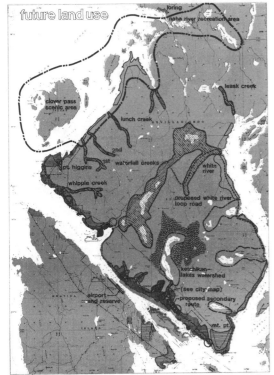

tionship between the linear form of the human settlement pattern and the verticality of the island's topography. The trees were graphically represented by simple vertical lines concentrated in various densities to achieve a sense of depth and shaping of the foothills immediately behind the city. Dots in the sky were used to simulate clouds common to Ketchikan and mask some of the upper elevations. The dots were also applied with varying densities to affect shaping. Buildings are outline shapes.

Land ownership establishes who or what entity controls what land. In Ketchikan, the majority of land in the city limits is under private ownership, the darkest value. City of Ketchikan lands were given the lightest value. The streets were left blank. Borough lands outside the city limits were hatched in a mid-value with a fine-point pen. (Common conventions often leave private lands white and make public lands darker values, but in this case private land ownership was an issue with the public.)

Diagrams represent the status of city policy regarding land use: existing land use (the base resulting from community action), existing zoning (the city policy on permitted uses, not necessarily in agreement with community actions), and future land use and directions for growth (that which the City aspires to achieve). House footprints were added for scale reference and orientation to the existing land use map.

Revillagigedo Island. The town form is linear and narrow, often no more than four streets wide. This elevation, drawn from a series of photographs taken from Gravina Island to the west, captures the rela-

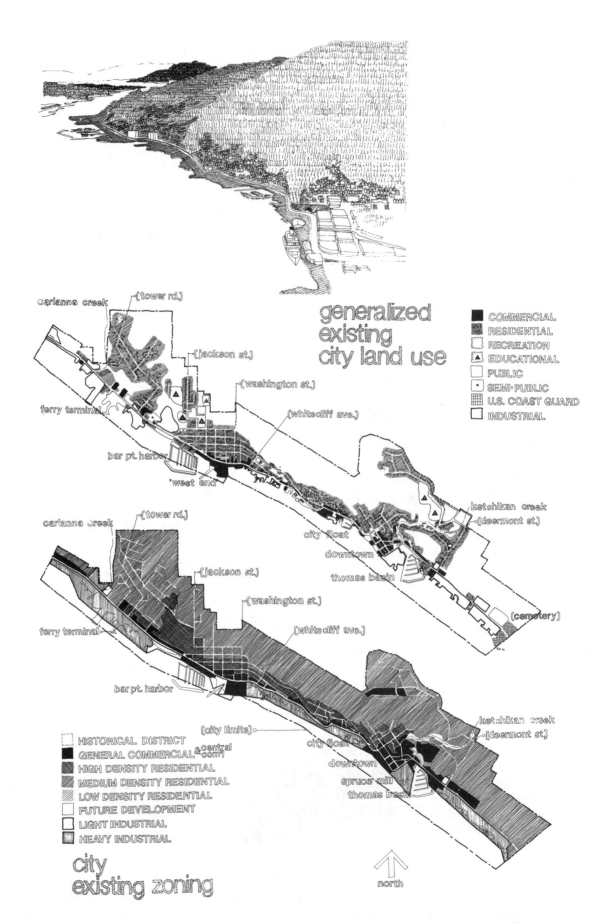

generalized
existing
city land use

■ COMMERCIAL
▨ RESIDENTIAL
▫ RECREATION
▲ EDUCATIONAL
□ PUBLIC
◉ SEMI·PUBLIC
▦ U.S. COAST GUARD
▢ INDUSTRIAL

carlanna creek
(tower rd.)
(jackson st.)
(washington st.)
(whitecliff ave.)
ferry terminal
bar pt. harbor
'west end'
ketchikan creek
(deermont st.)
city float
downtown
thomas basin
(cemetery)

carlanna creek
(tower rd.)
(jackson st.)
(washington st.)
(whitecliff ave.)
ferry terminal
bar pt. harbor
(city limits)
city float
downtown
spruce mill
thomas basin
ketchikan creek
(deermont st.)

▫ HISTORICAL DISTRICT
■ GENERAL COMMERCIAL & central com'l
▨ HIGH DENSITY RESIDENTIAL
▨ MEDIUM DENSITY RESIDENTIAL
▨ LOW DENSITY RESIDENTIAL
□ FUTURE DEVELOPMENT
□ LIGHT INDUSTRIAL
▦ HEAVY INDUSTRIAL

city
existing zoning

↑
north

6-7 City Maps.

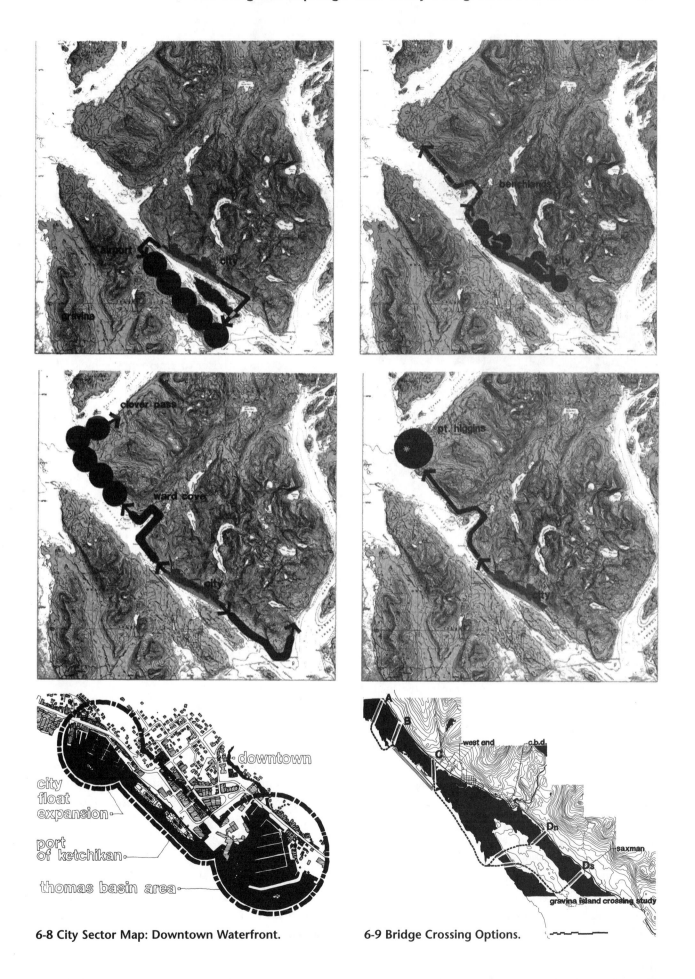

6-8 City Sector Map: Downtown Waterfront.

6-9 Bridge Crossing Options.

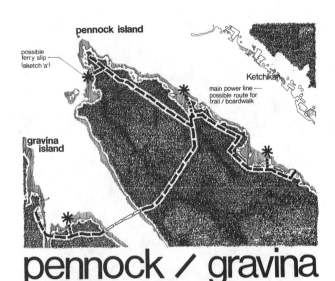

pennock / gravina

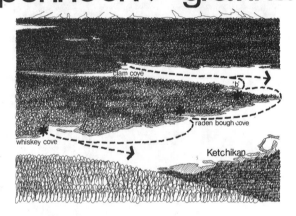

6-10 Vicinity Ferry Options.

The plan diagram is one of the most valuable means of communicating information to the general public due to the distillation of information into a readable spatial format usually with key biophysical reference shapes as a guide. Downtown Waterfront diagram emphasizes the water and wateredge with the darkest values and uses cruise ship footprints for scale, hatched buildings of the downtown for building density and scale, and a dark broken border to emphasize the area of study. The Gravina Island Crossing Study diagrams delineate bridge or hard water crossings as opposed to ferry crossings. Highly controversial in Ketchikan, these options were depicted with detailed topography and the existing road pattern for public reference and orientation. Another transportation issue was the local ferry system, vital to southeast communities. Ferry Location Diagrams needed to be uncluttered and simple. The diagrams contained water bodies, land masses and the city boundary as background reference. Added to

that base were the ferry sites and the proposed routes in white contrasted against the dark water for maximum contrast.

Selected Topical Studies Within the Townscape Place: Ketchikan Traffic Study— Traffic Patterns and Route Options, 1976

Introduction and Background

The Ketchikan tunnel along the Tongass Highway at the northern edge of downtown Ketchikan has long been a potential barrier to emergency vehicles if the tunnel is the site of a blocking accident or other mishap. No alternative route existed due to the water on the west side and the steep granite hill immediately to the east. Since 1924, ideas have been offered regarding an alternate route for emergency needs: the Hinselman Highway bypass in 1924, the Schoenbar bypass in the 1940s, and the Schoenbar bypass study in 1976.

This most recent Schoenbar bypass is a secondary route designed to alleviate existing and projected traffic problems as Ketchikan outgrows its one main street. The study was funded and coordinated by the Ketchikan Gateway Borough Planning Department in cooperation with the Alaska Department of Highways and the City of Ketchikan Engineering Department and co-authored by economist George Gee.

The study's purpose was to explore the highway options and present them to the Borough, State, and citizens of Ketchikan who would eventually be asked to approve the bypass. The final product was a technical planning document for public review with text, charts, and two- and three-dimensional diagrams. Basic route options are portrayed as overlays to a detailed topographic map, enabling the planner to draw only the options.

Three-dimensional sketch diagrams often portray vertical data in meaningful context better than two-dimensional diagrams. In these two route option diagrams, the adjacent land forms provide the scale

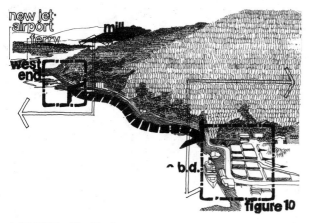

6-11,12 Traffic Study.

reference necessary to establish constraints for the route alignments. Looping horizontal lines are used to represent treed slopes and foothills, decreasing in size as the distance from the viewer increases. The route option arrow is the darkest value set against the light to medium-light background of hills and mountain forms. Only a few key building shapes are outlined for reference and orientation.

The same base aerial sketch is used to construct additional diagrams by drawing information on a mylar overlay, a photostat, or other quality copy of the original base. Notes can be hand-lettered on the drawing, traced from a letter guide, or pasted on using computer generated or film tape lettering. In this case, computer or lettering machine technology were unavailable on site and hand lettering was the most convenient and effective. Technical pens were used for the topography, and Graphos nib pens were used for the road system. Heavier weight technical pen points would also suffice for the roads. The water was darkened to provide movement to the drawing and emphasize the water/mountain relationship that causes the linear road network.

Place as Historic Artifact and Active Enclave: The Creek Street Public Facilities Design, 1984

Introduction and Background

Creek Street is a boardwalk neighborhood clustered along Ketchikan Creek south of downtown Ketchikan. Its history is a significant part of its present state: a neighborhood that existed as a native Tlingit fish drying encampment long before the Europeans arrived in the area. The creek is a source of rich folklore among the native peoples and its tales and myths are represented on many totem poles within the Ketchikan Creek corridor. With the arrival of non-native cultures to the area, sawmills, salting operations for the fishing industry, and the infamous "Street of Joy" or "The Line" created a built artifact of boardwalk and smaller woodframe clapboard houses on stilts winding along the creek at the base of a granite cliff to one side and the backs of downtown buildings on the other. It is a place defined by present day activities, history, the land and creek forms, an historic steel truss bridge, and Thomas Basin at the mouth of Ketchikan Creek. Salmon still spawn up the creek along with varieties of trout, viewed now by residents, shopkeepers, and awestruck visitors shielding themselves from the often blowing rainfall of southeast Alaska.

The purpose of the Creek Street Design study was to assess the location and possible improvements to the existing historic boardwalk and key publicly owned parcels of land along the creek. Proposals for new vehicular and pedestrian bridges were already being considered when the study began. A new

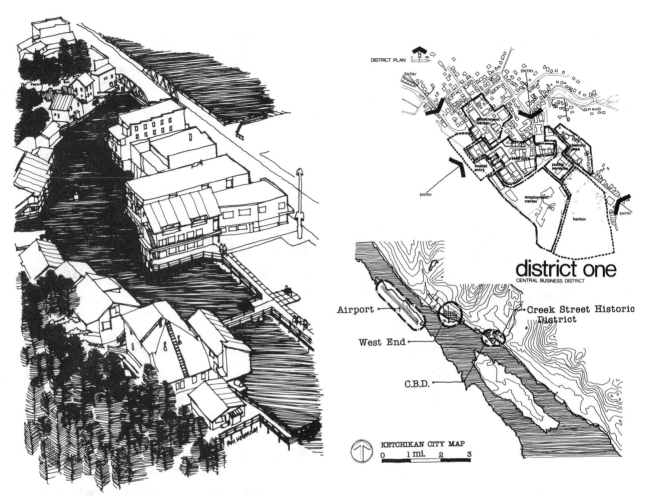

6-13 Creek Street. Outline drawings showing the core of the historic district and base plans for diagrams.

native-owned hotel and restaurant complex (now completed) was proposed and in progress with site work in 1984. A funicular connecting the Creek Street boardwalk and the resort was one of the program issues. The funicular is now complete and provides a vital link between the hotel and the creek. However, the study was expected to resolve conflicting opinions regarding the location of new bridges across the creek, completing the pedestrian connection from the hotel through Creek Street to the adjacent downtown.

The study required a visual and graphic analytical methodology for resolution of the boardwalk and bridge expansion. That methodology and the definition and subsequent minor alteration of the Creek Street place is the subject of this section.

Creek Street is immediately southeast of downtown Ketchikan with the downtown literally backing up to the creek edge on Ketchikan Creek, an his-

toric and still active king salmon spawning site. The Creek is a designated historic district located at the mouth of Thomas Basin as the creek enters the saltwater. A granite hill is the immediate east edge of the creek characterized by a 70-foot high tree covered steep slope; the downtown forms the west boundary with blank or inaccessible walls forming a two- to three-story edge along the creek. To the north the creek flows under Park Avenue and becomes the focal shape for a residential neighborhood bordering the creek as it spills out of the mountains. It is a mountain stream flowing through a linear residential area and literally cascading into an historic district and a business district before flowing under a steel truss bridge through Thomas Basin and into the waters of the archipelago. Places within places, all different, all connected, all sharing in the definition of one another.

The aerial oblique perspective expresses the

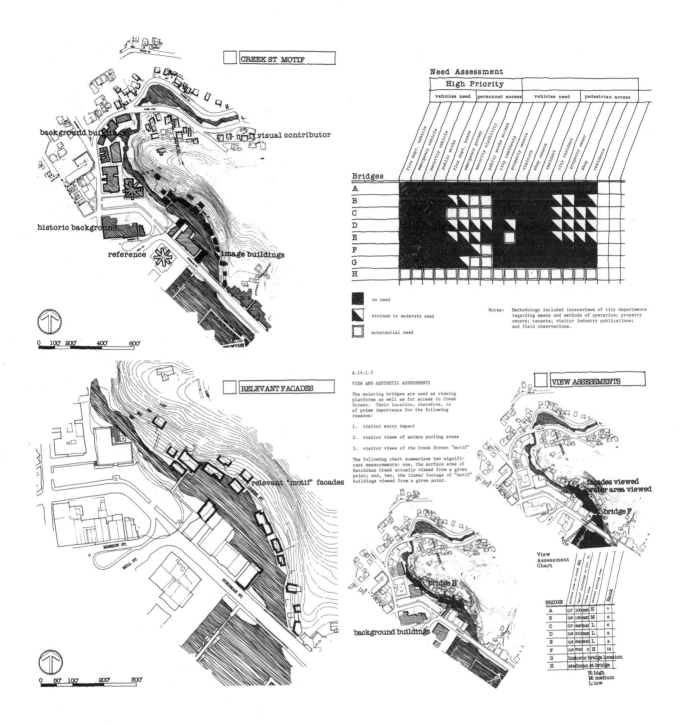

6-14 Creek View Evaluation Methodology. A graphic methodology was developed to evaluate the priority of possible viewpoints along the boardwalk based on the amount of relevant facades and the amount of surface area of the creek that could be observed from each potential boardwalk improvement site. Each potential view site was compared in an Evaluation Matrix distributed to the public at workshops. Taken as a part of a larger qualitative evaluation package, they provided a summary of the key qualitative features of the historic district: historic building facades, built-form contributions, the creek area itself, and the neighborhood and mountain background.

Creek Street and Its Visual Analysis. Use of contrast by line to highlight key areas of study. This series of visual diagrams represents an exploration for clues and context within the Ketchikan Creek neighborhood and Creek Street district. The analysis and public process was aided by the visual portrayal of building conditions, historic elements, view corridors, infrastructure, and many other conditions or parts that make up the creek corridor. Technical pens and Graphos nib pens on mylar constituted the majority of tools used. Pentel Sign pen also added heavier line weight values on some diagram.

buildings along the historic portion of the creek, focusing on the water area because of the proposed new bridges. The drawing was done with a technical pen on tracing paper with very little value, using the water surface as the strongest attraction to the eye.

The information series map-diagrams represent a larger number of diagrams that portray a sequential build-up of clues or conditions that have a bearing on the design outcome and influence and support designer decisions. All of the drawings were made with technical pen and india ink on tracing paper or mylar. Selected examples include:

Visual Access Windows. A location of possible view windows for pedestrians along the creek corridor and categorized by ownership type: public or private.

Land Ownership Status. The City- and State-owned parcels were of key importance for possible expansion and viewing areas, avoiding conflicts with private property owners.

Private Development. Locations of development being considered by the private sector, added with a Graphos pen and hatched where appropriate with a technical pen.

Relevant Facades. The historic character of the creek district was identified through the period building design of creekside structures as a basis for evaluating alternatives at a later stage of the design process. A Graphos pen was used to highlight with dark values the building outlines of "motif" facades.

Creek Street Motif. Views from the Creek Street boardwalk include background shapes of buildings and terrain not categorized in the historic district but key to the quality of the view. This diagram identifies, locates, and highlights those components of the background view that contribute to that quality. The key view elements include: the image buildings of the creek itself; historic background buildings; background buildings with no historic or architectural Creek Street-relevance; visual contributor buildings whose scale and design, while not historic or architecturally significant regarding the Creek, nonetheless add rather than detracted from the overall view; and the reference build-ings such as the library/museum, a contemporary structure of differing design and material character from the historic district.

Potential Projects. A basic map illustrating the projects generated through analysis and public participation workshops.

View Assessment Diagrams. Of particular importance for the political acceptance of the project recommendations was the bridge option selection methodology. Specifically, how did each bridge option impact the creek and its character and how defensible was each option test?

The graphic method employed was as follows:

• For each bridge option, a view window was drawn from the center of the bridge and from each end in each direction (up and down the creek);

• all water surface within the view window was highlighted in dark values so that it could be visually compared and quantitatively measured for area;

• the "motif" buildings viewed in the window were highlighted and measured based on the linear feet of frontage and/or sides visible in the view;

• the urban or background view was highlighted and measured in linear feet of exposed building side; and

• the natural setting exposed in the view was ranked according to a "high," "medium," or "low" exposure of mountains or water seen within the window.

Constructing the graphic assessment diagrams consisted of: Selecting a mid-viewing point on the given bridge or boardwalk expansion; drawing a view plane from that point out to the first corner or edge condition that would prevent the viewing plane from extending further; repeating it in the other direction (visualize a protractor with a 180-degree arc laid down on the view point with arrows pointing outward to define the view window or angle); and extending each view plane length until it also terminated in a blocking form. The water surface and building facades visible in the window are then highlighted and measured.

The view assessments assisted elected officials and laypeople in visually comparing the value of each bridge and boardwalk based on view potential given predetermined criteria such as historic buildings viewed in linear feet and visible creek surface. The project required a close involvement with the public, particularly residents, merchants, and landowners along the creek and citizens interested in preserving the historic aspect of the creek. Quick study sketches and final illustrative sketches were used as a means of visualizing the diagrams and plan concepts in three dimensions. Slidetrace was the primary method used to prepare base perspectives of existing conditions upon which new design ideas were overlaid. Quick studies were prepared on flimsy over the base perspective until the desired result was obtained and then a final ink sketch was prepared.

Once a basic sketch is drawn, it can be overlaid for quick alternative studies using the same base drawing.

Some sketches were done in the field, weather permitting, to portray a loose and conceptual character. These sketches were actually prepared with green and red Pentel Sign pens to highlight the treed slope and the boardwalk character. Their flamboyancy added to the public presentation by differentiating natural form from built form in vivid color.

Place As Historic Artifact:
Historic Stedman Facade Design Study for Historic Ketchikan, 1989

Introduction and Background

Stedman Street commercial district is immediately south and west of Creek Street, facing into Thomas Basin. The one- and two-story buildings on the east side of Stedman Street are pitched roof wooden

6-15,16 Creek Study Sketches and Site-Specific Plan Recommendations. Loose fast Pentel Sign colored-pen sketches were used in public workshops then translated to fine-point drawings for final reproduction.

6-17 Stedman Street Triangle. Sketch vignettes enable the public to view the three-dimensional outcomes of plan concepts.

structures with square parapet fronts with some trim and cornice articulation. This facade acts as an urban place "wall," defining the Thomas Basin area and serving as the entry to Creek Street from the south.

Historic Ketchikan is a non-profit group seeking to preserve and protect the historic and architectural heritage of Ketchikan. The Stedman Street facade group was singled out as a key group of buildings the restoration of which would aid the downtown's revitalization and that of Creek Street. Public meetings were held to inform the general public and enlist the ideas and support of business and property owners. Graphic visualizations were critical to increasing public awareness of the potential of the existing buildings. Since the study, most of the Stedman Street buildings have been restored and/or rehabilitated in keeping with the original design and character of the period.

The Stedman Street drawing relates the buildings to Creek Street, Thomas Basin, and the downtown area. It and the facade drawings were constructed with a technical pen and india ink, using layers of closely-spaced hatched lines to build value and focus in the drawing. Each of the facades[1] acts as a key link in a chain of buildings, creating an urban wall with historic character and consistency. The group of buildings has become a place along the Ketchikan waterfront as well as a linkage from one district of the waterfront to another. The buildings now contain gift shops, food stores, and a restored New York Hotel.

6-18 Proposal Drawing. Each proposed boardwalk improvement was highlighted on a plan diagram using stronger value outlines over fine line detail drawings.

stedman st. boardwalk

bayside hotel lookout

planter/bench

stedman st. triangle

[1] Some early design ideas were provided by Stephen Reeve, former borough planning director.

STEDMAN STREET STREETSCAPE *View North*

Before FOCSLE BAR *After*

6-19 A Stedman Street Historic Buildings. This pen and ink sketch places all of the to-be-restored buildings together as a single contextual element, a "wall" to Thomas Basin. Their significance lies in both their individual characteristics and in their relationship to one another.

6-19 B Foc'sle Bar.

HYATT BUILDINGS/STEDMAN STREET
Before

HYATT BUILDINGS/STEDMAN STREET
After

6-20 Hyatt Buildings "Before" and "After." Fine point pen and ink sketches of the buildings in their existing condition and after restoration.

6-21 Ketchikan Thomas Basin Commercial Center:
New Site Networks as Extensions of Existing Patterns.

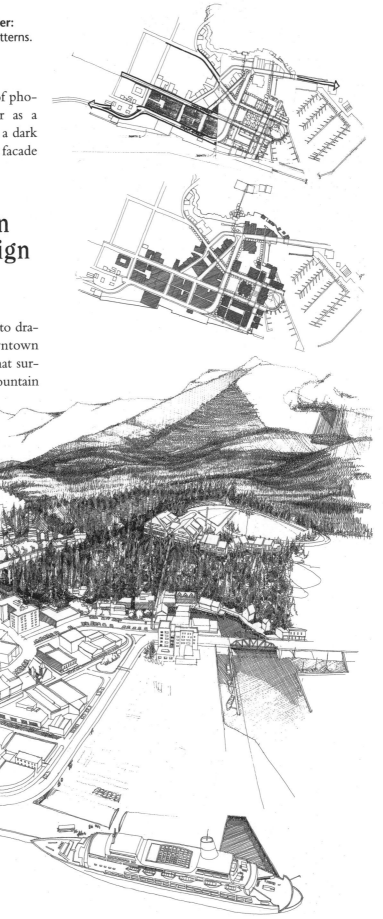

The drawing was sketched from a series of photographs taken on-site and pieced together as a guide. The background landscape was used as a dark value shape to highlight the lighter value facade group.

Ketchikan Thomas Basin Commercial Center Design

New City District: Spruce Mill Project

The composition of this drawing was chosen to dramatize the relationship between a downtown Ketchikan study site and the natural forces that surround it. Visualizing the built city in the mountain landscape put the site's location into perspective as a strategic piece of Ketchikan's downtown district. The study site became a fragment clinging to a small piece of filled level land at the foot of the coastal mountain range. The first aerial shows the study site as it exists, a vacant piece of waterfront land surrounded on two sides by the historic city downtown grid and the Creek Street Historic District, and on the other two sides by water of the Tongass Narrows and the Tongass Basin.

Background, Design Objectives, and Public Participation.

The study site, named for and occupied by a Spruce Mill that was destroyed by fire in 1976, was purchased by the city and cleared for development. The first building to take place was of a museum constructed on a donated parcel within

6-22 Spruce Mill Site, Ketchikan, Alaska.
The aerial view, drawn from a site aerial oblique photo, is set up to surround the blank site in the foreground with the natural and built forces that will shape the design proposal.

the middle of the study site. In 1992, development rights for the remainder of the site were granted to the Spruce Mill Corporation under strict design controls. An overriding concern of the Spruce Mill Development Group was to treat any design proposal of the study site as an opportunity to rebuild and support the existing historic downtown center. During the design process, visualizations of design proposals treated the site as a missing piece of the downtown, waiting to be connected to a surrounding historic context. With drawings that included the adjacent historical context, design proposals were keyed to what existed and a judgment could be made as to whether new development physically threatened or diminished the importance of the downtown.

Visualization of Proposed Character in the Design Process

Like many large scale development proposals, the exact building program was developed during the design process. Public input, financial constraints, and markets constantly shifted and with them specific design proposals. The visualization of proposed development had to be clear enough to communicate an understandable character to the layperson, yet open enough to accommodate future programmatic refinement of uses and their sizes. The aerial perspectives, showing various development proposals at different stages of the design process, are definitive enough to suggest building character, yet are sketchy enough to accommodate future change and development.

Study Site Connections to a City District

The two plan diagrams lay the basis for reconnecting the study site to the "mainstreet" network of the existing downtown center. The emphasis in one diagram is on the street corridor, or negative space as connector. This diagram connects the city street system by giving value to the extension of Front, Main, and X streets through the site to the water's edge, and introducing a new Market Street to connect Front Avenue to the south entry of the Creek Street Historic District. This street, parallel to Market Street, completes a proposed street structure on the study site consisting of six new city blocks, one of which incorporates the recently completed museum facility. The emphasis on the other diagram is on

building imprint, or positive space as connector. As a new preliminary building pattern, this diagram extends the building block pattern of the downtown into the study site.

Visualizing the Development of New Site Networks, Their Joints and Connections

The new street framework sets a logical and buildable order for development within the study site and three of its edges. The compositional complexity of the remaining water edge along Tongass Basin is visualized in these plan diagrams that explore alternative orders of building, open space and marina configurations resulting from the almost 45-degree relationship between the edge of the water and the city grid system. In these investigations, preliminary building organization is visualized simultaneously within a connective framework of public streets and pedestrian ways. The aerial perspective places one of the configurations within the preestablished street frame-work and the accompanying plan diagrams focus on developing detail within the joints and edges of the eccentric compositions. These scaled diagrams do not distinguish between inside and outside, but rather integrate a composition of exterior pedestrian and street connections as part of interior building organization.

Block Development Within a District Framework

The final study site framework of connected public streets defining new building blocks is outlined in the diagram. The diagram gives value to those special positional aspects of each block; corners, adjacencies to water or building edges, and special connections to activities that exist in the city. These are:

1. Cornerstone Block: The cornerstone of the framework, likely to be the first phase that continues the city's front street wateredge and provides a new cruise ship berth.

2. Corner Waterblock: This "promontory" block position has two water sides, Tongass Basin and Tongass Narrows.

3. Creek Street Block: This block has one water edge along Tongass Basin and is closest to the Creek Street Historic District.

4. Interior Block: The inland block borders Mill Street and three new streets of the pro-

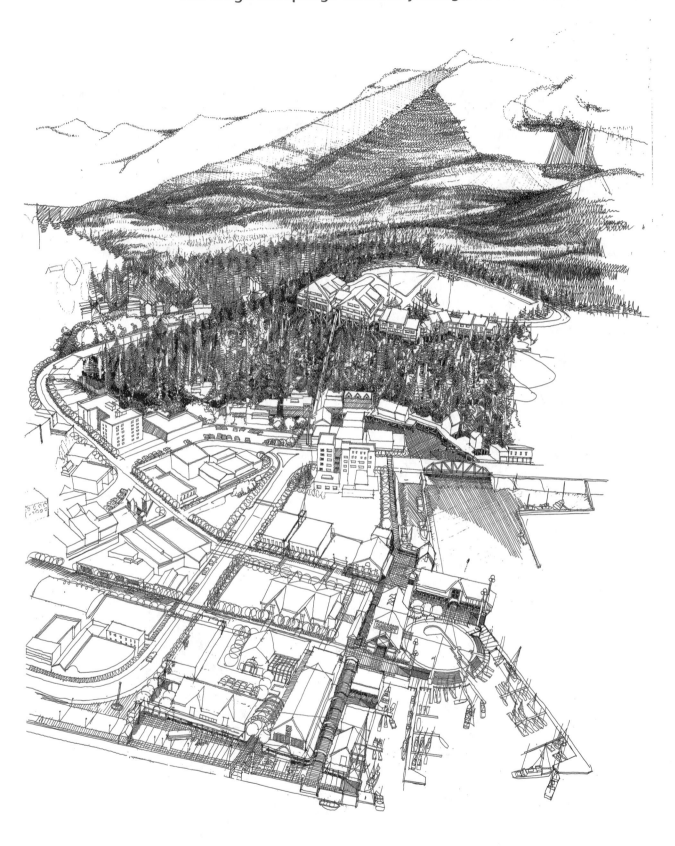

6-23 Ketchikan Alaska Spruce Mill Site Reorganization Scheme. The same aerial view is used to visualize various development schemes for the area. The drawing composition includes the historic block/street grid pattern that is extended into the site as a reference structure for exploring site design proposals. The structure includes existing street patterns, building massing and waterfront connections.

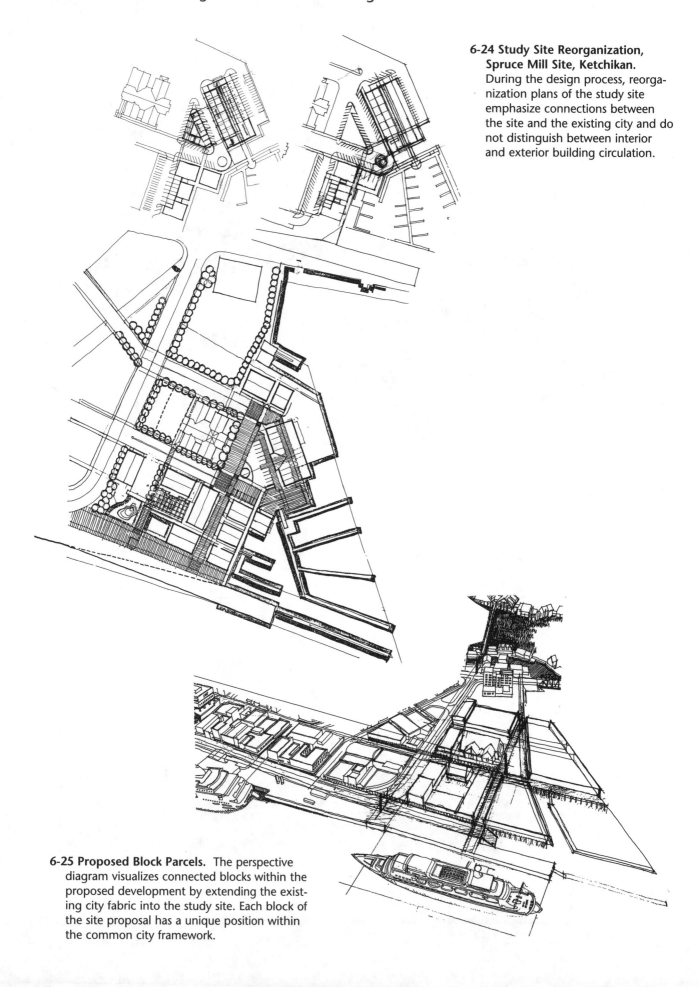

6-24 Study Site Reorganization, Spruce Mill Site, Ketchikan. During the design process, reorganization plans of the study site emphasize connections between the site and the existing city and do not distinguish between interior and exterior building circulation.

6-25 Proposed Block Parcels. The perspective diagram visualizes connected blocks within the proposed development by extending the existing city fabric into the study site. Each block of the site proposal has a unique position within the common city framework.

posed design framework. Most of the block was given to the construction of a new Museum and an area along Mill is held for its future expansion.

5. Parking Block: This inland block is defined by Mill and W Streets and the edge of the study site. Its narrow frontage facing the city and long dimension as a strip make it ideal for interim parking; a strip of new building could eventually front Mill Street.

6. Triangular Transition Block: The triangular block in the heart of the proposed design framework is formed by the shift of the water edge away from the city grid. The diagram treats its location as a type of keystone within the site composition. Two blocks front it and all blocks within the network touch it. Two of the triangle's points are the terminations of two city street extensions into the site.

Historic Building Typologies Within City Blocks

The historic building forms surrounding the Spruce Mill Study Site were visualized in simple line drawings as a way of informing the designers and public of previous building patterns; form, size, heights, and elevation patterns. These patterns are used as a basis for establishing new building structure in the study site that would relate to the historic downtown district. The drawings describe three basic types common to Ketchikan:

1. Free-Standing Pitched-Roof Buildings: These buildings commonly associated with

residential house forms, are some of the first buildings in Ketchikan. Many were replaced, some still exist, and others are scattered among other types.

2. Flat-Roofed Buildings: These buildings usually house commercial, retail, office, and manufacturing activities.

3. Parapet/Storefront Buildings: The western storefront facade type is common to the downtown area, expressing a heightened presence along important public streets. These buildings have both pitched or flat roofs behind their front parapets.

4. Civic and Public Buildings: There are a limited amount of public buildings with landmark silhouettes (churches, etc.).

The marquee element, common to most buildings in Ketchikan, is visualized as an element providing a continuity throughout the city. Most structures in Ketchikan offer some form of exterior rain protection overhanging the public sidewalk. The height and quality of the roof overhang varies, but the element does provide a logical connector to new development.

Proposed Building Typologies on the Study Site

The three-dimensional block diagram describes a possible relationship between the historic built form of the city and the proposed buildings on the six-block study site. The expansion of the existing SAPLIC museum, a free-standing pitched building already in the middle of the site, is the first new building to follow the principles outlined in the diagram. Along Front and Mill Streets, flat-top/parapet buildings are proposed on blocks that interface with historic parapet buildings. The proposed expansion of the pitched SAPLIC museum form happens between the existing facility and Mill Street. The expansion piece is a connector along the edge of the site, transitioning between the historic flat-top parapet buildings on Mill Street and the existing pitched-roof facility of the museum. The more finalized per-

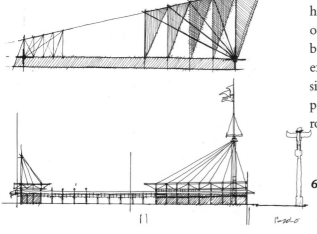

6-26 Triangular Keystone Block. The design of the keystone block of the composition, a focal point that terminates Main Street at the Water Edge.

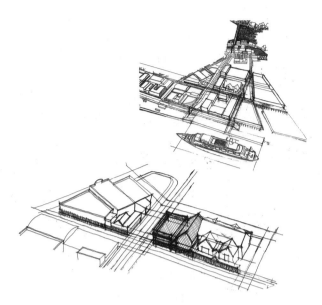

6-27 Proposed Museum Block Expansion With Historic Block Typologies. The diagram masses a building composition using the elements of historic block typologies, to transition between the downtown edge and new development within the study site.

spective, done for the Museum Board, focuses on the expansion along Mill Street, adjacent to the existing facility. The value of the drawing focuses on the Deer Mountain backdrop as a way of popping out the building silhouette and on the linear marquee that unites the different building types and connects to the downtown sidewalk system.

Rooms Within the Building, SAPLIC Museum. The understanding of a room as a place within a building, which in turn is a contributing piece of a larger district, which in turn, is part of the whole city is carried over through the reiterating of design ideas from scale to scale. The diagrams reiterate the position of the study site within the city, the museum block, and the building organization within the building block. The more literal perspective, done for the Museum Board, focuses on the immediate internal needs of the building program, exhibiting artifacts. In satisfying these requirements, the perspective describes other connecting ideas; an idea of how the room is made within the building by expressing a clear order of structure and an idea of the room's orientation within the city by placing the prominent Deer Mountain as an exhibit within the main museum room.

Buildings Within Blocks: Corner Waterblock/Creek Street Blocks

Proposed building form on the cornerstone and Creek Street Blocks emerges from perspective explorations along the Tongass Basin Elevation. The visualization places a computer view of a proposed hotel piece on the Cornerstone block within a traced slide of Ketchikan building context and its natural setting. In the final perspective, the presence of the existing building context serves as a reference for development of both the hotel on the Cornerstone Block and the adjacent housing form on the Creek Street Block. The resulting building form on the blocks is carried over from the former Spruce Mill and the residential scale of the adjacent free-standing, pitched-roof buildings of the Creek Street Neighborhood. Value and emphasis in the final drawing is placed along two edges that define the study site in perspective, one along the base of the mountain backdrop that defines the edge of the city and the other along the meeting of land and water.

Building Within Block: Cornerstone Block Development

Within the proposed study site framework, the plan diagrams focus on building development in the cornerstone block. During the design process, the precise development of the building program depended in part on the dimensional constraints of the block as visualized in the overall study site framework. The objective of all the new block designs was to maintain the continuity of the historical downtown building wall along its periphery while accommodating new requirements for parking and service within the block's center. The plan diagrams, freehanded to scale, explore ways in which alternative versions of new building programs can wrap around a required parking program, resulting in a block that has the outward appearance of the adjacent historic block pattern. The evolution of the plan and section diagrams represent the testing of partially decked levels of housing over ground-level commercial and office to two levels of office space over retail and commercial space on three sides of the block, a corner restaurant, and a free-standing pitched-roof building along Main Street to answer to the adjacent museum block.

6-28 Museum Expansion, Ketchikan, Alaska.

6-29 Museum Interior Connected To Deer Mountain Reference.

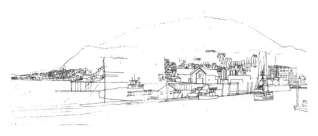

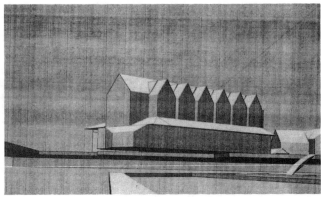

6-30 A,B,C Corner Waterblock Perspective Building Development, Spruce Mill Site. Proposed building impact along the waterfront is studied within the perspective of the traced waterfront context of the city. A computer massing diagram from the building plans is then traced and fitted into the perspective. The final presentation drawing gives value to the Deer Mountain backdrop of the city's water edge pier line.

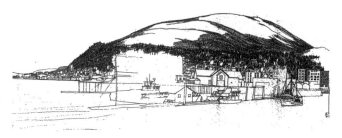

6-31 Corner Waterblock Water Edge Development.

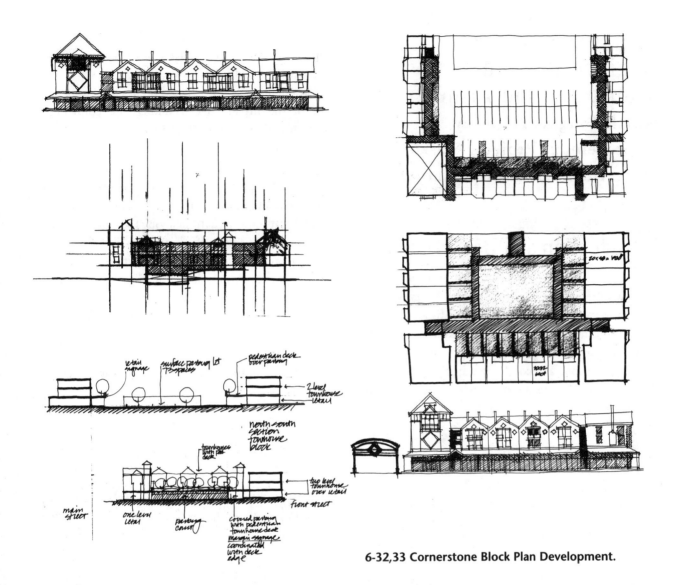

6-32,33 Cornerstone Block Plan Development.

Building Elevation and Continuity Within the Block

During the design process it is easier to think about building design in two-dimension, and usually building elevations and sections follow the resolution of a building plan. In this case, the historic elevation patterns along Front Street were visualized and extended into the study site early in the design process. Overlaid during the development of the block plan, section and elevation are the existing elevations of the City's Front Avenue Blocks. This drawing of historic front street is the basis for checking out new building dimensions and patterns along the adjacent new city blocks. Some buildings along Front Street are anonymous, one-story, flat-roofed structure with minimal architectural merit; others have elaborated false fronts with historic architectural merit. Together all buildings form a collective building block that defines Front Street as a place. The literal drawing of the existing Front Avenue Buildings is broken down into its abstract proportions and elements. The drawing reveals an existing pattern of three or four buildings per block with a larger (three- to four-story) building of historic value present in each block. The diagrams carry the patterns of individual building variation that happen within the continuity of the abstracted street wall and marquee element into the preliminary organization of the Cornerstone Block Elevations.

Visualizing Major Engineering and Transportation Projects:

North Tongass Highway Improvement Project, Alaska Department of Transportation, 1993

Introduction and Background

The Alaska Department of Transportation proposed to widen the existing four-lane North Tongass highway connecting the Alaska Marine Highway Ferry terminal in the north to downtown Ketchikan in the south, increasing the movement lanes from three to five. In addition, a second road improvement, the Third Avenue Extension, was proposed to be con-structed at a higher elevation to serve as an effective bypass for North Tongass. Ketchikan is a linear town form with a width of between two and six blocks, constrained by an immediate rise in elevation to the east of the urban edge. Buildings are constructed close to the existing roadway, in most cases with zero setbacks, and due to the lack of solid land, over piers along the waterfront. The changes to the town form would be significant with any major roadway improvement. Consequently, as a part of an environmental impact statement analysis, a public education component was identified with an initially strong urban form impact visualization section. More than twenty-five drawings depicting the impacts of the roadway construction and the changes to the town form were prepared and exhibited for the general public and a steering committee of community residents, property owners, and officials. A portion of those visualizations are described and discussed below.

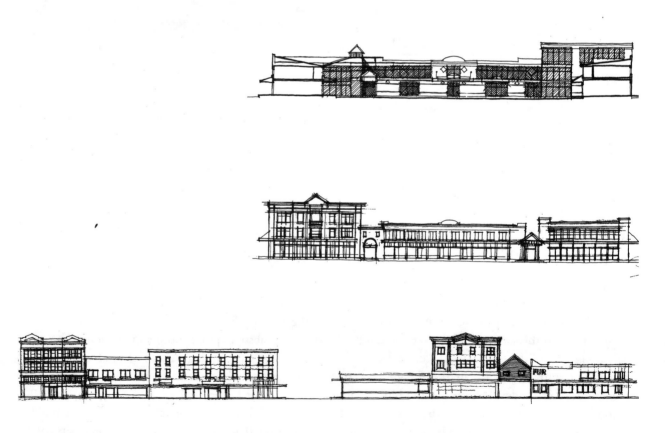

6-34,35,36,37 Cornerstone Block Section/Elevation Development. Front elevations of the cornerstone block are developed as a continuation of the historic main street facade. Dimensions, proportions, and patterns of the new block are referenced from visualizing historic building elevation patterns.

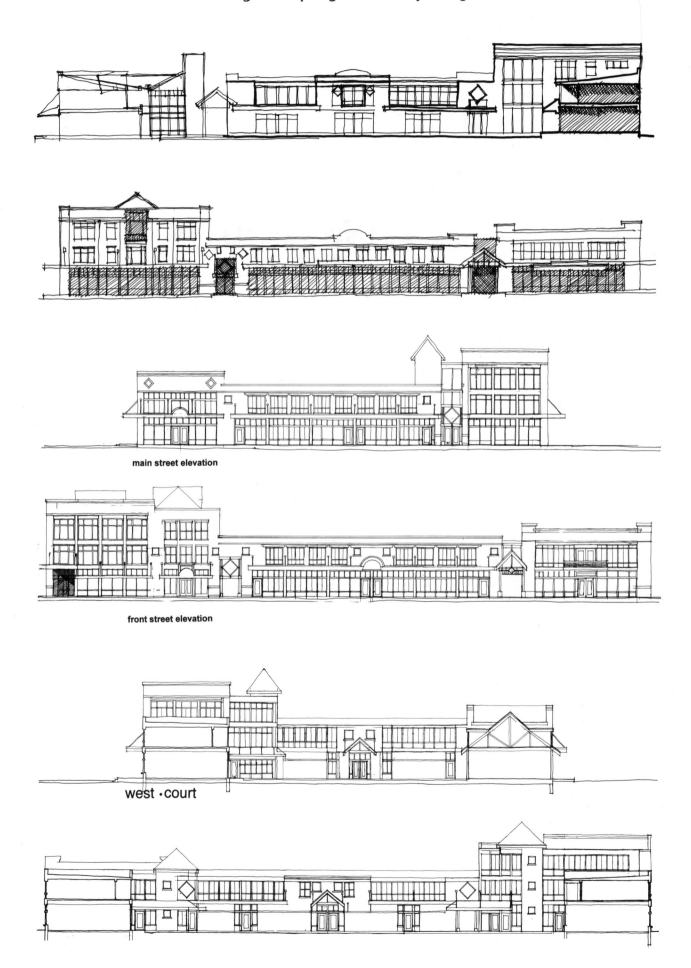

main street elevation

front street elevation

west · court

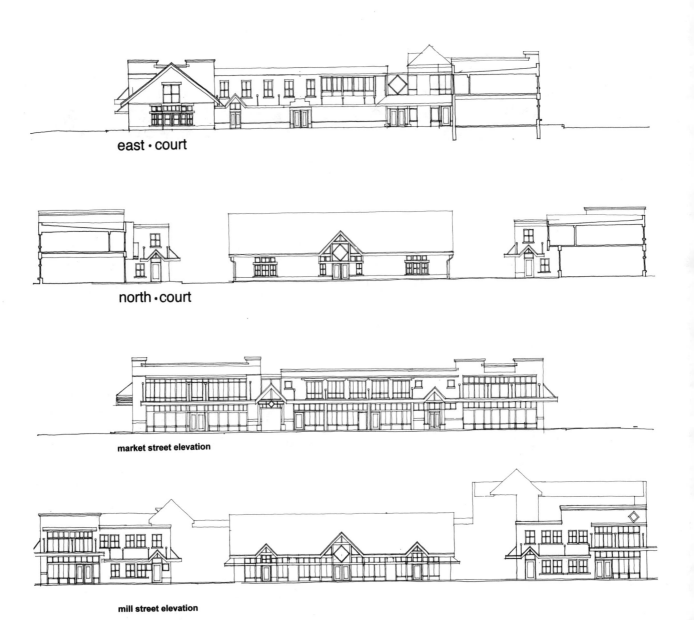

east · court

north · court

market street elevation

mill street elevation

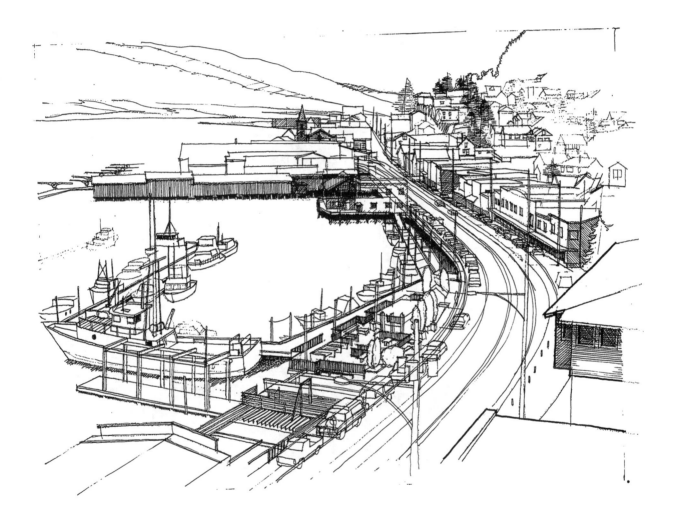

6-38,39 North Tongass Highway Improvement Series: Establishing Context
Understanding and Impacts of Change.

6-40,41 Tongass Highway Study, Ketchikan, Alaska.

7 Ish River Case Study

Introduction and Background

The Ish River case study encompasses an area within the Cascadia Bio-region extending from the U.S./Canada border on the north, formed by the State of Washington and the Province of British Columbia, to the southern Puget Sound area in the vicinity of the City of Olympia, Washington. The term "Ish River"[1] refers to the many native named river valley/watersheds in this area, such as the Stillaguamish, the Snohomish, and the Duwamish.

The Study Communities

The study explores means and methods of visualization in a series of public planning and urban design projects within five communities of different scales, physical settings, and issues, all related and connected by their eco-region. All of the projects required a public awareness approach through the public participation process. Active citizen participation utilized the extensive use of graphic visualizations with an emphasis on the relationships between the area's human settlements and the surrounding multi-layered natural context. Issues of study include pre-comprehensive plan *visioning*; Growth Management Area *urban design outcomes* visualization; *design guidelines*; *town planning*; and *waterfront revitalization* feasibility. The study communities include: the city of Bellingham, population 52,000, located within the Nooksack River drainage; the City of Kent, Washington, a railroad/agriculture community of 38,000 people enveloped in the Seattle suburbanization pattern; the City of Puyallup, another railroad/agriculture town undergoing suburbanization, population 16,000, located in the Puyallup River valley at the base of Mount Rainier; the Town of Vashon, population 3,000, an unincorporated settlement within urban King County and located on Vashon Island in Puget Sound immediately southwest of Seattle and north of Tacoma; and, the City of Bremerton, a waterfront community on Sinclair Inlet in Puget Sound 55 minutes by ferry west of Seattle, population of 35,000 people, home of the Bremerton Naval Shipyard and gateway to the growing Kitsap Peninsula.

Ish River Eco-region

Ish River represents an eco-region composed of the drainages that serve an inland saltwater system connected to the Pacific Ocean by the Strait of Juan de Fuca on the south end of Vancouver Island and by Queen Charlotte Sound to the north. The U.S. portion of this inland waterway extends south from Canada to Olympia, WA. It is this southern section that is referred to as Puget Sound, characterized by mainland fragments now islands within the sound, created as major land masses separated from the North American coast.

The northern portion of the Sound is characterized

---

[1] The term is attributed to poet Robert Sund of LaConner, Washington.

**7-1 Cascadia Bio-region.
Ish River Eco-region.**

by a series of coastal bays
(Birch, Lummi, Bellingham, Samish, Padilla, and Skagit); and, by island groupings such as the San Juan Islands, Fidalgo Island, and the Whidbey-Camano Islands. North of Camano Island the coastline is structured by two major river systems, the Nooksack River north of Bellingham and the Skagit River in the Mt. Vernon area to the south. Communities within the northern Puget Sound share a cross-border coastal culture with Canada rich in water-oriented commerce, art, and resources. The eco- and metro-regions are a part of the definition of their activities, urban forms, and planning and design aspirations for the future. The City of Bellingham, an evolved amalgamation of five timber and fishing towns along Bellingham Bay, is the dominant U.S. city in this area and is closely related geographically, economically, and culturally to Canada, 20 miles to the north.

The central portion of Ish River and Puget Sound is occupied by the Seattle-Tacoma metropolitan area, extending along the eastern shoreline of Puget Sound and interspersed with the Snohomish River on the north, the Snoqualmie and Sammamish rivers to the east, and the Duwamish, Cedar, Green,

and Puyallup rivers emanating from Mount Rainier on the southeast and south of the metropolitan area; and Bainbridge Island, Vashon Island, and the Kitsap Peninsula to the west of Seattle. The rivers and their valley eco-systems and the inlets and bays of the salt-water play an important form-generative role for this eco-region. Bremerton is a 55-minute ferry ride east to downtown Seattle and a bit more than an hours drive. Vashon Island is less than a two-mile ferry ride south to Tacoma and less than a four-mile ferry ride east to Seattle. The cities of Puyallup and Kent are ten miles or more southeast of Seattle and Tacoma in the Puyallup and Green River valleys, respectively, on line with Mount Rainier.

Shared Objectives

The five case studies undertook recent planning and design actions responding, in most cases, to the requirements of the State of Washington Growth Management Act. Common and central to each community's efforts was the effectiveness of constructive communication among all participants in the planning/design processes and the use of the results of that process in making design decisions. Public participation as authorship of the processes was the highest priority in at least two of the communities. Authorship comes with awareness and understanding of issues as a means of reaching a workable consensus—agreement to abide by the results of the process even if there is individual disagreement on its final outcome. In another community, Bremerton, a task force required use, cost, and design testing of concepts related to the difficult development strategies of a city-owned parcel. In addition, and particularly important to the people of the Pacific Northwest, is the issue of environmental sensitivity and responsibility, identifying and testing possible impacts on the environment from growth-related density increases and accompanying spin-offs such as traffic, pollution, wetland loss, etc. Out of all of these concerns comes an added concern: What can be added to the efforts of a conventional quantitative planning process to better influence built-form quality? And, given the recognition for an additional layer of detail in the search for quality of the built environment, what kind of design guidelines, required or negotiated, can each community effectively and realistically develop to ensure compliance with the plans and policies that represent the community preference?

The Bellingham Case Study, Bellingham, Washington

Regional Connections and Influences

Eco-regions Within the Bioregion: Bellingham

The Cascade Mountains River Valleys and Coastal Streams.

The geographic and ecological systems of the Pacific Northwest are often stronger determinants of human settlement patterns than the politics of jurisdictional boundaries. The border between the U.S. and Canada lies 17 miles north of Bellingham Washington, yet human settlement and movement patterns are more dictated by the courses of the Nooksack and Fraser rivers, which combine to create a flat plain rapidly being settled by the two countries, and the numerous coastal edges and streams connecting the mountains to Puget Sound. These river systems typify the western Washington and western British Columbia settlement pattern: river systems flowing west out of the mountains creating broad alluvial plains, that support interconnected habitat systems, each with a definite and distinct local ecology. Such plains have historically attracted human settlement based on historically plentiful food and habitat resources, providing a nurturing basis for multi-layered cultures for thousands of years.

Settlement Patterns Within the Eco-regions

The network of rivers, valleys, alluvial plains, and their communities is recorded as a network with rivers and transportation routes delineating the evolving pattern using a USGS map as a base.

Bellingham is an evolved composite of five resource-industry-based towns that emerged along the edge of Bellingham Bay. These towns developed at the mouths of rivers and streams along the bay, constrained to the east by the foothills of the Cascade Mountains and Mt. Baker. Their connection to the water's edge is an integral part of their settlement patterns and culture. Smaller eco-systems, nested or connected together to form the larger Nooksack River system, add final form, structure and organization, to the city's built pattern with Squalicum, Whatcom, and Padden Creeks.

7-2 Puget Sound Area.

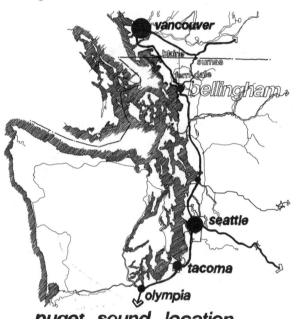

puget sound location

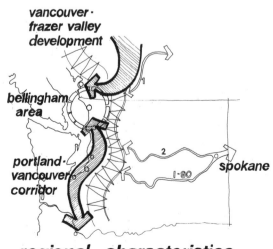

regional characteristics

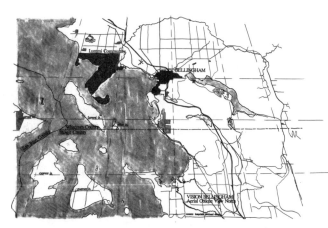

7-3 Bellingham Region. Bellingham, Washington is more closely related to the Vancouver British Columbia geographic area than to Seattle and the Puget Sound Basin.

Settlements, City Sectors, Neighborhoods, Project Areas, and Sites

All of these scales and settlement patterns are extensions of the regional place as context and serve as the personal place and context of the area's inhabitants. They are discussed in detail within the individual case studies that follow: Visions for Bellingham—a public participatory process for the entire city to establish approaches and directions for change for the comprehensive planning process; and West Bakerview Neighborhood—a neighborhood scale project with design guidelines or relationships.

Project One: Metropolitan Scale

Visions for Bellingham:
Establishing Approaches and Directions for Change Prior to the Planning Process

In Washington state, the 1990 Growth Management Act specified that communities update their comprehensive plans in order to address the pressures of growth occurring in the state, particularly along the Interstate Five corridor. In Bellingham, the Comprehensive Plan required updating to meet the needs of the 1990s: population increases, changes in lifestyles, economic opportunities along the coast, and the need to address the conflicting values associated with development and natural features protection.

The city debated a number of approaches to use for goals setting and decided on one that evolved a public awareness of "community," a sequential self-education process rather than one that asked people to select pre-existing image-preferences from outside of the community. The selected process consisted of a five-session conference format with 250 committed local residents extending over a three–month period. The sessions were designed to involve the conferees in a learning process about their community from the history of the early settlements, to the landform and drainage basins, to the types of neighborhood housing and parks. Participants were asked not to "conceptualize" about the future until they had accumulated better awareness of what the community was in terms of physiography, history, culture, and design.

Three hundred participants were selected[2] from activists and voter registration records. Invitations and questionnaires were sent to 14,000 voters; more than 500 people expressed an interest in the process, and 250 people accepted the charge to attend and participate in all five conferences. Thus, Visions for Bellingham became a goal–setting endeavor that involved a cross–section of the community within the limits of the voter record selection method.

The direction-setting process had one additional component that marked a departure from earlier similar processes: It contained a visualization methodology that assisted the participants in assessing goal-outcomes on a broad but recognizable community scale. Remember, this is a prelude to the comprehensive plan-updating process, not the plan-making stage; but "goals-setting" too often can become an ambiguous wish list. The visualization methodology formed the backbone of the conference communication format, providing participants

---

[2] The Department of Community Development, led by Director Patricia Decker, enlisted people from voting records, community groups, pro and con planning groups, residents, and property owners.

with three-dimensional interpretations of emerging concepts or goal preferences.

The five conferences were designed around five steps as means of understanding the community. Step one was an introduction to the process and a historic overview of when and how the community developed and for what major reasons. This step was characterized by a slide-discussion session that moved participants through their history with spatial references. Step two was a presentation and discussion of the underlying and dynamic ecology of the natural landform, from mountain and vegetative cover to watersheds and habitat streams. Step three was the design of the built environment: local and regional examples in order to increase a local appreciation for what design meant to local residents. Step four increased understanding of local issues, differing agendas, and different opinions regarding the state of the community: a first step in building consensus and agreeing to disagree within that consensus. Step five set the foundation for the visions of the city that the participants wanted as their home, finally arriving at goals that were spatially referenced, that built on the four previous steps instead of selecting fantasies and/or borrowed ideas from other communities that have little or no application to Bellingham.

Relating Vision to Built Form

During the visioning process, drawings proved an effective means of portraying the settlement patterns and three-dimensional built form within the larger physical surroundings, with particular emphasis on the relationships between settlement and the streams and open-space corridors that connected the mountains to the Puget Sound. The drawings were prepared prior to each conference and in some cases slides were made of them for large group display. Drawings were used as exhibits around the edges of the larger meeting space and used by small group discussions for reference and orientation. The following diagrams helped the conference attendees visually perceive their community, evoking in many a new-found appreciation for its order, structure, and valued natural assets.

In **Metropolitan Settlement Pattern** and **Bellingham Aerial Oblique**, two- and three-dimensional visualizations set the stage for public

7-4 Metropolitan Settlement Patterns. A solid/void graphic depicts the abstract settlement pattern of Bellingham.

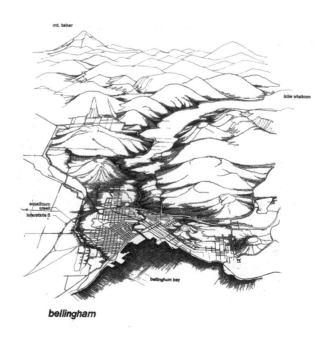

7-5 Bellingham Aerial Oblique. Drainage patterns, watersheds, streets, terrain, and development patterns all are integrated in the oblique for public reference and orientation.

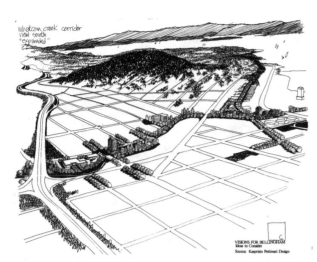

7-6 Whatcom Creek and Open Space Corridors. A felt tip pen drawing that highlights only the street network, major topographical features, and the creek corridors for public awareness of urban watersheds.

understanding of growth and development patterns. The aerial oblique was the most successful of the drawings, serving as a birds-eye view and making the issues more real and grounded. Neighborhood street patterns were visualized with closer-view USGS based aerial diagrams; creek corridors and transportation networks were highlighted in similar fashion, with the drawings eventually focusing in on the downtown, in panoramic and aerial views. Semi-abstract perspectives were also useful in portraying broad concepts and issues without venturing too far into specific design studies, with just enough detail to elicit comment and reaction from the attendees regarding the preservation of stream corridors, the compaction and enhancement of downtown, and the

issues of linear commercial development along the Guide Meridian state highway which eventually connects to Canada some 18 miles north.

During the five-conference event, the drawings were used over and over to remind, stimulate, and reference people as they worked through the development of goals for the community vision; identifying the key issues and controversies that the comprehensive plan needed to deal with in its objectives and policies. The conference was able to reach a consensus on an overall vision and goals with significant points of disagreement remaining, particularly between those seeking to protect natural features such as salmon habitats, wetlands, and open space areas, and those seeking less control and more dispersion of the settlement pattern for economic reasons.

The visioning process, if keyed to the settlement patterns and natural feature assets and workings of the land through visualizations, can advance the planning and negotiation process by testing ideas spatially and *in context*; differing substantially from earlier goal-setting processes where issues and concepts were discussed amid anonymous databases. Lastly, well-intentioned goal-setting processes, labelled as visions yet without spatial representations of visions, can often be vague, characterized by divergent opinions based on each reader's different interpretation of the same text. With visualizations, the capability for the public to critique and respond to the shape and pattern impacts of abstract ideas and goals is enhanced and made real. It is more clear what is preferred and what is not preferred. Visualizations

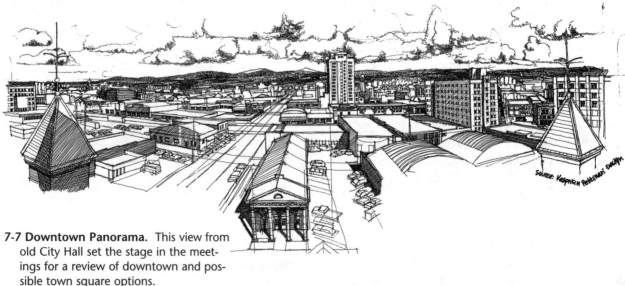

7-7 Downtown Panorama. This view from old City Hall set the stage in the meetings for a review of downtown and possible town square options.

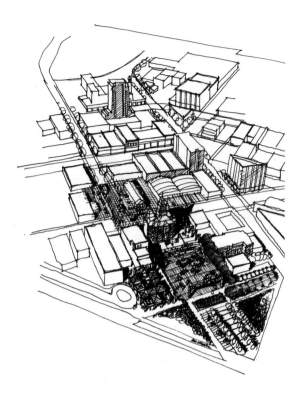

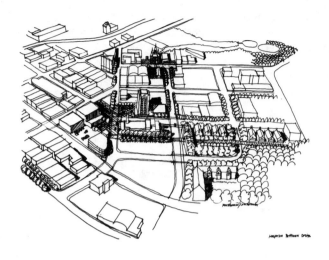

7-8 Town Square Aerials. Additional ideas taken from the public conferences were quickly sketched, providing more than one point of view and demonstrating implications of using public rights-of-way to expand a town square concept around the City Hall/Museum.

7-9,10 Town Square Vision Series. Quick sketches focused discussion on the site and features for a town square, in concept.

7-11 Connection to Mountains and Sound. Using the creeks and the historic center to structure the urban pattern.

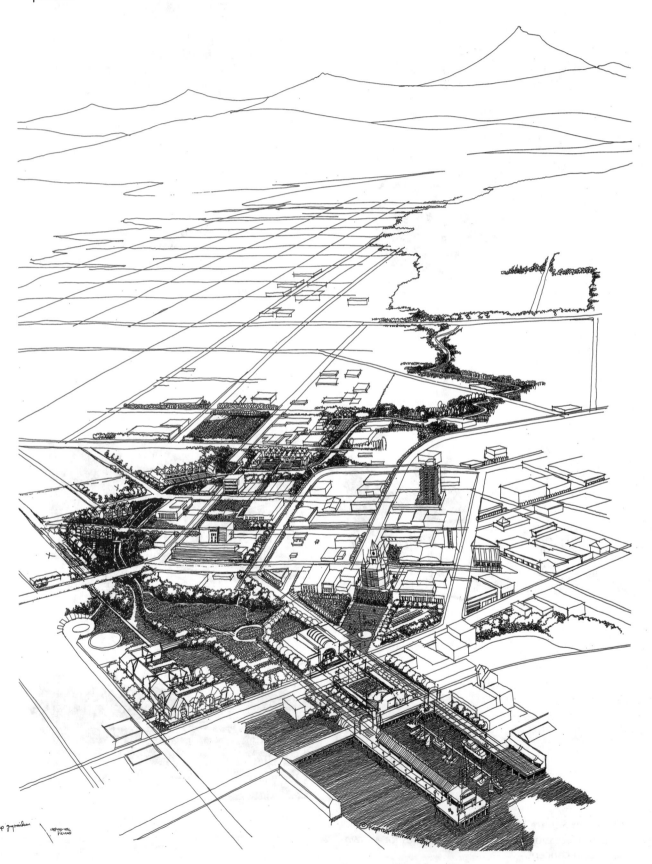

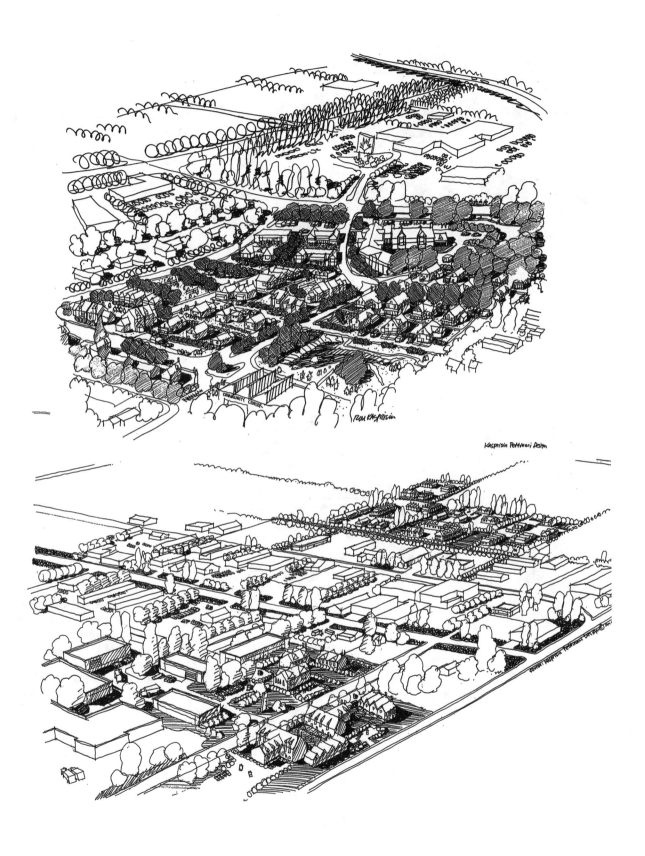

7-12 In-town New Neighborhoods. Gravel quarries and edge parcels all presented opportunities for new in-fill housing. Concerns during the vision process regarding the scale and character of higher density developments led the team to quickly vision mixed-unit and building-type arrangements around small protected open spaces for the conferencees' discussion and consideration.

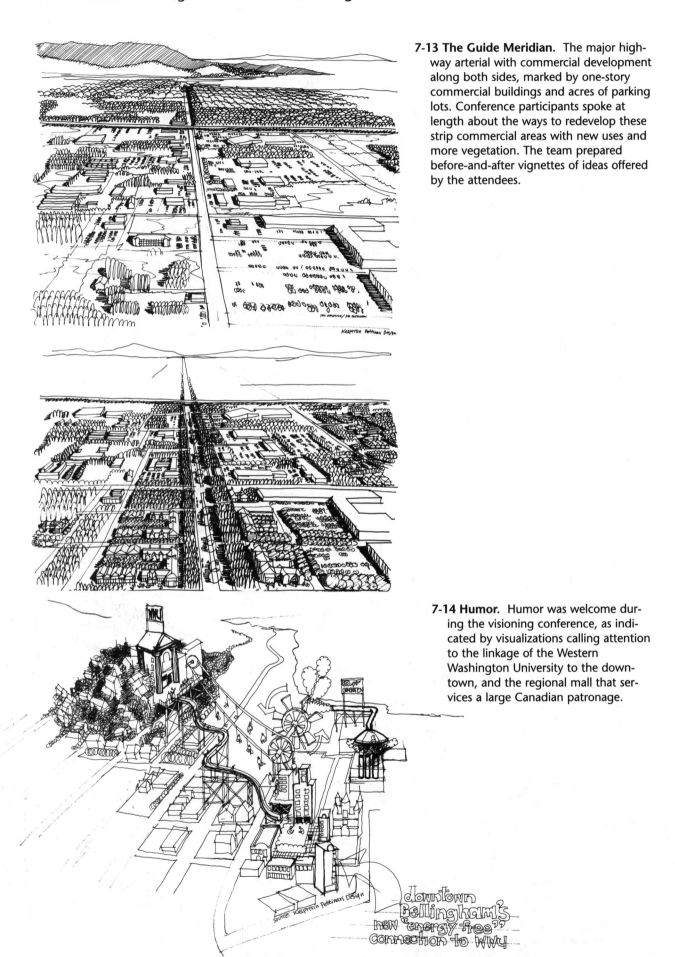

7-13 The Guide Meridian. The major highway arterial with commercial development along both sides, marked by one-story commercial buildings and acres of parking lots. Conference participants spoke at length about the ways to redevelop these strip commercial areas with new uses and more vegetation. The team prepared before-and-after vignettes of ideas offered by the attendees.

7-14 Humor. Humor was welcome during the visioning conference, as indicated by visualizations calling attention to the linkage of the Western Washington University to the downtown, and the regional mall that services a large Canadian patronage.

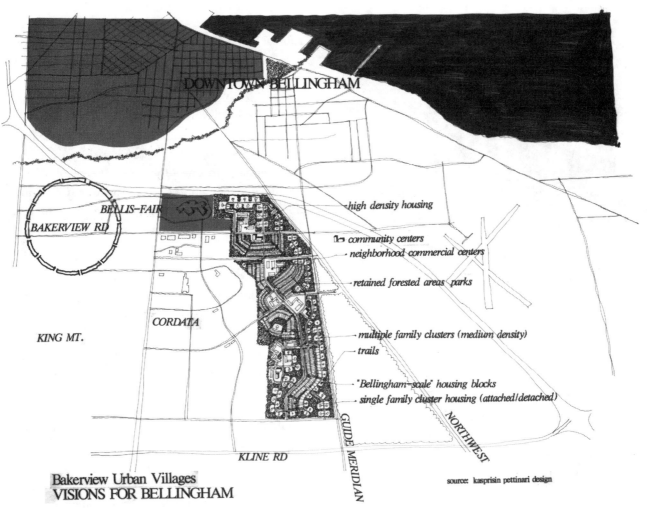

7-15 West Bakerview Neighborhood Location Map. The map locates the neighborhood within the metropolitan area and in relationship to the Bellis Fair Regional Mall on the outskirts of Bellingham. The mall has been a catalyst for change in the surrounding area, from traffic congestion to the filling of wetlands to changes in land values in surrounding neighborhoods. Local participants were so focused upon their property-value relationships and encroaching regional retail facilities that some had lost a perspective of the emerging neighborhood around their properties.

act in consort with the written descriptions and intentions of vision.

Project Two: Neighborhood Scale

West Bakerview Neighborhood: A Master Plan and Design Relationships

The West Bakerview neighborhood is a rural area in the midst of an urban suburban edge transition phase, an area impacted by the construction of a regional shopping mall and the associated development of new office, retail commercial, and medium density housing on a single-corporation-controlled tract of land, formerly the Wilder Ranch. As seen in the diagram, the Bellis Fair Mall regional shopping center is located on the northern edge of Bellingham at an interchange with Interstate Five, 17 miles south of the Canadian border and in close proximity to the Vancouver B.C. metropolitan area. Due to economic differences between the U.S. and Canadian currency, particularly in price structures, the Bellis Fair Mall and other stateside shopping centers in the vicinity attract Canadian consumer activity. The mall land use and land value patterns have placed pressure for change on the surrounding rural residential areas

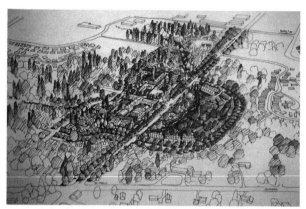

7-16 West Bakerview Aerial Oblique. The aerial oblique sketch locates the proposed neighborhood center along West Bakerview Road north on the urban--suburban fringe of Bellingham.

in the form of increased traffic, changing land-use patterns reflected in the expanding regional retail area, and changing land values making single-family detached housing densities uneconomical for land owners. The City of Bellingham undertook a study[3] to prepare and facilitate a public participation process that would result in a neighborhood re-creation strategy, focusing on the following key elements:

- traffic and pedestrian circulation;
- a system of parks and open space;
- location of neighborhood and regional commercial areas;
- relationship of the neighborhood to surrounding areas and street patterns;
- design guidelines and/or relationships for multi-family housing and related services; and
- economic viability of different uses and plans.

The component of the neighborhood plan that is highlighted in this case study is the design guidelines or relationships. This aspect of the plan is critical to the assemblage of the parts of a new neighborhood based on the fact that there is no single large landowner or developer for the 240-acre study and based on the assumption by the design team that development may occur in increments of smaller

properties, less compatible with finessed master plan approaches and more closely related to real development scenarios. The design team pursued a strategy of design relationships based on a concept of connected increments, the piecemeal construction of a neighborhood whose individually developing parts are related by a series of relational guidelines to form a whole. Therefore, three planning/design activities are integrated in one process: a concept of a larger coordinated neighborhood structure and organization; a design understanding of the program and parts of one site design; and a relational connection of one site to others.

Design Relationships and Visualization

The use of drawing as a language in West Bakerview applied to both the development (and testing) of design relationships and their communication to the City and property owners/developers. In the design relationships, two areas of connected increments became the focus of the study: the first, a proposed neighborhood center, consisted of mixed office, retail, and residential uses; and the other arrangements of multiple family housing complexes promoted diversity in both design and tenancy as well as connectedness to form larger related neighborhood segments.

The master plan allocated commercial uses and residential densities per specified areas and an overall circulation network to service those uses. The preferred master plan's effectiveness (and that of any master plan) is directly dependent on the strict adherence of all property owners and/or developers to the designated circulation network, landscape, and building locations and footprints, which can be unrealistic with multiple ownership. Consequently, given the existing parcel configuration, narrow and elongated lots measuring 165 feet by 1,320 feet, and the individual or smaller accumulated parcel development sequence, two principles for design quality were applied and tested as an inter-site development strategy.

[3] "West Bakerview Neighborhood Plan," Land Use Designations and Urban Design Guidelines for Mixed Use Residential Neighborhoods in Bellingham; City of Bellingham, Planning and Community Development, Dennis Tate Associates, Kasprisin Pettinari Design.

Principle One

Anticipate connected increments, where the design guidelines are focused on the relationships among or between adjacent developments as well as within each development.

Principle Two

Rely on the outcome of the connected increment process for overall design quality, rather than on a pre-determined master plan product outcome that assumes cooperation among diverse and different property owners.

Principle one, connected increments, uses existing City development codes for site and architectural design preferences and requirements and extends them to apply to adjacent sites. Methods to accomplish this include: edge-condition relationships requiring visual and/or physical connections between two adjoining sites; movement system connections and cooperation (i.e., a pedestrian trail or promenade connecting one site to another in a perpendicular fashion or along a common property line); building massing relationships based on the principle that, given development one's massing, then development two's massing is complementary or reflective; and through interactive landscape design as opposed to buffered or screened landscape configurations.

Principle two, design as process outcome, sets forth relationships of connection for the developer and designers relative to each part and its connection to adjacent development rather than requiring a reaction on their part to rigid pre-determined master plan product expectations that can have little or no means of success in multiple ownership applications.

The design guidelines[4] or relationships are divided into mandatory and negotiable (not optional) categories. Mandatory applies to the protection of ecosystems and major neighborhood-benefiting design or layout configurations such as circulation systems or building orientations or open-space hierarchies. Negotiable guidelines are those that are required but flexible with factors that can change from site to site

and adjacent-increment-order-responsive situations. As an experiment with these principles and their implications to the city staff, elected officials, and laypeople, the study produced a series of phased-increment visualization or example scenes, and *connected* development visualizations as a part of a larger public awareness process.

The following is an excerpt with some modifications in terminology from *West Bakerview Neighborhood Plan* illustrating the important connection between written policy/guidelines and visualizations.

Design and Development Guidelines

Site Planning

Intent

The West Bakerview study area has large areas that are relatively untouched and natural, with extensive stands of trees, gently rolling topography, and a natural unclassified drainage system that includes wetlands. Intensive development can occur in this area in the future, changing its overall appearance, and having the potential to change functions of the natural systems. To minimize adverse impacts to these systems and to maintain the unique character of the area, any designs for development must work with the existing topography, preserving existing stands of vegetation, and in general minimizing disturbances to the land. Views to Mount Baker are another natural amenity of the study area and are to be accommodated wherever possible.

Guidelines

Grading or significant earth movement of any type is to be minimized throughout the study area, and is prohibited within 50 feet of the centerline of the Open Space Corridor, unless the grading work is directly related to the enhancement of the Corridor.

Existing topography is to be utilized to its fullest potential for solar orientation, views, and aesthetic interest.

---

[4] These guidelines are for discussion purposes only and require local involvement and modification prior to application to a specific place and jurisdiction.

7-17 Aerial Oblique Blow-up.

A complete wetlands inventory is to be performed in the study area to ascertain its exact locations and boundaries.

Wetlands protection and mitigation will occur in accordance with the regulations established by the U.S. Army Corps of Engineers and the City of Bellingham. In general, wetlands are treated both as natural engineering functions of the landscape and as amenities for development, and their removal or significant alteration, except as enhancement, is not permitted.

Whenever possible, existing vegetation should be maintained in the design of new developments preferrably as patches or clusters for improved habitat.

Multi-family Residential Guidelines

Intent

The design guidelines and relationships are intended to develop a neighborhood character through its built form for multiple-family residential developments. The guidelines provide a diversity of building types as well as building designs. A key strategy consists of arranging the mix of building types around collective open space in a manner representing a small village or hamlet. This prevents a single building type from dominating the neighborhood and provides effective open space for the residents. The guidelines have the following components:

Housing types:

- three-story double-loaded corridor buildings;
- two-story single-loaded corridor buildings;
- two-story row- and/or townhouses, each with separate and private open space courtyards or yards; and
- units with common porches where appropriate.

Open space:

- commons or quadrangle-type arrangement for collective space;
- courtyards or yards for row- and/or townhouses;
- pedestrian promenade or trails to link one development phase to or along adjacent phases; and
- retention of all trees in rear or sideyard setbacks and 50 percent of all trees in front yard setback, or 50 percent of all trees within buildable area of site, whichever is greater.

Parking:

- cluster parking lots throughout development instead of one large lot configuration;
- underground or under-building parking is preferred where feasible; and
- limit garages and carports to 30 percent maximum of total required exterior surface parking spaces, or one garage or carport space per unit regardless of the number of bedrooms per unit, and no garage or carport for studio units— share parking spaces with adjacent commercial facilities where feasible.

Building design:

- pitched roofs with dormers, skylights, or other features that provide a shape break in the roof line;
- break facade plan at regular or rhythmic intervals using repetition with variety rather than

monotonous and continuous flat facades;

- use upper story setbacks at corners or sideyards where light and sun exposure are appropriate; and

- articulate entries with canopies, porches, entry hoods or other weather-protection forms.

Guidelines and Relationships

Growth pressure in many Pacific Northwest communities is occurring at the urban-suburban fringe, that place where rural countryside is experiencing increased freeway access and regional shopping centers, with lower-density residential developments, and highway-oriented strip commercial uses. Rules are needed to coordinate development practices, public and community-benefit needs, private market aspirations, and natural features and systems protection. This section presents a series of development rules or principles in three-dimensional model format for review, discussion and consideration by public and private interests participating in the growth activities within this area.

Development Rules or Principles

Development rules or principles are directions and conditions for implementation of growth related activities within a specific area. The rules are divided into two categories: Mandatory Guidelines (required), and Development Guidelines (required and negotiable).

Mandatory Requirements

Mandatory requirements are development actions that must be complied with in order to implement a certain built-form pattern. They set aside certain ground rules deemed necessary to achieve public directions, objectives, and policies for a given physical area of the city.

Development Guidelines

Guidelines are standards or principles which are used by a city to supplement mandatory requirements, permit bonuses or incentives, or provide site-specific evaluation of overall requirements. Guidelines are required in intent and flexible in their application, providing the public and the private sectors with a basis for discussion and negotiation as a response to neighborhood objectives, site and environmental conditions, and market factors. They are flexible and interpretive provided that a development proposal can offer an equal or greater action to meet the intentions of the guideline.

Portrayal of Development Guidelines: Example Scenes

As a means of providing the layperson with examples of what the guidelines represent, the West Bakerview model uses three-dimensional diagrams, or "scenes" to depict various ways in which the guidelines can be interpreted. The scenes are not architectural solutions: They are models which represent open space utilization, placement and treatment, pedestrian connections and facilities, and varieties of building types. These scenes demonstrate development intentions and challenge the private sector to respond with equal or greater design applications.

The Old/New Suburban City

Regional Connections and Influences

The City of Puyallup is located near the southern edge of the Ish River eco-region and its Puget Sound trough. It is situated in the Puyallup River alluvial plane, one of the major river drainages emanating from 14,400-foot high Mount Rainier 28 miles to the southeast. The city is situated on the south side of the river as it enters a levee system coursing northeast through the Tacoma industrial flats into Commencement Bay and Puget Sound.

The City of Puyallup is a community of 24,000 people located in an historic agricultural valley northwest of Mount Rainier experiencing the growth pressure spill-over from the Interstate Five urban corridor between Seattle on the north and Tacoma on the east. The city's landform is characterized by a flat alluvial plane, with the older city center and adjacent urban development, the Puyallup Fairgrounds, active farmlands, and diminishing but still extant salmon habitat streams. It is also characterized by the South Hill valley edge with new residential subdivisions and shopping malls located on the hill slopes and upper plateaus, the area of signifi-

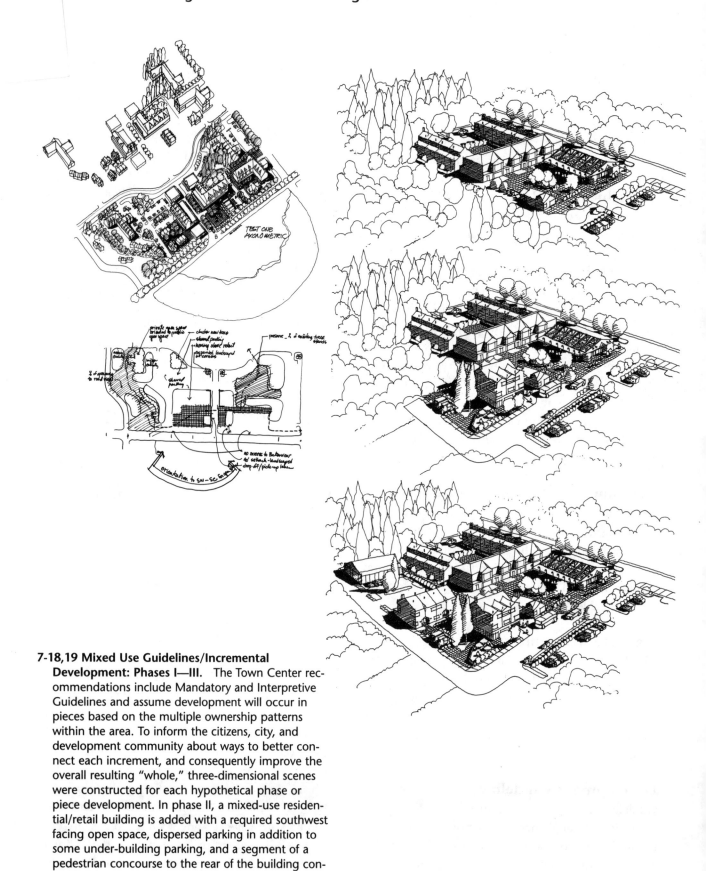

7-18,19 Mixed Use Guidelines/Incremental Development: Phases I—III. The Town Center recommendations include Mandatory and Interpretive Guidelines and assume development will occur in pieces based on the multiple ownership patterns within the area. To inform the citizens, city, and development community about ways to better connect each increment, and consequently improve the overall resulting "whole," three-dimensional scenes were constructed for each hypothetical phase or piece development. In phase II, a mixed-use residential/retail building is added with a required southwest facing open space, dispersed parking in addition to some under-building parking, and a segment of a pedestrian concourse to the rear of the building connecting it to prior phases. Phase III adds a mixed-use development consisting of separate townhouse units and a one-story retail commercial building, both with shared parking. The townhouses are required to locate on the connecting pedestrian concourse.

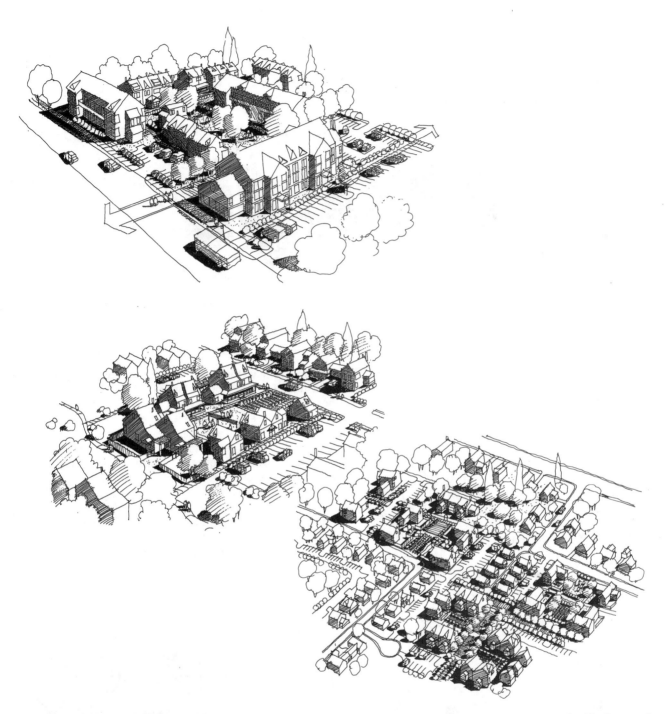

7-20 Multiple-family Housing Mixed-Building Type.
The City Council requested ways to influence a diversity of resident profile and neighborhood scale. Design cannot regulate or dictate occupancy profiles exactly but can influence the profile through a diversity of unit and building type, providing a range of housing for single people of mixed ages and families. In the three-dimensional design guideline scene, three building types are exemplified for the public and the development community: double-loaded corridor three-story multiple-family-unit buildings, with handicapped tenant sections; single-loaded corridor two-story walk-up multiple-family-unit buildings; and two-story grade-level-entry attached townhouse- or rowhouse-type buildings all arranged around useable common open space and with dispersed parking lots along the perimeter of the cluster.

Multiple-family Housing Mixed-Cluster Type: Commons. The aerial oblique sketch diagram guides development toward a configuration containing single-family detached units, single-faily attached units, duplexes, and single-family detached units with accessory or "granny" flats, for diversity of scale and market. The "commons" concept of open space encourages a hierarchy of centered or clustered open spaces, including a community open space ranging in size from one to two volleyball courts (and out-of-bounds areas), fenced private and individual open-space plots, and covered private or shared open-space porches or verandas.

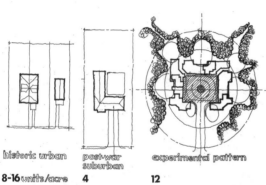

changing patterns

historic urban   postwar   experimental pattern
                  suburban

8-16 units/acre   **4**   **12**

7-21 Multiple-family Housing Mixed-Cluster Type: Clusters of Clusters. Each commons cluster is shown in relation to other similar clusters, encouraging a street-oriented yet contained open space configuration. This design serves as an alternative to the popular small lot, alley in back, single-family detached developments of traditional neighborhood design, which can use more surface area for paved surfaces. The diagram demonstrates different building type mixes within each cluster. The aerial oblique is an excellent format to demonstrate the possible combinations of cluster commons housing arrangements and their fit with single-family detached small lot developments. Diversity of building type and connection of cluster or piece to piece are critical instructions within the drawing concepts.

7-22 Puyallup in Ish River Country. The context is defined in relation to the central Puget Sound area and its Puyallup River watershed. The graphic uses hatching and distance radii to add reference and orientation.

7-24 Puyallup Urban Area Solid-Void. A solid-void map indicates the extent of town settlement pattern.

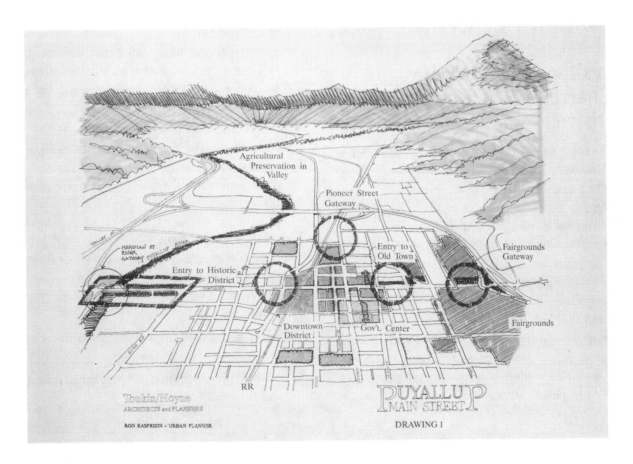

7-23 Mount Rainier, the Puyallup Valley, and Puyallup Urban Area. A fast and loose aerial oblique sketch completed on-site in a Main Street Design charrette locates the valley in relation to its source, the mountain, and adds the Puyallup settlement pattern with a simple street grid. Colored marker was applied to the back of the tracing paper.

cant new growth and a suburban-type commercial center competing with the older downtown.

In western Washington, Puyallup is noted for the annual fair held at the fairgrounds immediately south of the downtown, attracting over 1,000,000 people each year. The historic economic and cultural base for the community lies in hops, berries, rhubarb, and flower bulbs, grown in the rich and fertile alluvial plane, which enticed European settlers and native American and Japanese farmers. The region's child population is growing. New science and light industry, one-half acre residential subdivisions on the valley floor and wooded slopes, suburban parking and site-development standards impacting the historic downtown, and increased traffic congestion are changing all at once rural and small-town community.

Project One: Historic Downtown Center

Puyallup Downtown Design Charrette: The Downtown District

In January of 1992, the Puyallup Main Street Association undertook a week-long design charrette[5] to generate design concepts for the historic downtown center with active and on-going participation of the public, property and shop owners, the City of Puyallup, and the Main Street Association. The charrette studio consisted of a storefront on the Meridian Street and occurred from a Sunday evening sit-down introductory dinner with the design team and stakeholders through to the following Friday evening with a major presentation of concepts and strategies for all interested and concerned citizens. The design team worked in the studio in public view and with public interaction during the daylight hours; visited sites, buildings, property owners and merchants as needed; met in the evenings with committee members and key persons to brainstorm and review findings; and, beginning Thursday, visualized the final recommendations and policies for the public presentation. Team members were accommodated in local motels for the duration of the on-site charrette.

Charrette Process

The design (and planning) charrette included:

- review of the community's and downtown's history and development patterns from available past studies and planning activities;
- meeting the stakeholders in an informal setting;
- touring the city and downtown district to determine their conditions and opportunities;
- setting up a visible and accessible public studio space;
- meeting with local residents, business people, city officials, and staff to discuss issues and ideas;
- identifying and determining the positive and negative aspects of the cityscape, making written and graphic recommendations, and outlining an implementation strategy; and
- identifying specific projects for the city, the Main Street Association, and private stakeholders to undertake to initiate and maintain improvements to the quality of the built environment.

Key Issue Selection

The design team reviewed the many issues outlined by the stakeholders and other participants and selected ten key issues for focus during the week process. They included:

- traffic and parking improvements in the retail core area;
- historic preservation at the Meeker Mansion and the retail core;

---

[5] The Puyallup Main Street charrette was funded in part by the Washington Main Street Program and sponsored by the Board of Directors, Puyallup Main Street Program. Team participants included Les Tonkin, historic preservation architect; Ron Kasprisin, urban designer; Barbara Oakrock, landscape architect; Vicki Scurri, urban artist; Richard Dickens, economist; David Kylie, traffic planner; Lynn Johnson and Steve Burstein, City of Puyallup; and David Secord, Puyallup Main Street.

- gateways or entries to the downtown;

- renovation of storefronts and downtown buildings;

- improvements of sidewalks, streetscapes, and signage;

- cultural and transportation connections with the fairgrounds;

- public art at the Meeker Mansion, fairgrounds, and gateways;

- re-adaptation of existing buildings and complexes for contemporary uses;

- spatial organization concepts to connect the downtown and maintain its compactness; and

- marketing strategies for downtown.

Levels of Recommendations

The charrette produced three levels of project prioritization and responsibility:

Level One: shorter-range projects with high impact and immediate start-up actions exemplified by ordinance and code changes; loan assistance programs for private sector building renovation/restoration actions; and, selected city-sector improvements such as streetscape trees, sidewalk patterns, etc.

Level Two: medium range, two- to three-year actions and projects that are based on initial political, property owner, or other changes prior to implementation. Examples include the completion of the ongoing civic center master plan prior to taking action on improving Pioneer Park and the downtown pedestrian connections to it.

Level Three: long-range projects and actions that are dependent on less stable political and economic factors such as a new cultural arts center and a transit center for downtown connected to a multi-county commuter rail program.

The charrette process is a creative work format that is characterized by intense review of information and site conditions. It is a high-energy brainstorming opportunity for design professionals and laypersons working together, and is an opportunity to express ideas and concepts in fast sketch-type graphic visualizations that benefit both. The following examples summarize the process graphics and the concepts inherent in and through their crafting.

Elements of the Downtown

Downtown Puyallup is an older established and compact commercial center that contains specialty shops, financial institutions, restaurants, personal and business services, and remnants of early (1930—1940) automobile dealership buildings. The central district is bordered by high-intensity newer automobile dealerships that comprise part of the approaches to the historic core. The Puyallup River is one-half mile separate from the downtown core.

The Burlington Northern Railroad, in an east-west alignment, effectively divides the downtown in two, with frequent train traffic in and out of the Tacoma area and port. The northern downtown segment is smaller and less stable than the southern segment but has quality and compact building stock, some dating to the 1890s with articulated and contributing architectural features. The southern segment contains the banks, primary retail core, government complex, and fairgrounds. The main intersection is Meridian (north—south) and Meeker Street, complemented by the Meeker Mansion (1890) at the east end of the downtown core.

The downtown area is eroding as a compact pedestrian-friendly center due to the addition of on-site parking lots with new or refurbished commercial buildings. It is in competition with the South Hill Mall, serving new residential areas up on the plateau, and suffers from an identity crisis due to the surrounding strip auto dealerships that characterize the outskirts of the downtown area. On the plus side, the streets are narrow, pedestrian in scale, and well travelled with commuter traffic that must flow through the core area. Buildings contain significant architectural style and articulation, and the civic complex expansion and the fairgrounds improvements help reinforce the function and level of activity of the downtown for the long term.

Design Recommendations

Design recommendations and strategies for implementation include the following:

- establishment of a Historic District and a Business Improvement Association in the downtown commercial core as the management frameworks for public and private sector implementation actions;

rehabilitation designs for storefronts and buildings within the downtown, ranging from contextual paint-up and fix-up activities to new or expanded building construction;

• purchase and demolition of a vacant furniture store adjacent to and obstructing the view of the Meeker Mansion along Meeker Street;

• incorporation of the Meeker Mansion into the proposed Centennial Park;

• construction of the first phase of a streetscape sidewalk pattern per the team artist's design recommendations;

• removal of all off-street parking requirements for commercial and office uses within the designated historic district;

• designation of an open space network throughout the downtown district, connecting existing buildings and new in-fill building projects; and

• focus of attention on the city gateways, now dominated by strip automobile dealerships with zero-setback built-form, as a means of strengthening the visibility and credibility of the historic commercial center.

Design Visualization

Design visualization begins with the valley, its settlement patterns, and the valley "walls" that include majestic Mount Rainier. This quick-sketch communicates the essential parts in a larger diagrammatic context, drawn with a Pentel Sign pen on tracing paper and back-colored with wide tip markers. Time and speed are critical to set this drawing up as a base tool. Buildings, trees, and smaller street networks are filtered out so as to highlight the basic patterns of information.

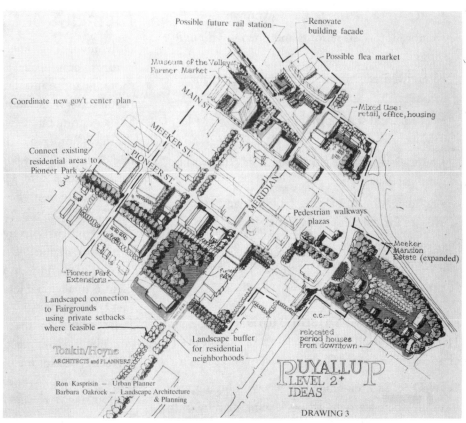

7-25 Sketch Overview. An axonometric aerial sketch provides an overview of the older downtown area, highlighting key projects and the connections among them. The sketch was drawn with a felt-tip pen (Pentel Sign pen), completed on-site and colored with marker. Only the perimeter block building outlines were drawn in to focus on the target areas, reducing the extra lines of block building interiors. Blow-up views of the same overview sketch can provide additional visualization diagrams from the same drawing. Each key or target project becomes a separate visual statement.

In the hour prior to the public presentation, a simple diagram was outlined and photographed (in slide form) as a visual aid identifying projects and phasing. It identifies landscaping treatments, facade-renovation areas, pavement-improvement areas, and a new historic district.

To further increase the public's appreciation and awareness of physical recommendations within the existing downtown built-form context, an axonometric aerial visualization, Level 2 Diagram, was developed from a base plan with building footprints at one inch = 100 feet. A choice was made to filter out as many potentially interrupting background lines as possible, resulting in block patterns that consisted of outer block edges without the interior

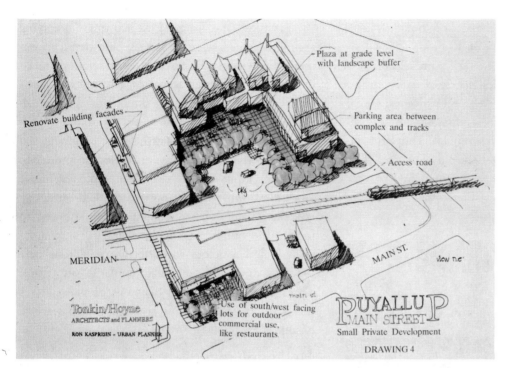

Renovate building facades

Plaza at grade level with landscape buffer

Parking area between complex and tracks

Access road

Renovate building facades

MERIDIAN

Tonkin/Hoyne
ARCHITECTS and PLANNERS

RON KASPRISIN - URBAN PLANNER

Use of south/west facing lots for outdoor commercial use, like restaurants

MAIN ST.

View n.e.

PUYALLUP
MAIN STREET
Small Private Development

DRAWING 4

7-26 In-fill Sketch and Meeker Streetscape Sketches. A quick felt-tip pen sketch with color added to the reverse side of the flimsy tracing paper, suitable for public presentations. These sketches are two-part processes: one, a Pentel sketch on flimsy trace for review with client; and two, a technical pen illustration for inclusion in the public report document.

building roof lines. Key buildings and buildings surrounding spaces to be highlighted were outlined in their entirety, with shadows. The intent of the visualization was to highlight key open space networks within a larger built-form context, in a quick and loose format. Colored marker was applied on the back side of the tracing paper drawing, muting the higher-intensity marker colors. Different Pentel Sign pens were used for the drawing, alternating among points that had various levels of wear on them, from new sharp-pointed tips to more worn, broader, and drier tips.

Quick-sketch techniques also proved advantage for site-specific studies in a tight time frame (one hour or less) where key context, scale, site relationships, and landscape forms were the focus. Small Development is an axonometric aerial diagram drawn with a Sign pen. It is an outline drawing of existing buildings with new in-fill buildings set around pedestrian space, noted with a grid ground plane pattern. Landscape forms are kept simple, and major shapes are shadowed to provide value differentiation. The outer edges of building shapes across perimeter streets are provided for the viewer's orientation and reference.

Eye-level perspectives and plan sketches of pavement patterns combine to inform the public regarding placement and scale of ground patterns and street trees, and more detailed pattern configurations at key intersections as in Meeker Street Meridian.

Project Two: Design Guidelines

City Image Study: Introduction

The City of Puyallup upgraded the city's Comprehensive Plan in accordance with the requirements set forth in the State of Washington's Growth Management Act. As a part of that effort, the city desired to develop urban design scenarios focusing on residential and commercial/industrial land uses, preparing prototypical development patterns for selected sites and addressing the relationship between the natural and built environments. The prototypes were to be communicated in readily understandable graphic images to the public and a steering committee illustrating design policies that underlay each scenario.

The public participated in three workshops and an open-house exhibit, providing feedback and ideas regarding the prototypes. Each workshop was attended by about fifty people. The first involved a slide presentation and preference survey regarding design and scale issues for housing and commercial uses. The second and third presented and explored design changes to existing sites as a means of developing design policies that were preferred by the public. The final open house enabled the public and task force to review the process and products of the study as a means of finalizing approval of design policies.

The city staff and the design team selected ten study sites for a detailed design test of concepts and development constraints. Five sites involve residential development types and five represent commercial development. Each contains physical and land-use conditions that exist within the Puyallup area. The residential site studies are highlighted in this case study.

Test Sites

Residential Study Sites

Site One: Agriculture land preservation within new residential development

Site Two: Existing single family residential block in-fill.

Site Three: Wooded sloping site with single family character.

Site Four: Multiple family residential development adjacent to existing single family developments.

Site Five: Rural/urban transition areas with large lot development to preserve rural character.

(Sites One through Three are used as examples:)

Approach

To introduce the project to the public and the Comprehensive Plan Steering Committee, the city staff and design team conducted a visual preference workshop, reviewing slides of housing types by density and commercial developments in Puyallup and other Puget Sound communities for public information and conducting a survey of the design preferences of those in attendance. Based on that information, the team began a design assessment of the ten selected sites for study.

Each site was assigned an existing underlying zoning designation, including use and density parameters and special biophysical considerations to be included in the design scenarios. The team prepared conceptual designs for each site at one inch equals 200 feet. These scenarios were reviewed by city staff and presented at public workshops for comment and modifications. Site plans were revised according to the public input and were again presented at public workshops until a consensus was reached on design guidelines and policies. Graphic methods used to inform the public of guidelines and recommendations included before and after aerial-oblique perspective drawings and diagrammatic site plans. Three-dimensional sketch diagrams provided close-up views of housing clusters and types to serve as examples for public reference.

Methodologies

As in many urban design studies for smaller communities, in-depth explorations and analysis need to be completed in shorter durations with limited budgets. In addition, the public involvement process is well attended and requires visualization material to be effective. The designer can benefit by visual thinking methods that allow for a plurality of alternatives to be generated and tested quickly and illustratively. This section describes and depicts a number of methodologies that enable schematic site plans, diagrams, and perspectives to be used in the cognitive process. Relying only on two-dimensional site studies and a final illustrated plan because budgets are small may be efficient but not effective. In many ways, these examples underscore the potential for working in three dimensions more than in plan as ideas are developed and tested.

Site-Planning Templates. In the agricultural preservation site study, *templates* were used to generate general site planning and design concepts quickly and in presentable fashion. Templates are a pattern of objects or shapes that represent design and development components. They enable the designer to prepare concept site plans that incorporate building typologies and the supporting services for those buildings (i.e., parking and open space). A scale of 1 inch/200 feet was selected for the conceptual studies. In a one-acre square, drawn at the selected scale, a number of building typology footprints were

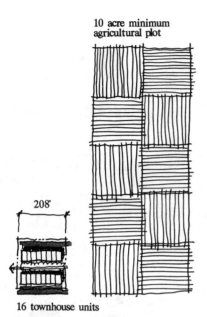

10 acre minimum
agricultural plot

208'

16 townhouse units

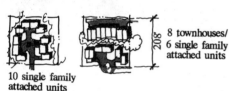

10 single family
attached units

8 townhouses/
6 single family
attached units

208'

7-27 Agriculture Site Program Templates. Two-dimensional templates of residential cluster developments fitting a one-acre square, and ten-acre agriculture fields were prepared prior to the conceptual site plan studies. These templates were placed under the tracing paper to quickly portray certain densities and unit configurations.

7-28 Conceptual Footprint Diagrams. Using the templates, alternative concepts were quickly developed for public review and exploration. Color with pencil added to the visualizations' effectiveness in the public workshops. Six of these diagrams were completed with enough detail to begin discussions on impacts with the public.

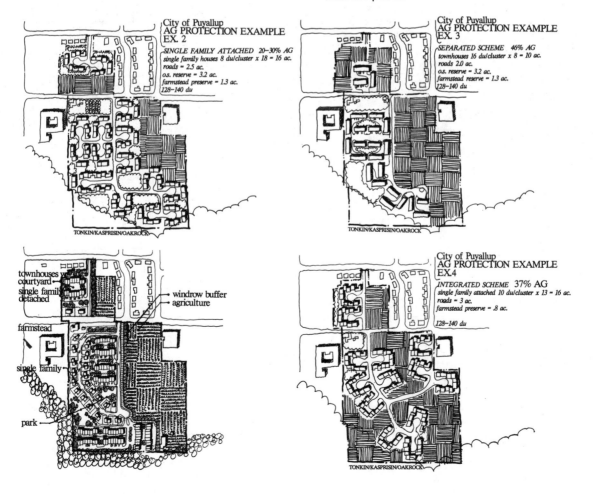

City of Puyallup
AG PROTECTION EXAMPLE
EX. 2

SINGLE FAMILY ATTACHED 20–30% AG
single family houses 8 du/cluster x 18 = 16 ac.
roads = 2.5 ac.
o.s. reserve = 3.2 ac.
farmstead preserve = 1.3 ac.
128–140 du

TONKIN/KASPRISIN/OAKROCK

City of Puyallup
AG PROTECTION EXAMPLE
EX. 3

SEPARATED SCHEME 46% AG
townhouses 16 du/cluster x 8 = 10 ac.
roads 2.0 ac.
o.s. reserve = 3.2 ac.
farmstead reserve = 1.3 ac.
128–140 du

TONKIN/KASPRISIN/OAKROCK

townhouses w/
courtyard
single family
detached

farmstead

single family

park

windrow buffer
agriculture

City of Puyallup
AG PROTECTION EXAMPLE
EX.4

INTEGRATED SCHEME 37% AG
single family attached 10 du/cluster x 13 = 16 ac.
roads = 3 ac.
farmstead preserve = .8 ac.

128–140 du

TONKIN/KASPRISIN/OAKROCK

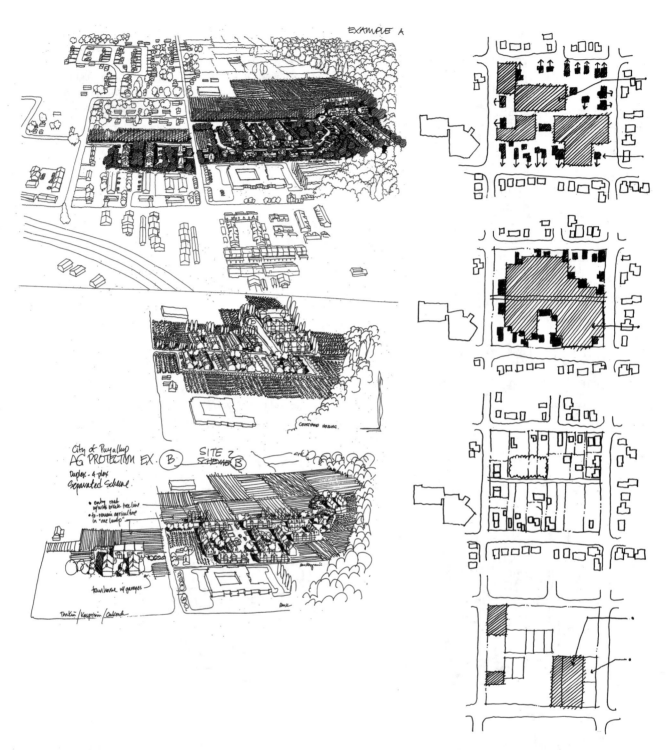

7-29 Beginning to End: the Sketch. From a slide view taken from an airplane, a perspective footprint base is first cut; followed by a massing sketch; followed by a more articulated building features sketch; followed by a "dress rehearsal" where all of the major parts are combined for a rough draft. Options are explored in the three-dimensional format. The final visualization is a technical pen and ink drawing using a fine-point tip. The background shapes set scale and existing development patterns. Shadows are used to pull out building masses; agricultural "scribbles" are used to add texture and value as a surrounding "shape."

7-30 Block Conditions Diagram. This series of two-dimensional diagrams summarizes physical conditions on an in-city block proposed for new residential unit in-fill. Solid-void, hatching, and outlining are all used to make the diagrams useful for public review.

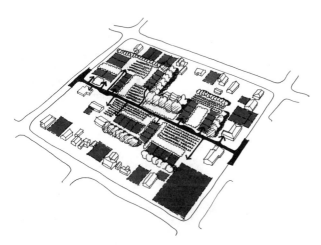

7-31 Block Diagram Explorations. One advantage of working from a three-dimensional format is the relative ease in laying out footprint options not unlike working on a two-dimensional plan. The perspective block is divided proportionately into a perspective grid, then used as a base for exploring new forms. Relations of buildings to open space to parking access are clearly indicated in diagram; this base then provides a perspective plan for raising vertical dimensions.

drawn in with parking and open space elements, providing the designer with a workable number of units by building type (townhouse and single-family detached and attached) that could be accomodated in one acre. Conceptual layouts were developed, each with a different approach regarding the overall road pattern and differing configurations of agricultural lands—-lands that might be preserved in a working manner with surrounding or adjacent residential development at four units per gross acre for the site. Given these starting points, the templates were used as an underlayment so that one-acre squares could be drawn on the site plan in various arrangements fitting to the road and agriculture patterns to determine the number of units possible by building typology; followed by a more detailed tracing of the footprints within the squares to add building components to the site plan. This enabled six different site development options to be conceptualized in a brief period of time with enough information for public comment, critique, and elaboration.

In the single-family residential block in-fill study

site, a perspective sketch was used as the base for multiple options. The sketch was drawn from an aerial oblique slide of the study block in Puyallup. Using a perspective grid allocation for the block to gain an estimate of block dimensions, the designer prepared multiple options for residential in-fill using pea-patches (common garden plots), the service alley, and various cluster typologies to develop alternatives presentable to the local residents at a public workshop. Colored pencil was quickly added to the sketches, the basic presentation form for this site.

In the wooded site study, templates were again used to determine general development patterns that were less intrusive to the heavily treed site, meeting a city objective of determining comprehensive plan policy for steep slopes where erosion reduction was desired through an increased retention of existing trees. More detailed analysis of this issue is necessary based on the preliminary directions and policies developed from the schematic explorations. One success of the study included the growing awareness by the public and the development community of the footprint impacts on the site's conditions of one housing typology compared to another, i.e., single-family detached on larger lots vs. single-family detached and attached in clusters.

These investigations were made prior to the development of the comprehensive plan detail, investigating the spatial impacts of planning policy, and developing policy from the site-development testing process using building typology templates and free-hand sketch studies.

Kent Growth Management Visualizations

Background and Overview

The City of Kent, in the process of a staff-generated comprehensive plan update[6] to meet State of Washington Growth Management requirements, sought a public information visualization tool to

---

[6] This project involved a close working relationship with planning department personnel Fred Satterstrom, Linda Phillips, and others as visualizations of shape and pattern were developed and critiqued for relevancy of density and form.

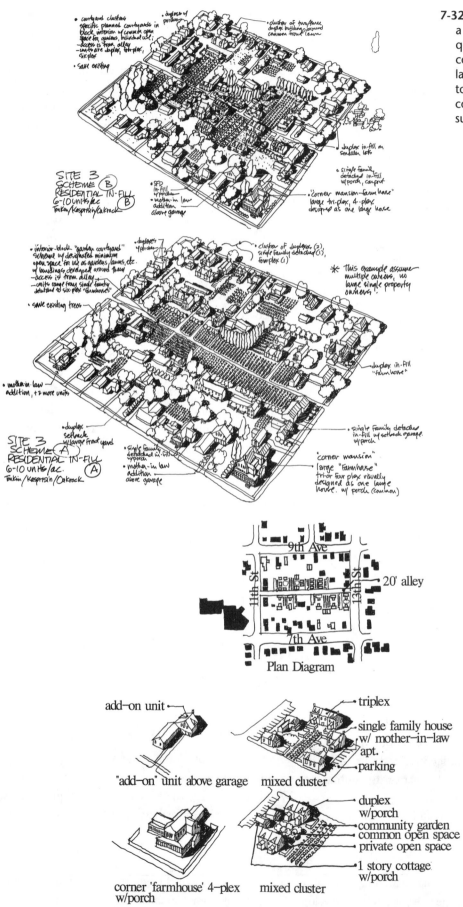

7-32 Sketch In-fill Studies. Using a felt-tip pen, the designer can quickly add scale, architectural components, open space types, landscaping, and parking access to the three-dimensional plan to construct a draft perspective suitable for public review.

SITE 3
SCHEME B
RESIDENTIAL IN-FILL
6-10 Units/ac.
Tonkin/Kasprisin/Oakrock B

SITE 3
SCHEME A
RESIDENTIAL IN-FILL
6-10 Units/ac.
Tonkin/Kasprisin/Oakrock A

9th Ave

11th St

13th St

20' alley

7th Ave

Plan Diagram

add-on unit

triplex

single family house w/ mother-in-law apt.

parking

"add-on" unit above garage   mixed cluster

duplex w/porch
community garden
common open space
private open space

1 story cottage w/porch

corner 'farmhouse' 4-plex w/porch   mixed cluster

7-33 Sketch In-fill Blow-up.

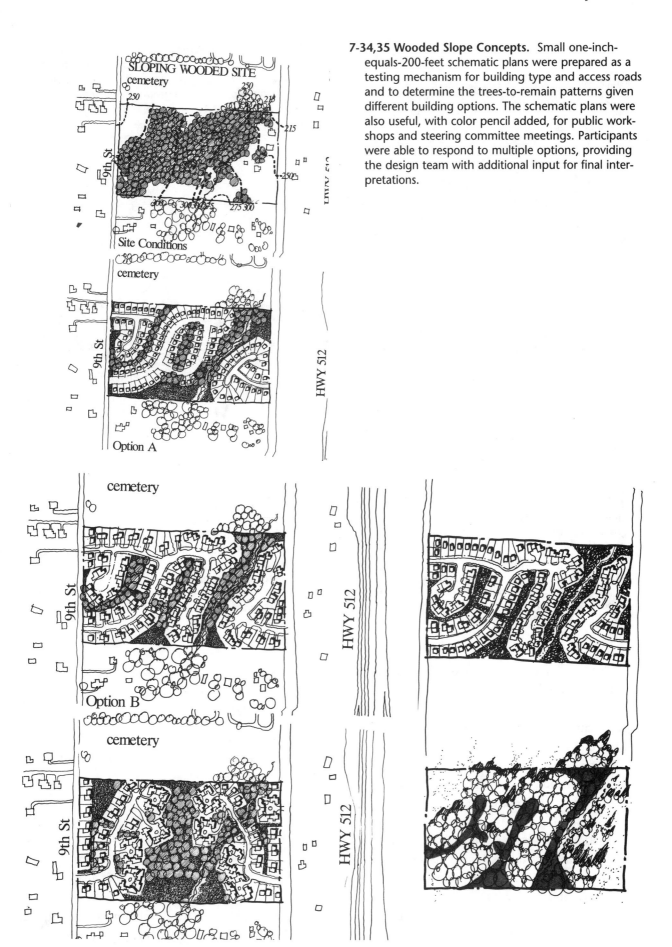

7-34,35 Wooded Slope Concepts. Small one-inch-equals-200-feet schematic plans were prepared as a testing mechanism for building type and access roads and to determine the trees-to-remain patterns given different building options. The schematic plans were also useful, with color pencil added, for public workshops and steering committee meetings. Participants were able to respond to multiple options, providing the design team with additional input for final interpretations.

7-36 Final Wooded Slope Guidelines. The final drawing resulting from workshop input was drawn with a technical pen and inserted into the original base aerial oblique drawing. The ground plane was darkened in value to contrast the house forms.

7-37 The "Ghost." Mount Rainier is the southeast backdrop to the Kent valley communities, powerful in its dimensions, yet often overlooked by the busy activity on the ground and often obscured by the misty rainfalls of the Pacific Northwest. It is a dramatic land form aspect of Kent's context that stands for much more—the source of watersheds that supply the valley with life-giving waters, habitats for salmonoid fishes, and sustenance for the remaining agricultural industry. When the water quality goes, so does the valley and its communities. The views of the mountain act as a reminder of both the beauty and majesty of the northwest and of the fragile and critical functioning of its landform, and are therefore included as important urban context images.

depict various scenarios and densities being considered for adoption. Two areas were selected for the exercise: downtown and an area called East Hill, which is saturated with under-utilized shopping centers and highway strip malls.

The visualizations provide a two-fold vehicle for planning evaluation of alternatives. First, they provide the staff with a testing procedure, working with the urban design consultant, by which to craft the form manifestations of described public policy, reviewing and editing the urban designer's interpretations of the staff's descriptions and information. Second, they provide the public with a visualization, subject to the usual "this is only a test" clarifiers, that can elicit ideas and comments about what policy means and how

they can engage in the growth management process with an evolving understanding of what policy means in built form.

The Downtown Kent series of drawings included both a conceptual design overview of the downtown area, developed from plans, interviews, and work sessions with staff, and zoning and design guidelines, and a visualization of building types, building intensities, and scale issues with shapes and patterns that are reasonable as assumptions of future development within the parameters of the growth management guidelines. The value of this intense and short duration type of project lies in its ability to be critiqued both during and after the process of visualization.

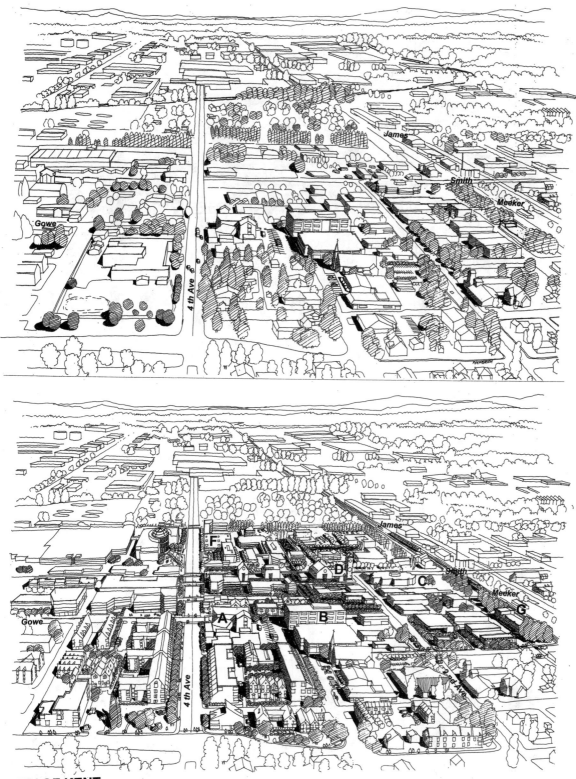

CITY OF KENT

DOWNTOWN
Preferred Alternative
Visualization

1994

View North via 4th

Legend/Reference

A City Hall
B Centennial Building
C Library
D Performing Arts Center
E Justice Center
F Borden Site
G BN RR

Please Note:
This visualization is a conceptual illustration only, drawn to convey general bulk, scale, and intensities of future mixed use development.

Source: Kasprisin Pettinari Design

7-38 Existing Downtown Aerial Oblique and Growth-management Scenario Oblique: Mixed Use. With staff assistance, the existing context was developed from an aerial oblique slide.

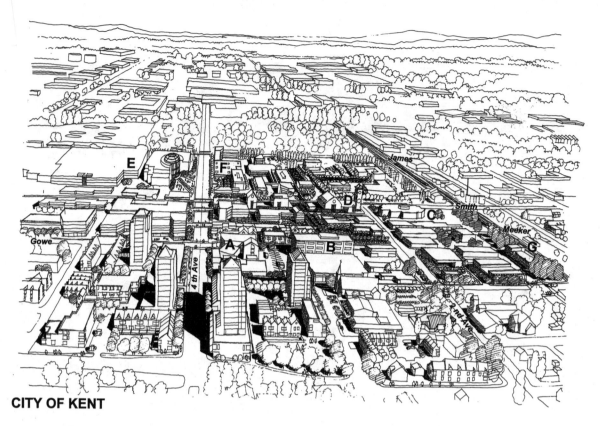

CITY OF KENT

DOWNTOWN
Urban Center
Visualization

1994

View North via 4th

Legend/Reference

A City Hall
B Centennial Building
C Library
D Performing Arts Center
E Justice Center
F Borden Site
G BN RR

Please Note:
This visualization is a conceptual
illustration only, drawn to convey
general bulk, scale, and intensities of
future mixed use development.

Source: Kasprisin Pettinari Design

7-39 Growth Management Scenario Oblique: Urban Center and Urban Center Splice. Using the *Mixed Use Scenario* as a base drawing, changes in intensity represented by higher-density building forms were drawn as transparent overlays to the base. These were copied, cut out, and spliced over a copy of the first base (mixed use) and reprinted, producing a second scenario, Urban Center, with much less time expended. Multiple options were quickly executed for public review and comment.

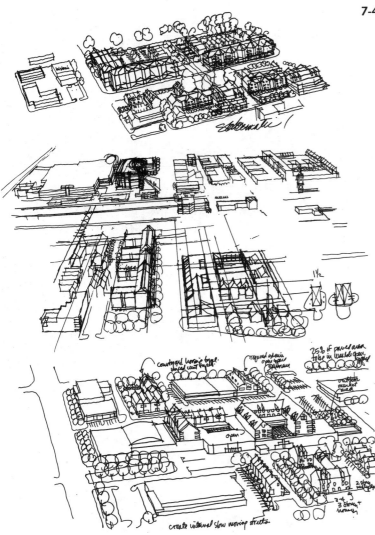

7-40 Study Sketches for Downtown Kent.
These sketches, part of the preliminary drawings from another view not finalized, exemplify the type of three-dimensional design process possible when the oblique is established as a base. Distances and proportions can be accurately estimated using the block grid as a reference point and comparing the perspective grid to a quantifiable and measurable base map.

City staff were able to articulate land use and development-intensity issues more clearly as rough drafts of the aerial oblique sketches were presented and assessed at work sessions. The very act of selecting a view of the downtown can have ramifications on what is focused on and what is made less critical in the receding perspective. The process essentially acted as a testing mechanism for planning concepts and urban-design guidelines as the drawings were made.

In the East Hill drawing series emphasis was placed on generating ideas for the private sector for ways to transform existing and under-utilized shopping centers, where parking lots and retail buildings had become so dispersed that no pedestrian orientation or semblance of a compact activity center remained. City staff were exacting about the message in the drawings: in-fill development characterized by mixed-use with retail commercial on the ground floors and residential above, interspersed with pedestrian open space. The retail ground floor image was critical and even at the large aerial oblique view had to read clearly for the public.

These drawings are vision drawings with a site-specific message of development intent rather than detail. The city took a risk in spatially representing policy for the public, realizing the many different ways the drawings could be interpreted. The public responded enthusiastically because they had reference, orientation, and access to an interpretation—something to respond to, something to help them translate written goals and policies into a spatial example of impacts and implications in a setting they could recognize.

The perspectives are suitable for mounting on foam-core boards for public meetings to stimulate, instigate, and inform.

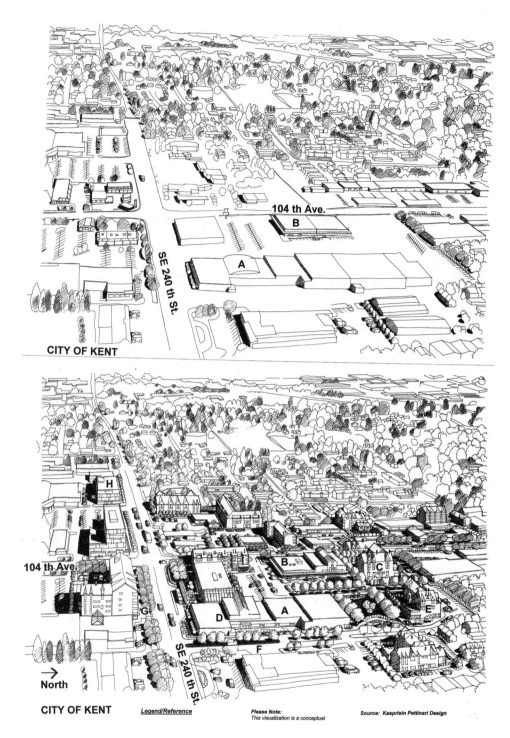

104 th Ave.

B

SE 240 th St.

A

CITY OF KENT

104 th Ave.

H

G

B

C

D

A

E

F

North

SE 240 th St.

CITY OF KENT   Legend/Reference   Please Note: Source: Kasprisin Pettinari Design
This visualization is a conceptual

7-41 East Hill Existing Context Oblique. Prepared by a graduate planning student in the office, the before or existing oblique sets the existing conditions for a later residential high-density in-fill study of over-developed highway-oriented retail malls along arterials in Kent, Washington.

East Hill Mixed Use Scenario. In-fill development scenarios for the retail shopping centers were developed in three dimensions based on a number of key criteria: small increases in retail uses, specifically at the ground floors of new residential developments;

remodelling of existing retail facilities to make them more people-oriented and less auto-oriented; new in-fill located around small open space courts or parks, absorbing some of the parking lot areas as standards are lowered from six spaces per 1,000 square feet of gross leasable floor area to three spaces per 1,000 square feet (standard changes now occurring within the urbanized Seattle-Tacoma area); and the creation of slow-moving service roads within the private developments. All line work is done with fine-point technical pen on tracing paper; a Pentel Sign pen was used to lightly outline major building forms adding just enough differential value.

Project Three: Small Town Design Standards

Vashon Town Plan Zoning and Design Standards

Background and Overview

Vashon is an island community of 10,000 people located in Puget Sound south of Seattle and north of Tacoma. It straddles King and Kitsap counties, a rural enclave in an urban county (King). On the island are numerous smaller unincorporated towns, one of which is the Town of Vashon, a crossroads commercial service center for the island residents which contains a residential population. Water shortages, development pressures from Seattle and Tacoma, and a different life-style all combine to make an interesting and challenging approach to a town plan and zoning and design standards. A summary of the community's sentiments toward the future of the town can be stated as follows: *Vashon is a contemporary small town, content with its hodge-podge form and style, wary of "design" success that could lead to increased visitor attrac-*

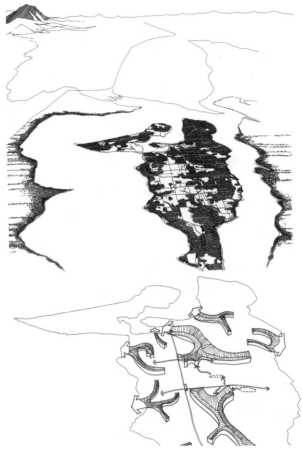

7-42 Vashon Island in the Puget Sound.

7-43 Vashon Small Scale In-Town Residential.

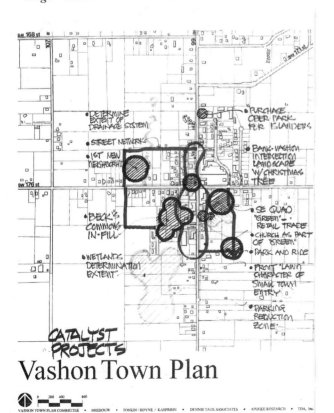

CATALYST PROJECTS

Vashon Town Plan

VASHON TOWN PLAN COMMITTEE • BREDOUW • TONKIN/HOYNE/KASPRISIN • DENNIS TATE ASSOCIATES • APOGEE RESEARCH • TDA, Inc.

Vashon Town Form

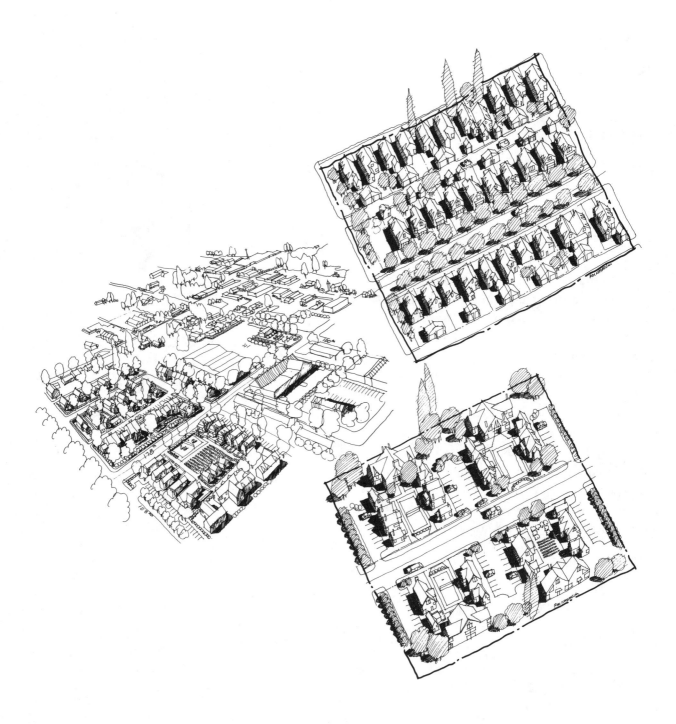

7-44 Two axonometric drawings of the same site provided a format for illustrating two acceptable residential configurations for the community. In *Small Parcel Subdivision*, 32 single-family residences were located on a four-acre tract, using neo-traditional principles (alleys, small lots, and street frontage orientation of pedestrian activity). In *Commons*, the same four acres were configured with a cluster of diverse building types: multiplex homes, multiplexes, single-family attached and detached units, and cottages; a common open space area equal in size to one volleyball court plus out-of-bounds; individual open space areas for each unit, contiguous to each; one side of the commons oriented to the primary pedestrian street or major sidewalk leading to that street; shared parking perpendicular to the street; and protected open space between each commons development.

7-45 Vashon Farmsteads. Areas around the built-up town are agricultural in use and/or character. With changes in zoning and a desire by residents to retain the scale and function of rural farmsteads, the *Vashon Farmstead* standard was developed to include the following characteristics: retain existing farmhouse (or primary original residential structure); provide a common access drive for all units on site; retain a front-yard setback consistent with adjacent and nearby setbacks; provide shared parking; provide for diverse small-scale housing types, within allowable zoning density, including multiplex rehabilitation of existing homes with single-home appearance maintained; single-family attached and/or detached homes to rear of primary farmhouse; cottages in similar arrangements; and a tillable area maintained on-site.

7-46 Vashon Multiplex Homes. The axonometric examples represented ways of providing additional units within a single family home appearance.

Vashon Cottages. These cottage options, a minimum of 160 square feet in size, provided an accessory unit resource for developments so that affordable housing and life-increment housing are made available within the community without constructing homogenous one-unit-type-lower-income "ghettos" in compounds.

tions, and determined to be a real functioning town, limited in its growth, providing real services to the people and friendly in its way of living.

Town meetings, workshops, open exhibits, and detailed work sessions were a part of the process. They were well attended and community-based regarding direction and ideas. The consultant design team[7] worked as co-participants with a planning committee to forge an innovative approach to small town design, seeking to avoid suburbanization and franchisement of the town. A critical issue was the jurisdiction and regulation of zoning and land use by King County, a larger government entity located east of and including Seattle and dealing with a large geographic area not similar to the island community. The design standards and the Special District Overlay attached to the new zoning ordinance also needed to meet a county objective of being applicable in other rural town centers throughout the county, a significant challenge for all concerned.

The following sequence of visualizations summarize a lengthy and complex process of public involvement and urban design. The final project has been accepted and adopted by the Vashon Island Community Council.

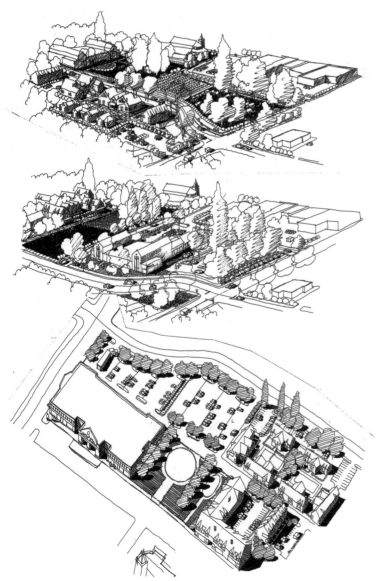

7-47 Large Lot Commercial Development. This visualization dealt with a common challenge for small towns---the development of a large single-owner commercial complex with on-site parking, potentially disruptive to the compact and pedestrian nature of smaller towns and cities. The characteristics illustrated in the axonometric include: (1) modulation of large building faces to reduce scale impacts; (2) mezzanine windows above storefront windows; (3) building entryways with insets or protected outdoor spaces; (4) no blank walls (defined); (5) orientation to a primary pedestrian street; (6) orientation to a pedestrian walkway that leads to a primary pedestrian street; (7) provision of useable open space equal to 40 percent of the paved parking and service street square footage, exclusive of landscaping and pedestrian areas ("A" and "B"); (8) combining adjacent open space requirements for even larger "public-use" space; (9) total open space oriented toward a historic or local feature of significance such as a public or semi-public building; and (10) a pedestrian walkway at curb height in parking areas. The diagram also visualizes the relationship of the large lot development to adjacent different use developments: (11) retail commercial on the ground floor of residential buildings; (12) residential units and/or office uses on upper floors; (13) building orientation to major open space features; (14) side and/or rear yard parking; (15) multiplex on site perimeter; (16) common internal open space for cluster tenant use; (17) multiplex homes; and (18) perimeter parking areas.

[7] Pam Bredouw (planner), Les Tonkin (architect), Dennis Tate (resource background), Ben Frerhicks (economist), Ron Kaprisin (community design), working as an interdisciplinary team.

Project Four: Waterfront Feasibility, Bremerton Waterfront

Design and Economic Development Exploration

Downtown Bremerton, Washington is situated on Sinclair Inlet in Puget Sound, a one-hour ferry ride west from Seattle. It is home to the Bremerton Naval Shipyard and a major modal split port for Seattle–bound commuters living in Kitsap Peninsula. It has one of the last undeveloped downtown waterfront parcels of land in any of the major Puget Sound cities, a lingering opportunity made difficult in part by the military related economy and the flight of downtown businesses to outlying malls. The city desired to assemble a Request For Proposal (RFP) for the city-owned site as a way of enticing the private sector to develop it. As a part of that RFP, the city requested that an economic and design feasibility study be conducted to determine the uses appropriate for the site, their extent and characteristics, and the preferred design guidelines that could influence the physical configuration of uses on the site and

improve its connections to the older downtown.

Of key importance to the larger study was the urban design/architectural testing of economic and political feasibility issues. The study team worked through initial plan diagrams, site sections, and economic scenarios to establish a point of beginning for discussion with a task force committee. A model was constructed for the site and used to study eight different massing studies, each accompanied by a financial feasibility analysis. As ideas took shape on a generalized level, axonometric studies were prepared as a means of testing open space organizing elements, uses and view relationships, parking and retail relationships, and connections to off-site activities and the downtown.

The use of drawings, models, and diagrams enabled the design framework to evolve over a number of months, resulting in a city-supported Request For Proposal and design and economic guidelines. The integration of quantitative economic analysis and design visioning and massing visualization provided a basis for making difficult decisions. The design schemes were viewed as explorations of design opportunity rather than final architectural solutions.

For speed and quality, all drawings were made with a Pentel Sign pen on Clearprint tracing paper.

7-48,49,50,51,52 Bremerton Waterfront Revitalization Series. This series of doodles and axonometrics represents an urban design and economic analysis for a key city-owned downtown waterfront block. In a search for a feasible package with which to attract developers, the team used various visualization formats to test economics, politics, and functional needs related to the site design.

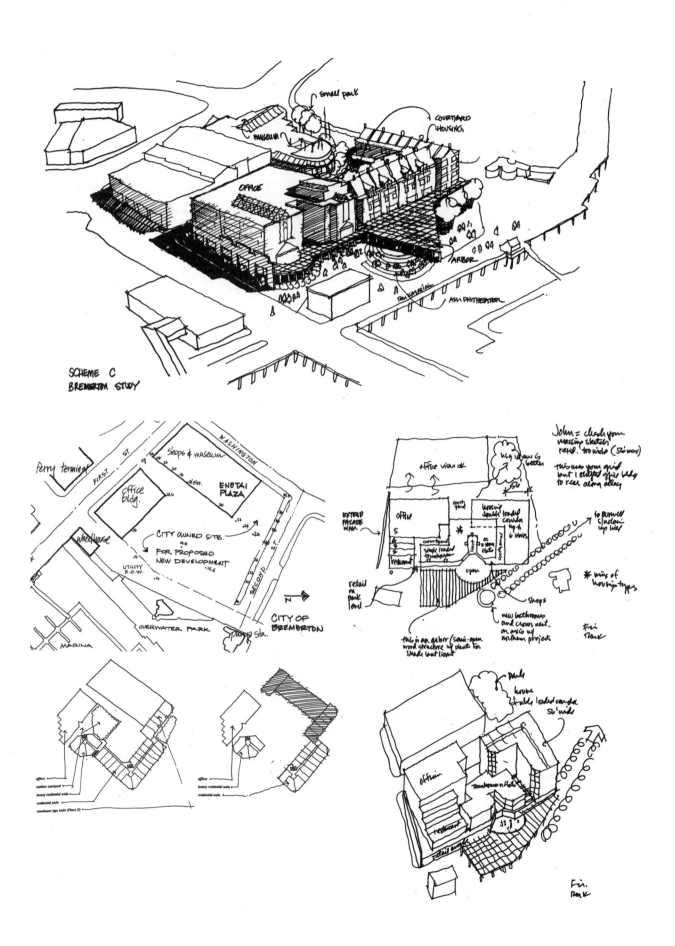

SCHEME C
BREMERTON STUDY

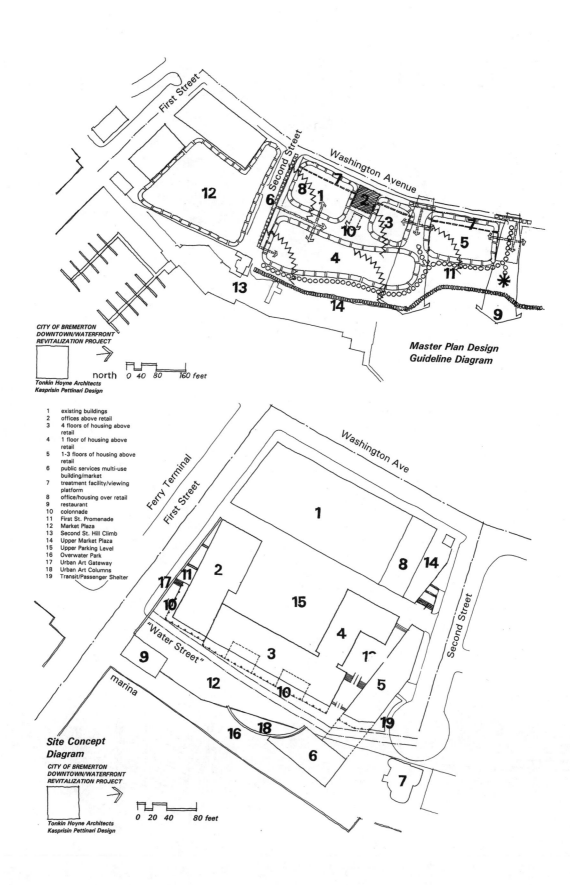

CITY OF BREMERTON
DOWNTOWN/WATERFRONT
REVITALIZATION PROJECT

north   0 40 80   160 feet

Tonkin Hoyne Architects
Kasprisin Pettinari Design

**Master Plan Design
Guideline Diagram**

1   existing buildings
2   offices above retail
3   4 floors of housing above retail
4   1 floor of housing above retail
5   1-3 floors of housing above retail
6   public services multi-use building/market
7   treatment facility/viewing platform
8   office/housing over retail
9   restaurant
10 colonnade
11 First St. Promenade
12 Market Plaza
13 Second St. Hill Climb
14 Upper Market Plaza
15 Upper Parking Level
16 Overwater Park
17 Urban Art Gateway
18 Urban Art Columns
19 Transit/Passenger Shelter

**Site Concept
Diagram**

CITY OF BREMERTON
DOWNTOWN/WATERFRONT
REVITALIZATION PROJECT

0 20 40   80 feet

Tonkin Hoyne Architects
Kasprisin Pettinari Design

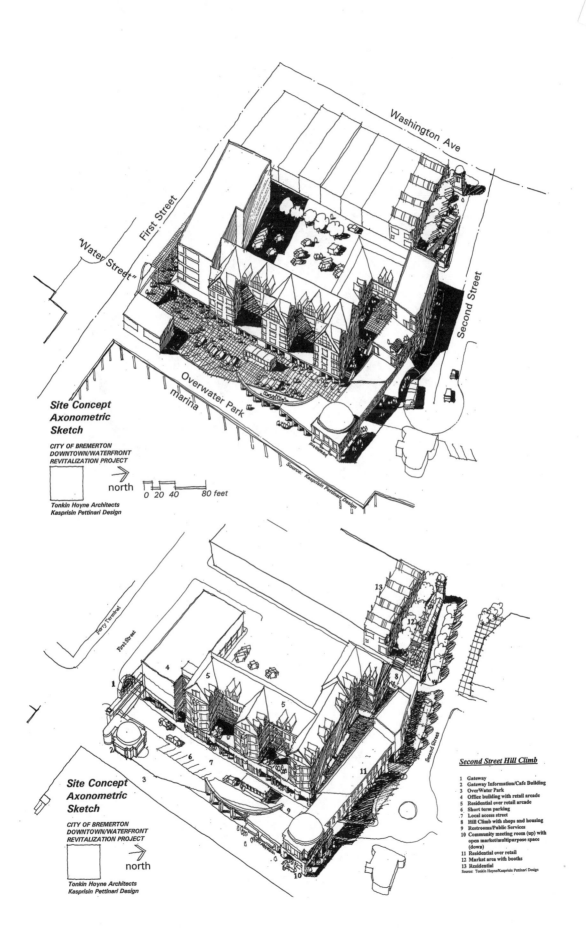

Site Concept Axonometric Sketch

CITY OF BREMERTON DOWNTOWN/WATERFRONT REVITALIZATION PROJECT

north

0 20 40 80 feet

Tonkin Hoyne Architects
Kasprisin Pettinari Design

Source: Kasprisin Pettinari Design

Site Concept Axonometric Sketch

CITY OF BREMERTON DOWNTOWN/WATERFRONT REVITALIZATION PROJECT

north

Tonkin Hoyne Architects
Kasprisin Pettinari Design

Second Street Hill Climb

1   Gateway
2   Gateway Information/Cafe Building
3   OverWater Park
4   Office building with retail arcade
5   Residential over retail arcade
6   Short term parking
7   Local access street
8   Hill Climb with shops and housing
9   Restrooms/Public Services
10 Community meeting room (up) with
    open market/multipurpose space
    (down)
11 Residential over retail
12 Market area with booths
13 Residential

Source: Tonkin Hoyne/Kasprisin Pettinari Design

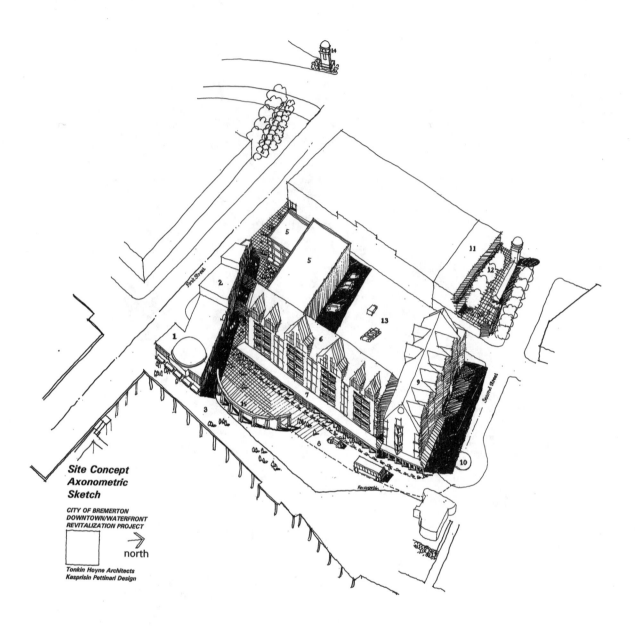

Site Concept Axonometric Sketch

CITY OF BREMERTON
DOWNTOWN/WATERFRONT
REVITALIZATION PROJECT

north

Tonkin Hoyne Architects
Kasprisin Pettinari Design

8 Cowlitz—Willamette Case Study

Introduction/Background

Visualizing the natural container in which the metropolitan area grows carries an understanding of its limits, and reshapes attitudes toward any project within those limits. The aerial view is over Portland, Oregon, the metro area that developed in the center of the Willamette-Cowlitz Eco-region at the intersection of the Willamette and Columbia Rivers. The street grid on the flat plain is cradled by the natural boundaries of the river intersection: the wide expanse of the Columbia River on the east, its flood plain and the narrower Willamette River winding along a west hill edge.

When growth obliterates boundaries, the opportunity for creating defined places is destroyed; city and country become one as they both lose their distinction. Portland's compact historic center grew along the Willamette River, stopping at the edge of the west hills. Over the course of a century the city expanded: east across the Willamette River, south on the plain of the Willamette Valley, and west over the hills toward the foothills of the Coastal Range. Today the city of Portland receives a very small 3–5 percent of the metro growth. Most new development expands along the metro periphery into the forest and farmlands surrounding the city.

Drawing Value

Drawing composition and value is chosen to clearly illustrate the interplay of the built settlement pattern within the natural limits of the eco-region. Along the horizon, the Cascade Mountain range and its Mount Hood landmark at the edge of the eco-region is included as the first reference. The second order is the boundaries that define the metro area and give it an identity as a place. These include the surfaces of the Columbia and Willamette Rivers, their edge topography, and the settlement pattern of transportation lines that have subdivided the grid into subdistricts.

Citizen Participation and the Planning/Design Process

In 1947, the State of Oregon adopted the statewide planning goal dealing with urban growth. Goal 14

8-1 Cowlitz-Willamette Eco-region Within Cascadia.

227

8-2 Metro Settlement Within Eco-region "Room," Portland, Oregon / Vancouver, Washington. The aerial places the metro area within its natural container. The drawing composition and line value emphasize those forces that have shaped the settlement pattern; the joining of the Willamette and Columbia Rivers in the foreground, the West Hill and Cascade Mountain boundaries in the background.

8-3 Urban Growth Boundary: Portland, Oregon. The urban growth boundary around the Portland, Oregon metro area is intended to contain urban sprawl. It sets the scene for the reuse of vacant and under-utilized lands within the city as well as densification around alternative public transportation modes.

required each city to adopt an urban growth boundary, "in a cooperative process between a city and the counties that surround it." An urban growth boundary typically creates an area that encircles a settlement. To amend the boundary, a city must comply with the exception requirements from the statewide planning goal, calling for a review of alternatives.

As an alternative to the expansion of the growth boundary that encircles Portland, the Department of City Planning has developed, through various ongoing programs, strategies for densifying the city. The local chapter of the AIA, the Department of Architecture at the University of Oregon, and neighborhood groups have participated in these efforts, and three are outlined in this case study. These include the Northwest Triangle R/UDAT study sponsored by the American Institute of Architects and two neighborhood studies conducted by the Regional Rail Program and the Cities Livable Program, both within the Portland Planning Department.

Visual Thinking Within the Citizen Participation Process

Visualization is used in several ways and at different stages during the public participation process. Drawings are done to both initiate and direct public participation, as well as to respond to it. The process begins with two-dimensional views that quantify existing character and conditions of study sites, and ends with three-dimensional sketches describing the fit of alternative design concepts within a given concept.

A recurring theme during the visualization process is the appearance of a particular study site within its larger context. For the public, the idea of establishing a place within a place is first an orientation device for locating the study site. Later and more importantly in the process, visualizing the study site up the scale ladder reveals opportunities for connecting new development to the surrounding context.

Rebuilding a City Center District

In April 1983, the local chapter of the American Institute of Architects invited, through the Regional/Urban Design Assistant Team (R/UDAT)[1] program, a number of professionals from across the country to visit Portland and conduct a study of a large parcel of strategically located land within the city center area. The team was given the charge to study the area and make recommendations to help the citizens better understand the potential value of the relatively unknown area of the city and to develop ideas that would spark discussions about its future.

Visualizing Existing Conditions and Character

The aerial drawing and diagram places the size and relation of the study area to the city center. The study area is visualized as a large, unconnected "hole" within the city fabric, strategically adjacent to both the city center and the edge of the Willamette River. It is the boundaries and the edges of the district that are a focus of the drawing. The north boundary of the district, the Willamette River, receives the most value as it swings around the site to form the east edge of the city. The backdrop of the city center and the West Hills that form its west and south boundaries also receive value. This drawing was used as a base to visualize five alternatives, each based on a different assumption, that contained reasonable opportunity for development of the area. As more was learned about the study district, it became known as the Northwest Triangle, containing five subdistricts, separate in function, urban character, and density of activities.

8-4 "Northwest Triangle" Study District, Portland, Oregon. The study site, an abandoned and under-utilized industrial/railroad district, is visualized as a large void strategically located between the city center and the river. Boundaries of the study district are emphasized by the most value in the drawing: the Willamette River as it swings north along the site to form the east edge of the city, the south boundary, the city backdrop, and the West hills boundary. The drawing is used as a base to visually explore and develop alternative proposals that are referenced to the existing city structure.

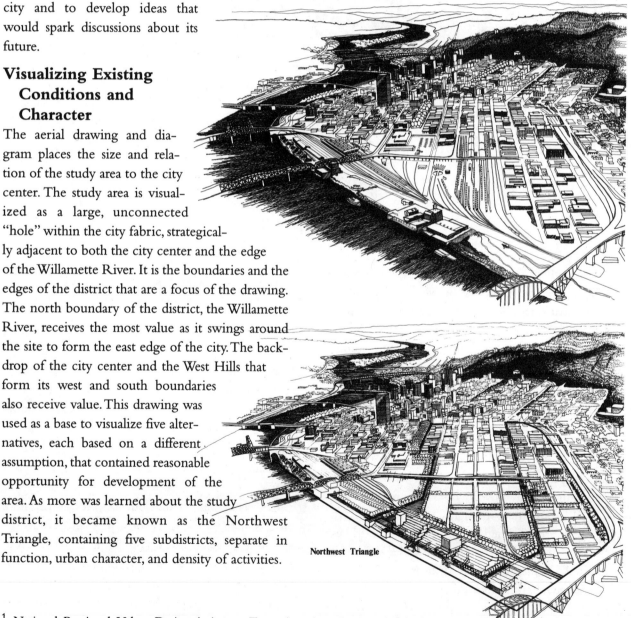

Northwest Triangle

---

[1] National Regional Urban Design Assistance Team, American Institute of Architects. Warehouse/Waterfront District Study, Portland, Oregon. Published: *Last Place in the Downtown Plan*, 1983.

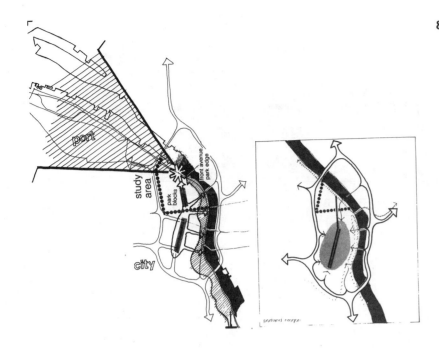

8-5 Study-Site Location Diagram. The two-dimensional plan diagram reduces complex information regarding the study site's strategic location to its most basic relationship with the city center, its street grid and park block system, the historic river course, and the contemporary freeway system that encircles and feeds the downtown. Selected pertinent information is carried by the diagram: site size, shape, and the suggestion of extending an important public connection, the existing downtown park blocks through the study area to the river's edge.

8-6 Development Scenario in Plan, Northwest Triangle District. Two-dimensional plans can describe two-dimensional size, but give limited information regarding site character, scale, and spatial relationships between parts and their context.

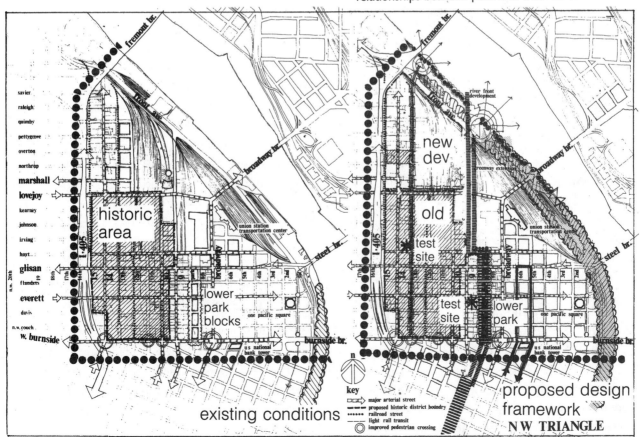

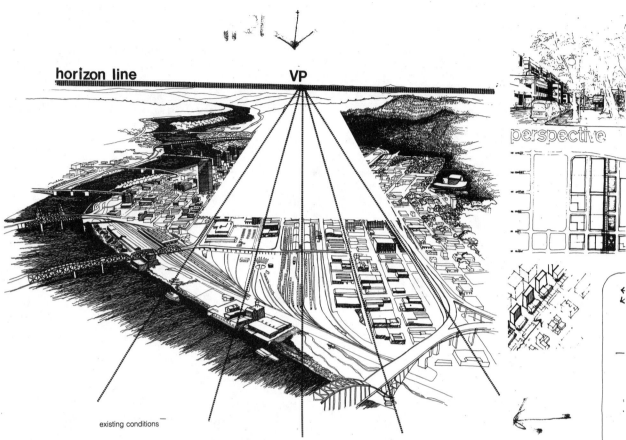

horizon line   VP

perspective

existing conditions

8-7 Perspective Framework from Existing Photographic Slide. Setting up a perspective drawing composition is not an arbitrary decision, but can be a conscious move to "see" certain relationships and to facilitate exploring new organizations. A single vanishing point organizes the perspective framework of the aerial view. It is used to measure and construct alternative design scenarios in the district that relate to the existing historical grid.

Visualizing New Networks of a City District

The aerial-base perspective illustrates one of the development scenarios in the Northwest Triangle. The drawing treats the historic city center not only as a backdrop, but as reference structure. From the drawing structure itself, street connections and building fabric are projected into the previously undeveloped study site. The extension of public street systems into the Northwest Triangle District are a key recommendation of the study team. They include: extending the historic park block sequence that presently stops north of the study district to the waterfront; extending the existing public waterfront park along the Willamette River into the site; extending 13th Avenue within the abandoned warehouse district as a pedestrian way through the site and to the waterfront; and extending the existing downtown transit mall that stops north of the district

to the railroad station. Drawing value is placed along the edges and boundaries of the new framework to define the district and link its five subdivisions to the historic patterns of the city. The highest emphasis is given to the city's Park Block system which is extended through the Northwest Triangle to the Willamette River. The architecture of new development is only suggested in city block form.

Urban Park Block Subdistrict

These diagrams focus on potential development organization within one of the Northwest Triangle's subdistricts, the Park Blocks. The identity of this subdistrict is firmly established through its historic built character. From the drawings of general historic building form that defines the park blocks as a subdistrict, in-fill principles are extrapolated.

8-8 Park Block Subdistrict Building Design Principles. Diagrams of a student test to develop new building principles within the proposed urban design framework.

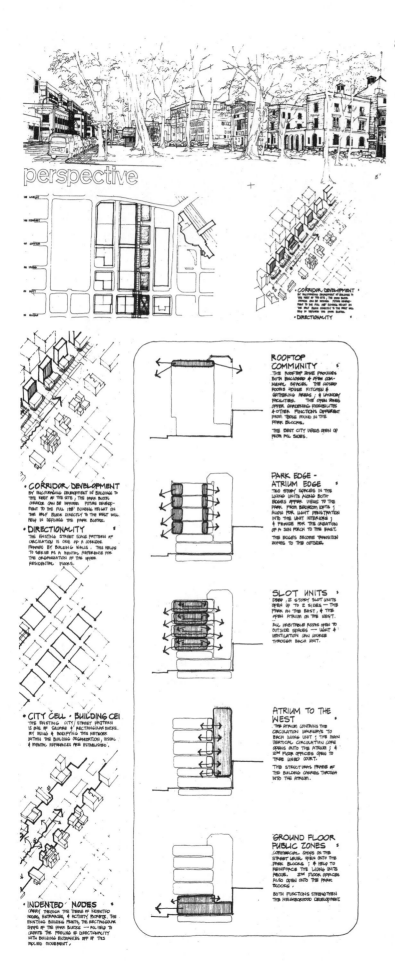

perspective

ROOFTOP
COMMUNITY
THE ROOFTOP ZONE PROVIDES
BOTH ENCLOSED & OPEN COM-
MUNAL SPACES. THE CLOSED
ROOMS HOUSE KITCHEN &
GATHERING AREAS ; & LAUNDRY
FACILITIES. THE OPEN ZONES
OFFER GARDENING POSSIBILITIES
& OTHER FUNCTIONS DIFFERENT
FROM THOSE FOUND IN THE
PARK BLOCKS.

THE BEST CITY VIEWS OPEN UP
FROM ALL SIDES.

PARK EDGE -
ATRIUM EDGE
TWO STORY SPACES IN THE
LIVING UNITS ALONG BOTH
EDGES OFFER VIEWS TO THE
PARK, FROM BEDROOM LOFTS ;
ALLOW FOR LIGHT PENETRATION
INTO THE UNIT INTERIORS ;
& PROVIDE FOR THE CREATION
OF A SUN PORCH TO THE EAST.

THE EDGES BECOME TRANSITION
ZONES TO THE OUTSIDE.

SLOT UNITS
DEEP, 2 STORY SLOT UNITS
OPEN UP TO 2 SIDES — THE
PARK ON THE EAST, & THE
OPEN ATRIUM ON THE WEST.

ALL HABITABLE ROOMS OPEN TO
OUTSIDE SPACES — LIGHT &
VENTILATION CAN COURSE
THROUGH EACH UNIT.

ATRIUM TO THE
WEST
THE ATRIUM CONTAINS THE
CIRCULATION WALKWAYS TO
EACH LIVING UNIT ; THE MAIN
VERTICAL CIRCULATION CORE
OPENS ONTO THE ATRIUM ; &
2ND FLOOR OFFICES OPEN TO
TREE LINED COURT.

THE STRUCTURAL FRAME OF
THE BUILDING CARRIES THROUGH
INTO THE ATRIUM.

GROUND FLOOR
PUBLIC ZONES
COMMERCIAL SHOPS ON THE
STREET LEVEL OPEN ONTO THE
PARK BLOCKS ; & HELP TO
REINFORCE THE LIVING UNITS
ABOVE. 2ND FLOOR OFFICES
ALSO OPEN ONTO THE PARK
BLOCKS ;

BOTH FUNCTIONS STRENGTHEN
THE NEIGHBORHOOD DEVELOPMENT

• CORRIDOR DEVELOPMENT
BY ENCOURAGING DEVELOPMENT IN BUILDINGS TO
THE WEST OF THE SITE ; THE PARK BLOCK
CORRIDOR CAN BE IMPROVED. FUTURE DEVELOP-
MENT TO THE FULL 180' BUILDING HEIGHT ON
THE HALF BLOCK DIRECTLY TO THE WEST WILL
HELP IN DEFINING THE PARK BLOCKS.

• DIRECTIONALITY
THE EXISTING STREET SCALE PATTERN OF
CIRCULATION IS ONE OF A CORRIDOR
FRAMED BY BUILDING WALLS . THIS HELPS
TO SERVE AS A MENTAL REFERENCE FOR
THE ORGANIZATION OF THE UPPER
RESIDENTIAL FLOORS.

• CITY CELL • BUILDING CEI
THE EXISTING CITY STREET PATTERN
IS ONE OF SQUARE & RECTANGULAR BLOCKS.
BY USING & MODIFYING THIS NETWORK
WITHIN THE BUILDING ORGANIZATION, VISUAL
& MENTAL REFERENCES ARE ESTABLISHED ;

• INDENTED NODES •
CARRY THROUGH THE THEME OF INDENTED
NODES, ENTRANCES, & ACTIVITY POCKETS. THE
EXISTING BUILDING FRONTS, THE RECTANGULAR
STEPS OF THE PARK BLOCKS — ALL HELP TO
CREATE THE FEELING OF DIRECTIONALITY
WITH BUILDING ENTRANCES OFF OF THIS
IMPLIED MOVEMENT ;

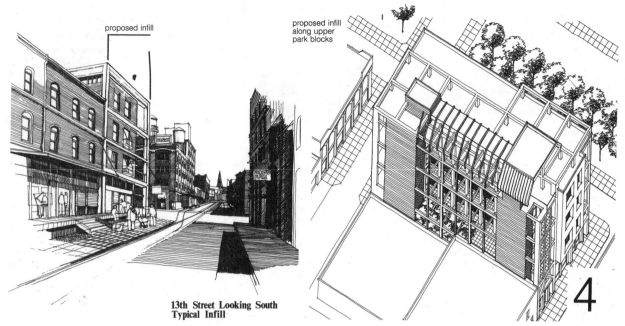

8-9 Architecture Test. The architectural designs test these principles along proposed pedestrian streets within the framework; the Park Blocks and 13th Street NW.

Subdistrict Principles: Stadium Proposal

Network reorganization at the district scale is interpreted very differently in another type of building proposal. A design scenario that locates a sports stadium in the rail yard subdistrict is visualized within the same network identified in the previous R/UDAT study. At the subdistrict scale, the unprecedented size of the stadium structure is mediated in a diagrammatic composition of existing and proposed building forms within the network of Park Block and 13th Avenue extensions to the river. This two-dimensional composition is then illustrated to create a more finalized presentation drawing, still emphasizing the public connections (Park Block and 13th Avenue) identified in diagram.

Neighborhood Districts Within the City

The aerial visualization sets the context for two cooperative efforts between the city and eastside Portland neighborhoods to visualize new development within districts. The drawing composition looks west over Portland and focuses on the vast grid of eastside neighborhoods in the foreground, bounded by the Columbia River on the right and the Willamette River moving across the center of the drawing. This is a simple one-point perspective with a single vanishing point placed along the horizon line on the distant edge of the Pacific Ocean. This drawing was done from tracing the foreground—the eastside grid—from a slide of a USGS map. Two vanishing points were found from the traced grid in perspective; one from parallel grid lines extended to find the single vanishing point along the horizon line and another from diagonal lines extended from a square in the perspective to the horizon line. The diagrammatic structure of the drawing shows the horizon line lowered to minimize the drawing size and focus on the study sites in the foreground. The arbitrary bending of the vanishing lines to meet the one vanishing point along the lowered horizon line distorts only the far background. In this distant area beyond the hills of Willamette valley lies another valley, the Tualitin, where much of Portland's growth spreads west. This is however, another story. This aerial perspective focuses on study sites within the eastside grid.

Visualizing a Study Site Within a Neighborhood District

An infinite number of individual sites exist within the larger aerial city perspective. Each site is a story, complete in itself, viewed as the most important by those who know it and connected to all others. The first study site within Portland's eastside grid is along the edge of one of the district's few distinct features, Sullivan's Gulch. The gulch, a watercourse draining the higher eastside plain to the Willamette River was first occupied by a transcontinental railroad from the east, then Interstate Freeway 80, and finally Portland's first light rail line connecting the city center east to Gresham, Oregon. The aerial perspective of the study site, a small piece within the larger eastside perspective, has been blown up to reveal its particular story. The placement of Portland's first light rail line in the gulch with the Interstate Freeway creates station stops disconnected to adjacent neighborhoods. The heart of this particular study site is an opportunity site, an under-utilized highway maintenance center, that sits between an historic neighborhood commercial center at the intersection of Glisan Street and 60th Avenue, and a light rail station off the bridge over the gulch.

The drawing reflects the strong edge condition of the Gulch, containing the freeway and light rail line, by emphasizing the shadow created by the topographic differences between the floor of the gulch and the floor of the eastside neighborhoods. The large parcels of light warehousing and manufacturing buildings along the edge of the gulch, forming a barrier between the neighborhoods and the light rail station, are treated in the drawing as a void.[2] The Regional Rail Program was established so that the city of Portland, Oregon and its citizens could look at issues that affect the future of the metropolitan area's light rail system. Through its outreach program, information about light rail is provided to the public so that an active and informed constituency can be formed in the region. Studies of specific alignment alternatives in proposed corridors and the impact of potential development around existing and proposed stations is communicated to affected neighborhoods.

The effort of the Regional Rail Program's at 60th Avenue and Glisan Street visualizes the impact of raising residential densities adjacent to the light rail station within the predominantly single-family Center Neighborhood. The pattern of single-family homes that surround the study site is an important boundary feature of the drawing. The drawing gives its darkest value to the surrounding neighborhood fabric, contrasted to the whiteness of the center "void" and clearly shows the disconnection between the surrounding neighborhood and the light rail station. The study site is the first available opportunity to rebuild a neighborhood around the light rail station while providing new connections to the station area from existing neighborhoods. The aerial is a base map that will be overlaid with alternative proposals that explore redevelopment in the area.

Existing and Reorganized District Structure

Compared with the Westhills of Portland where a dramatic hill edge sets the scene for neighborhoods within a continuous park system, Portland's eastside is a relentless grid of streets. The major natural systems through the eastside grid are Sullivan's Gulch and the Mount Tabor area, where a clear sense of place is established by a freestanding butte within the flat city grid.

---

[2] The Livable City Project began as a result of a strategic plan spearheaded by 55 community leaders and adopted by the City in 1991. The project looks at ways to increase the city's share of metro growth from 3 to 5 percent to a goal of 20 percent while maintaining the quality of life in existing neighborhoods like the Hollywood district. The Livable City Project identifies growth concepts that could be applied throughout the city. These include development within existing neighborhood districts, Central City, around transit stations, along main streets, and in specific opportunity sites. The Hollywood project is one of three pilot projects that tested these growth concepts during the public outreach phase of the Livable City Project. The objectives of the project were to provide for a partnership of citizen advocates, landowners, developers, financiers and city staff to address specific in-fill development issues and achieve a consensus within the neighborhood on scale, character, and quality.

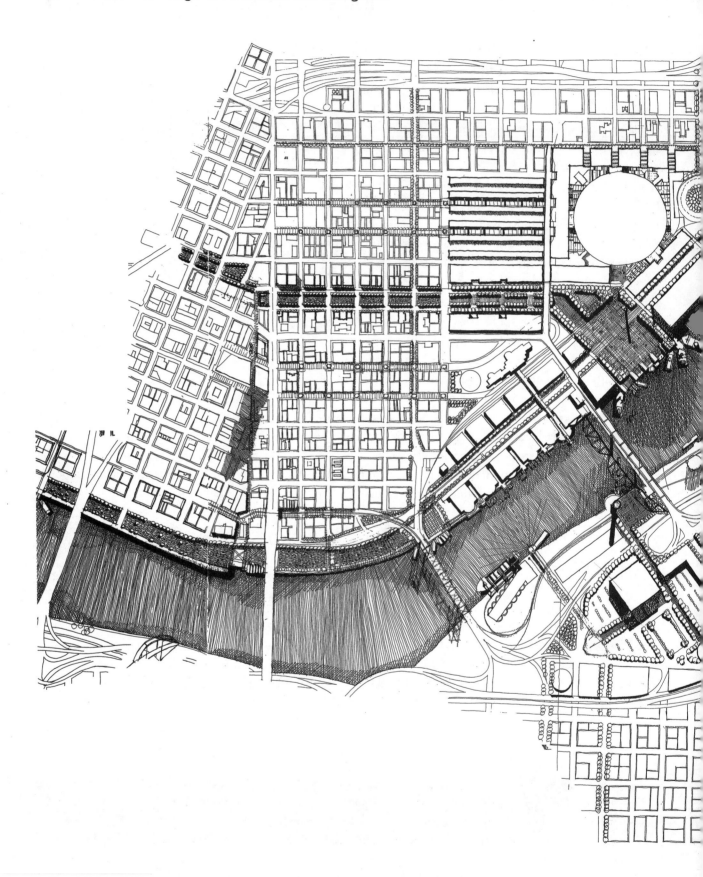

8-10 Plan Design of Stadium Proposal. The more finalized drawing of the stadium proposal carries over the principals of connection described in the study diagrams by placing rendering value along key streets and edges of the design framework.

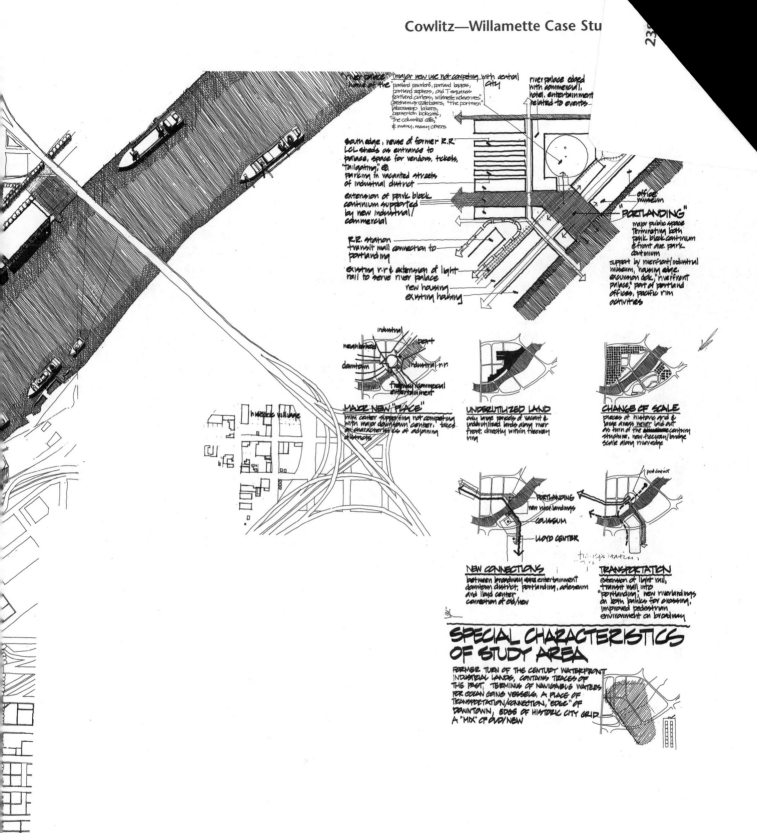

8-11 Design Framework for Stadium in Rail Yard Subdistrict: Northwest Triangle.
The diagrammatic plan describes another design district framework scenario that
explores the possibility of locating a major events facility in the study district. Basic
issues regarding the stadium proposal are singled out in individual diagrams, which in
turn are synthesized into a final diagrammatic framework that locates proposal
"parts" in relation to the river edge and the park block extension.

8-12 East Portland Aerial Perspective. The drawing sets the scene for study sites in the Eastside district of Portland, located in the immediate foreground of the composition. The drawing value emphasizes the edges of the district and details the vast street grid that characterizes the district.

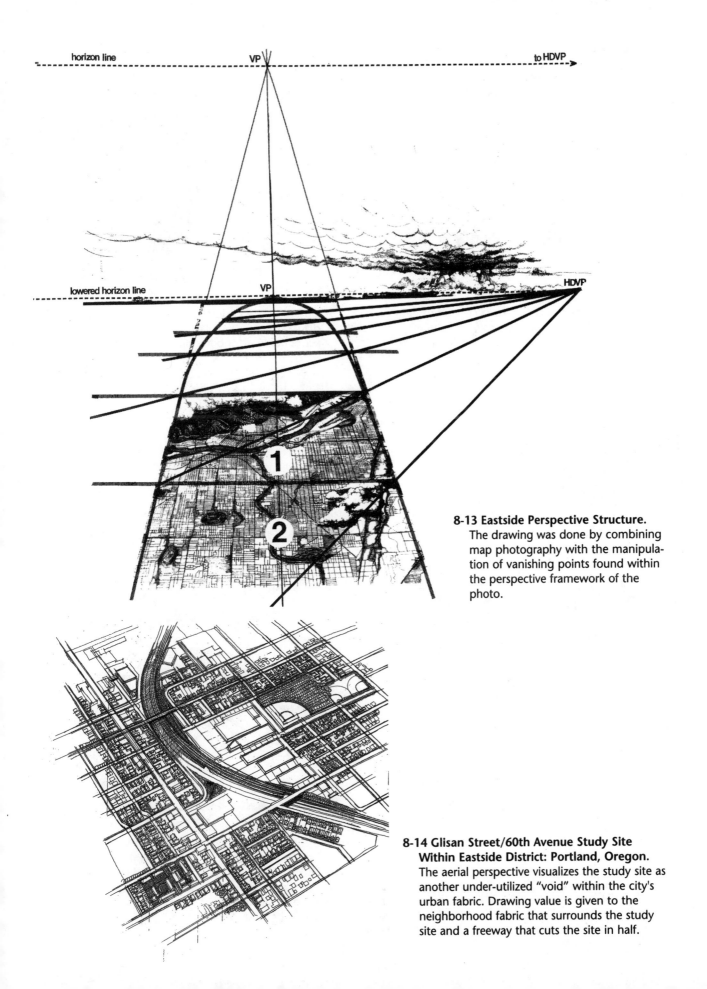

horizon line   VP   to HDVP

lowered horizon line   VP   HDVP

8-13 Eastside Perspective Structure.
The drawing was done by combining map photography with the manipulation of vanishing points found within the perspective framework of the photo.

8-14 Glisan Street/60th Avenue Study Site Within Eastside District: Portland, Oregon.
The aerial perspective visualizes the study site as another under-utilized "void" within the city's urban fabric. Drawing value is given to the neighborhood fabric that surrounds the study site and a freeway that cuts the site in half.

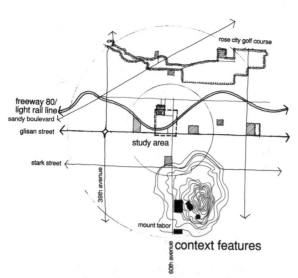

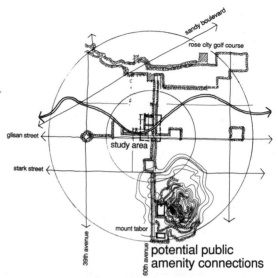

8-15A Study-site Context. The circle composition locates the study area at Glisan Street and 60th Avenue in the center of a quarter-mile walking-radius from the existing light rail station and highlights the relationship of the study site to key organizing systems: Glisan Street, a major arterial to the city center, the freeway/light rail corridor that passes by the site, and a network of public open spaces.

8-15B Study-site Pedestrian Connections. The circle diagram suggests pedestrian connections between surrounding neighborhoods and the light rail station.

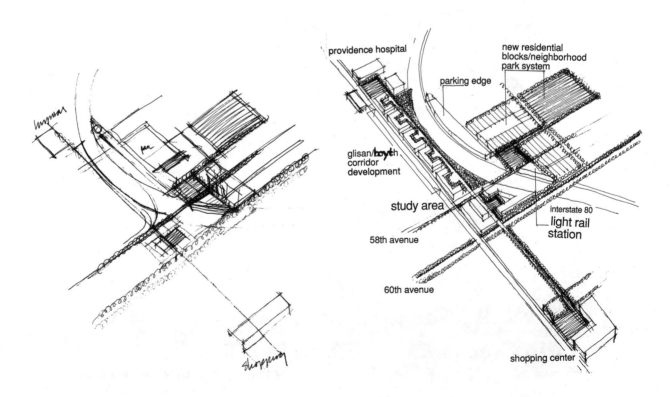

8-16 A,B Study-site Perspective Reorganization. The two-dimensional plan proposals are developed over the original aerial perspective of existing conditions. Initially, the rough sketch suggests a network of lines connecting key attractors to the study area: a city hospital, a shopping center, and a public open space system.

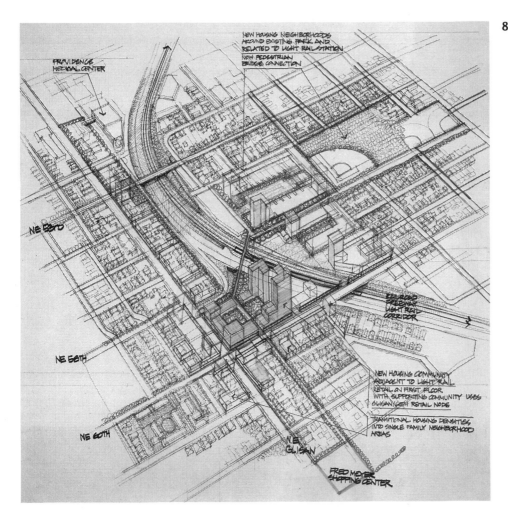

8-17 Study-site Perspective Reorganization of Glisan/60th Ave. Study Site, Portland, Oregon.

The series of diagrams examines the study site within the existing eastside grid context, and identifies potential linkages to existing and proposed open-space amenities. The circle composition locates the study area at Glisan Street and 60th Avenue, in the center of a quarter-mile walking radius of the existing light rail station, and highlights the relationship of the study site to key organizing systems: Glisan Street, a major city arterial connecting the site to the city center; the freeway/light rail corridor that forms the north boundary of the study site; and a network of public open spaces and buildings. The second circle diagram extends connections from the surrounding neighborhoods to the light rail station in the form of tree lined boulevards and pedestrian ways along 60th and Glisan. The two-dimensional plan of potential connections is developed in study perspectives over the original aerial perspective of existing conditions. Initially, the rough sketch **(1)** suggests a network of lines connecting key attractors to the study area (a city hospital, a shopping center, and a public open space system). A more developed view **(2)** of the same sketch gives it dimension and shows the form of new blocks of development. In a third step **(3)**, the same system of new pedestrian connections and supporting new building development are overlaid on the original aerial perspective. The generalized restructuring of the study site area was presented to the surrounding neighborhoods as a point of departure in discussing appropriate redevelopment within their district.

Development Character

Development impact is visualized in the heart of the neighborhood district at the intersection of Glisan Street and 60th Avenue. An existing view of the area includes a cluster of historic structures that still defines the intersection. From the visual structure of the existing view, perspective lines are extended until they meet at a vanishing point along the horizon line. The horizon line and the vanishing point are

8-18 A,B Proposal Development Impact.

then used as a framework within which new building heights can be accurately measured.

Study Site Within Neighborhood District

Continuing west along Sullivan's Gulch, this aerial magnifies the area around the next light rail station, Portland's Hollywood district. The composition of the drawing places the gulch off to the side and places Sandy Boulevard, the only major city street that cuts diagonally across Portland's eastside, at the center of the drawing.

The story is different here, with vacant blocks of land between the light rail station and a larger, more identifiable historic city district center along Sandy Boulevard on the north side of the gulch. In plan, the larger shaded circle represents a quarter-mile walking radius from a light rail station adjacent to the study site, a three-block area in the Hollywood district.

This large, under-utilized parcel of land along the existing light rail line, linking the eastside to the city center, is the topic of a joint pilot project of the Regional Rail Group and the Livable City Project.

The Hollywood pilot project, a potential model

for future planning efforts within the city, began with the selection of a steering committee composed of local neighborhood leaders, citizens, interested property owners, and business interests. Rather than starting with the constraints of traditional land use and zoning regulations, the steering committee was encouraged to develop a consensus for their "ideal" development and then let the city staff deal with the implications of regulation change.

Visualizing a Study Site Within a Neighborhood District

During a six-month period of weekly meetings, design principals for the study area were arrived at by visualizing alternative design proposals. The process of discussing and giving physical form to these principals began with blowing up the three-block study site within the previous aerial perspective in a series of successive steps. Each drawing step down the scale ladder adds more detail to a framework of connections identified during the previous drawing step. In the first step, the blown-up perspectives of the study site are of the same view; one is literal, showing existing conditions, and the other is an abstract diagram that identifies the three-block study site as a core area, a single piece within a larger system of related

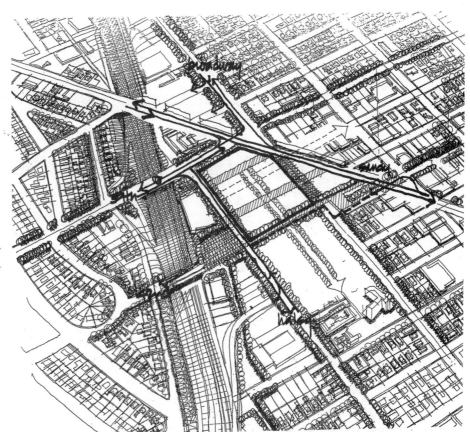

Core Area Development Guidelines

Clarify and balance vehicular circulation around the core area periphery.

1. Make 39th two way from Sandy to overpass. Allow right turn onto 38th from Sandy. Re-route some buses to 39th to take pressure off of 42.
2. Allow left turn onto 37th or 38th from Broadway.

Maintain public view/access corridors through area, especially between Sandy/Broadway and light rail station.

1. Maintain 40th and 41st in existing locations or relocate as needed by new development.
2. Possibly extend Weidler west through core area.

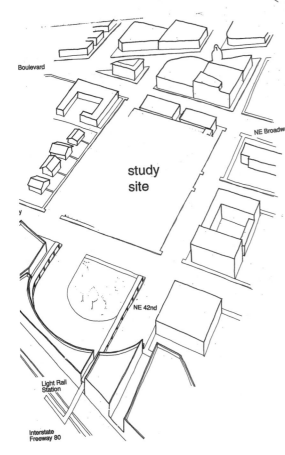

1/4 mile walking radius

8-19 Hollywood Neighborhood District, Study Site Within Neighborhood Connections. The aerial visualization stresses the position of the study site within a potential framework of neighborhood district street connections. Treed street edges are used to exaggerate the primary connections of the network and the circle places the site at the center of the quarter-mile walking-radius from its adjacent light rail station.

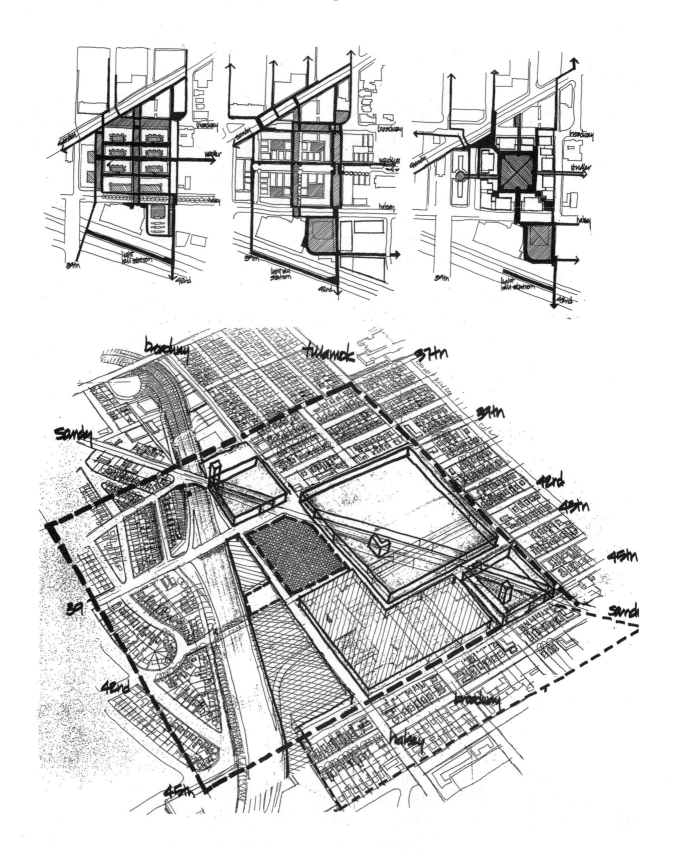

8-20 Study-site Subparts and Alternative Site Frameworks. The alternative plan views portray different design alternatives that link the study site to the surrounding neighborhood and the district's light rail station. Each alternative places a different importance on various parts of the framework, resulting in different block sizes.

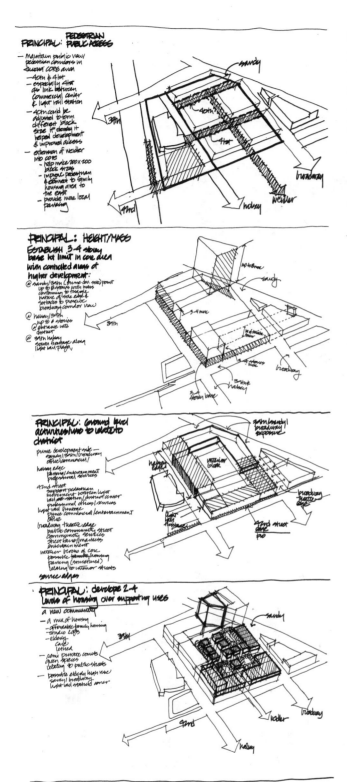

8-21 Visualizing Preliminary Design Guidelines: Hollywood District. The three-dimensional diagrams are the first step in translating public discussion into a set of individual design principles. The freehand drawings are done during public meetings to summarize discussions and decisions regarding design guidelines for new development.

subdistricts. Both drawings carried over from the previous aerial an understanding of surrounding subdistrict character, street hierarchy, and potential connections between new development on the study site and the surrounding neighborhoods. These drawings laid the basis for developing alternative design proposals that explored different building densities and envelopes, different use mixes, public open-space systems, and parking strategies. An overall objective of all proposed development scenarios was to support a better connection to the existing light rail station in the district and to create a development character that was sympathetic to the qualities of the existing neighborhood. Abstract diagrams were used to communicate preliminary concepts and later, these same views were turned into more literal and finalized drawings.

Drawings to Communicate Design Principles

The diagrams visualize the preliminary set of design principles that could connect a new development within the core area to the Hollywood district. These principals deal with pedestrian access through the area, new building height and mass, ground level uses and their relationship to the surrounding subdistricts, and new housing configurations. These visualizations are free-hand sketches done over a blown-up piece of the larger aerial perspective. The principles evolved during the citizen participation effort through a series of overlays, constantly changed until a finalized version emerged. The street system framing the core area is terminated in arrows implying connection and directionality. Within the street framework line weight and value is focused to bring out the pertinent aspects describing each principal. New building envelopes for the three-block study site are developed in a diagram that visualizes existing spatial conditions formed by buildings (or the lack of them) around the study site. Another diagram pulls out with shading important street connections through the study site and between the light rail station. Lastly a set of diagrams begins to organize pieces of architectural form and identifies ground-level activities that would appropriately connect to the surrounding subdistricts.

Finalized District Principals

The finalized core area development guidelines are a direct outgrowth of the preliminary visualizations.

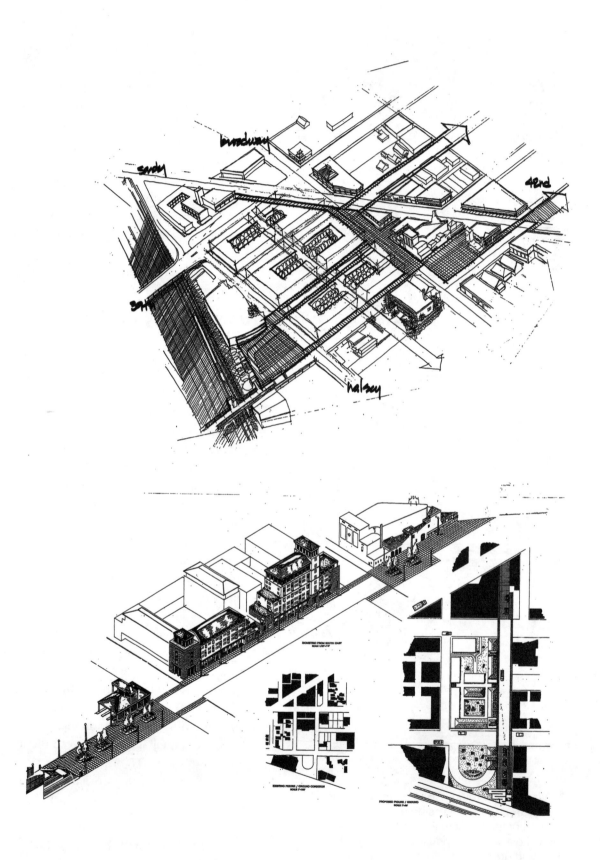

8-22 Pedestrian/Public Access and Open Space.

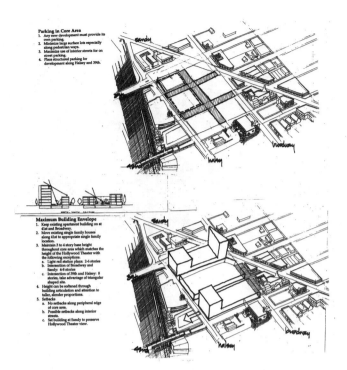

8-23 Building Height/mass and Parking Streets.

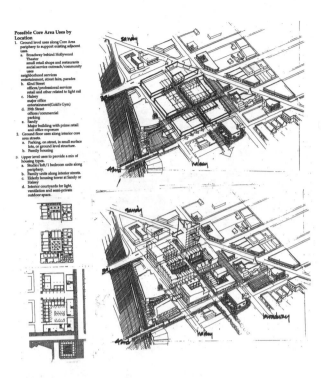

8-24 Ground- and Upper-Level Building Activity Relationship to the District.

The same aerial view is used with heightened line weight and value to further demonstrate the individual guideline. The guidelines are introduced by a new diagram that clarifies circulation and connections within and around the study core. In-fill within the resulting street framework is diagrammed to illustrate development guidelines along with small designs exemplifying the point of the design principal. The last plan drawing demonstrates some possible outcomes of the design principles.

A Small Community Within an Eco-region: Cottage Grove

The trunk of the Willamette River that passes through the metropolitan Portland area on its way to the Columbia River is created by a network of streams and rivers that reach out to drain the much larger eco-region room. Along these drainage branches, a network of smaller communities and towns grow. The aerial diagrams looks west over the main street of Cottage Grove, Oregon, a small com-

munity tucked into the foothills near the southwest corner of the eco-region, far away, yet connected to the Portland metropolitan area. The rendered line of vegetation diagonally across the drawing is the course of a north fork river, one of the tributaries that feed the Willamette River.

Cottage Grove developed along the north fork of the Willamette River. The city's main street visualizes the elements that create a sense of place and connectedness in the landscape for the community—the foothills, river, and forest edge. Like the Portland neighborhood, this study involves a community concerned with the future quality of their downtown, once a vital commercial and cultural center of surrounding neighborhoods. While the Cottage Grove community has strong feelings toward its historic downtown district, this center has slowly deteriorated with the city growing east along Interstate Five and the foothills of the Cascades. This deterioration triggered a planning effort by the city to raise the awareness of the public regarding their historic downtown while giving individual building owners

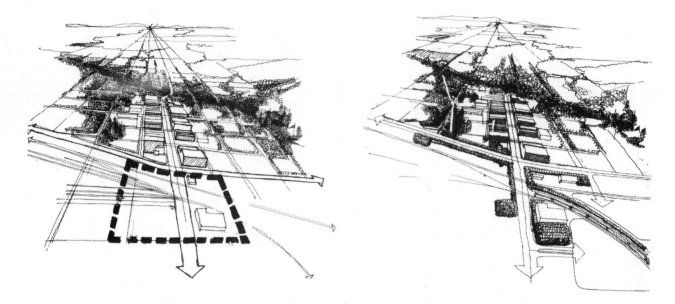

8-25 Downtown Cottage Grove, Oregon. The aerial sketch brackets the small downtown main street between parallel built and natural systems that connect it to the larger region. In the background, line emphasis is given to a segment of the natural network that organizes the historical settlement: the North Fork of the Willamette River. In the foreground, segments of later built connections, Highway 99 and the Southern Pacific Railroad, form the downtown's entrance. Restructured east downtown entry place is restructured with a new building and landscape edge.

concepts which could reestablish a sense of place in the downtown.

The process of visualization during the public participation process simultaneously included drawings along different points of the scale ladder. Aerial perspective and plans of the downtown area were used to describe overall design concepts at the city district scale while perspectives and elevations represented individual buildings and collective block facade concepts. Public perception of many older and deteriorated downtown districts is commonly a negative one, associated with forgotten buildings whose value has been obscured by years of deferred maintenance. During the public participation process, abstract line drawings of individual buildings removed reality for a moment to reveal the inherent positive style and character of historic downtown buildings. These same drawings were developed into further proposals with individual property owners.

Opportunities at the Downtown District Scale

The locations of proposed improvements were common to many communities whose sense of place has been lost over time to the automobile. These improvement areas included reestablishing a sense of city entrance and identification, improving the pedestrian environment and capitalizing on the proximity of adjacent neighborhood districts, reinforcing the identity and quality of the existing downtown building group, and reorganizing vacant lots, alleys, and city parking areas. At the city district scale, the plan diagram put into perspective parking and walking complaints by representing one- and three-minute walking-radius circles throughout the downtown area. The same aerial perspective that visualized the position of the historic town center in relation to the eco-region's landscape was used as a base drawing to study the spatial restructuring of the downtown's entry from the east.

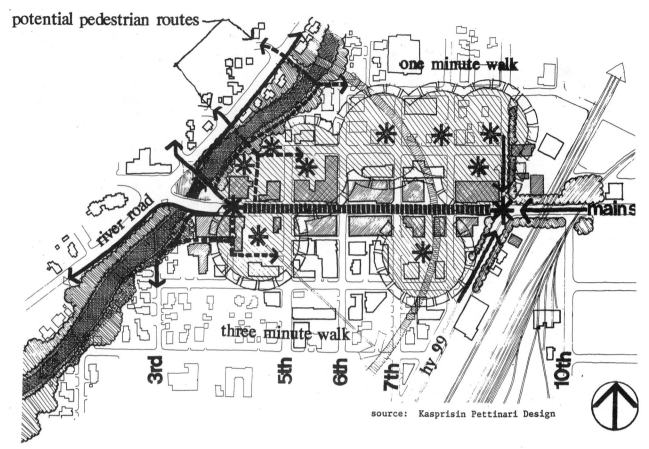

potential pedestrian routes

one minute walk

river road

mains

three minute walk

3rd   5th   6th   7th   hy 99   10th

source: Kasprisin Pettinari Design

walking radii from parking areas

8-26 Walking/Parking Relationships. At the city district scale, the plan diagram of one- and three-minute walking times puts into perspective common complaints regarding parking and walking distances.

City Entry

The dotted area in the aerial perspective, the east entry to the downtown, lacks spatial structure. Historically, the railroad station and city hotel formed a city entrance and terminated main street in the dotted area of the downtown aerial perspective. Presently the area lacks spatial structure. Streets have been widened to serve new commercial development, and existing historical structure is underutilized. The same aerial perspective is used to visualize the restructuring of this area with new building and landscape edges to serve the needs of an excursion train operation that runs from the outskirts of downtown into the mountains.

Two ground-level before-and-after perspectives done from the same view contrast the existing sense of non-place with a more developed and defined

possibility of a public street that introduces the city's downtown historic district. Another set of perspectives and diagrams visualize the restructuring of the opposite entrance end of main street by relocating a large, existing covered bridge into the area as a pedestrian crossing of Coast Fork. This river area is the original site of the town and has a pleasant, historic neighborhood character containing historic residences, a museum, city library, and the city hall. The covered bridge, abandoned from a logging railroad of another time pattern, serves as an entrance gate linking pedestrian walks into the historic river area.

Open Space

While Cottage Grove still maintains a critical historic building mass, like many communities, it has also experienced a substantial loss of buildings through

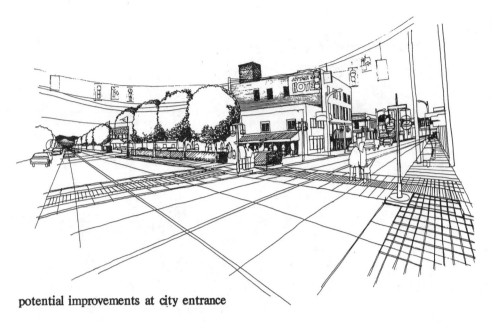

8-27 Town Entry. Two ground level before-and-after perspectives contrast the existing "void" of no place with a more defined public street room place that introduces the city's downtown historic district.

potential improvements at city entrance

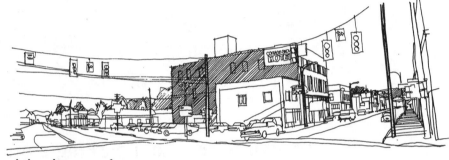

existing city approach

neglect, fire, and deterioration. The diagram visualizes built- and open-space patterns along the five-block Main Street. Some of the existing building walls adjacent to vacant lots along Main Street have been effectively used for advertising and the diagram identifies a limited opportunity for this activity, if actually connected to building use. Ideally, the former vacant building lots would become future building sites, realistically the in-fill process in a small community is very slow. A set of before-and-after perspectives contrasts existing to proposed interim designs for open spaces surrounding and fronting Main Street.

Visualizing Individual Building Design and Renovation

All but one of the original wood storefront buildings have been replaced along Main Street and today the strength of the downtown image exists in the common building wall of brick and masonry buildings. Throughout the public meetings, line drawings of existing downtown building elevations were used to both explore and communicate cleanup and restoration strategies and to recapture historic facade characteristics, were possible. The line elevations, done in ink on mylar, served as base maps for design renovation and future reference material. The elevation abstractions removed buildings from their literal context and revealed to some of the public, for the first time, the character and value of existing historic buildings. Ground-level perspectives visualized improvement in strategic building corner locations.

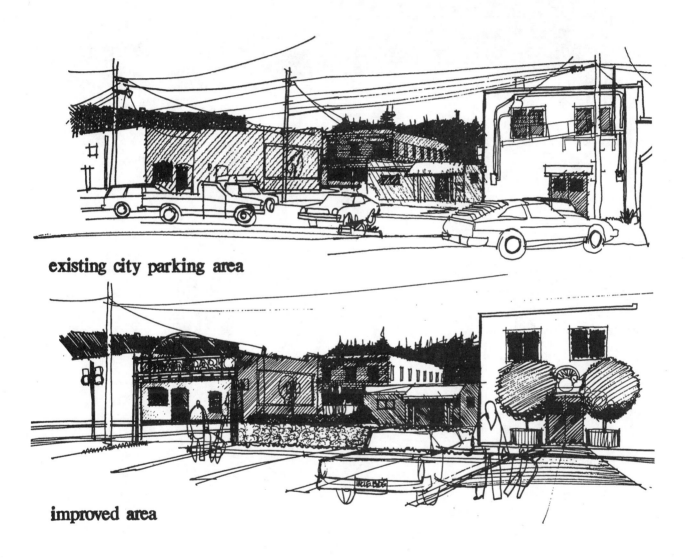

existing city parking area

improved area

8-28 Before-and-after views of City Parking Area.

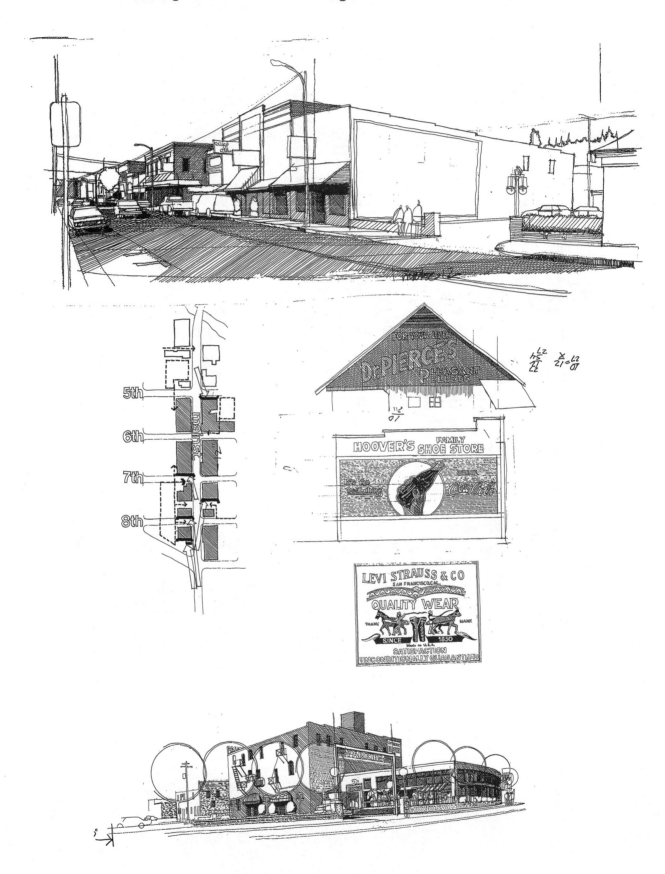

8-29 Vacant Lots and Exposed Building Wall Locations.

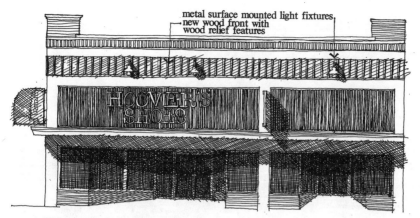

metal surface mounted light fixtures
new wood front with wood relief features

HOOVER'S SHOES Option One

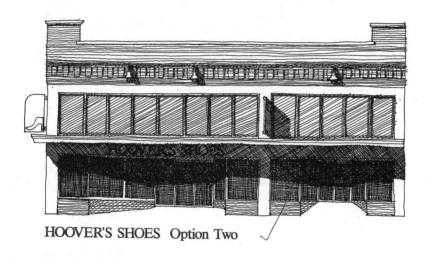

HOOVER'S SHOES Option Two

8-30 Building Renovation Proposal/Signage.

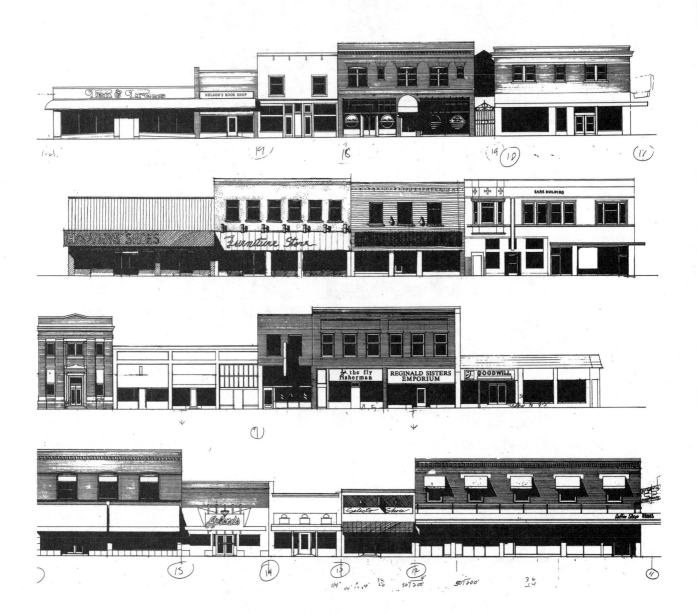

8-31 Building Elevation Proposal Recovery. Line elevations of existing historic buildings remove them from literal context and can reveal to the layperson for the first time the true character and complexity of their designs.

9 Clark Fork: Bitterroot, Missoula, Montana Case Study

Introduction/Background

In 1981, the City of Missoula, Montana enlisted the help of the National Endowment for the Arts in sponsoring a national design competition for the downtown riverfront corridor.[1] The objective of the competition was to raise public awareness concerning the city's future quality of life, to generate a master plan for the river corridor through the city, and to solicit designs for two specific sites along the downtown riveredge. These two sites were the vacant riverfront land immediately behind the historic city center and another vacant riverfront parcel fronting the University of Montana campus within the city. The citizens of Missoula were interested in reshaping their city's future and adopting a plan that would direct their efforts over time, as well as implementing an achievable demonstration project.

The design competition was held in two phases. From a first phase of open submission, five finalists were selected to continue on a second phase to be held for a week in the city itself. These submissions responded to a generalized set of programmatic needs and objectives identified by a citizens' committee working with the National Endowment for the Arts. During the second phase, initial design concepts were refined and presented to the public. These design concepts included both larger river corridor master planning concepts and two specific concepts for individual sites. A third phase of the competition was the selection of a single finalist and contract to implement the first phase: construction of the downtown site.

Visual Thinking Design Process

The design process included visualization at many different scales. These included drawings of the eco-region, the region, the city and its river corridor, and the selected study sites. Drawings were done not only for the required public process, but as a way of analyzing the existing environment and uncovering constraints and opportunities. From visualizations of

9-1 Clark-Bitterroot Eco-region Within Cascadia. The Clark Fork-Bitterroot Eco-region is along the eastern edge of Cascadia. The Clark Fork-Bitterroot watershed flows west via the Columbia River to the Pacific. The watersheds of eco-regions east of here flow east via the Missouri into the Gulf of Mexico.

[1] Caras Park, First Prize, Construction of National Design Competition for the Design of the downtown riverfront, Missoula, Montana. Sponsored by the National Endowment for the Arts and the City of Missoula.

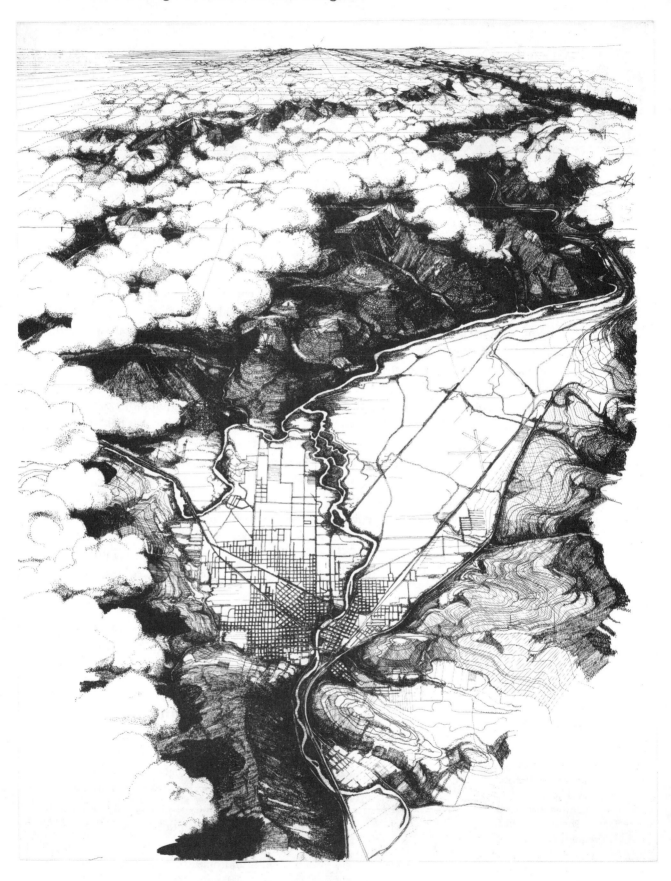

9-2 Settlement Within the Clark Fork-Bitteroot Eco-region: Missoula, Montana. The aerial
view emphasizes the course of the Clark fork as it flows through the settlement of
Missoula, Montana (in the foreground) to the Pacific Ocean. Drawing value emphasizes the
mountain edges that define the former bed of a great glacial lake where Missoula now sits.

existing conditions, design issues and basic proposals were distilled into diagrams that clearly communicated opportunities to the public. These diagrams were done along the scale ladder, from views of city relationships to the immediate study sites. Visualizations of final, developed proposals became tests that interpreted the ideas presented in the simplified framework diagrams.

Visualizing the Eco-region: Settlement Within the Region

Missoula is located within the Clark Fork/Bitteroot Eco-region, and the diagram describes the city's relationship to the irregular eco-region chamber defined by the valley floor, the sky, and surrounding mountain edges. The Clark Fork passes east/west through this place, eventually joining the Columbia River in Canada and draining into the Pacific Ocean. The Clark Fork, the historic trail of Lewis and Clark, is the spine that organized settlement in the region and is a major organizing factor in shaping Missoula. The aerial perspective looks west over the Clark Fork/Bitteroot Eco-region with the city grid of Missoula in the lower foreground and the Bitteroots, the west edge of the eco-region, vanishing in the background. The Bitteroots are the first wave of mountains, set perpendicular to the passage of the Clark Fork river and the transportation lines that follow it: two transcontinental railroads, Highway 12, and, most recently, Interstate 80. The City of Missoula developed along the Clark Fork at the mouth of Hellgate Canyon, a formidable landmark at the east edge of the city flanked by Mount Jumbo and Mount Sentinel. The Clark Fork rushes through the canyon and across a broad plain before disappearing into the Bitteroots. The flat valley plain, once the bed of a great prehistoric lake, became the site of the city and today provides convenient sites for most growth.

River District Within City Settlement

Drawings elaborate on the form of the Clark Fork as a major organizing element at the city settlement scale. The Clark Fork, a wild mountain river prone to

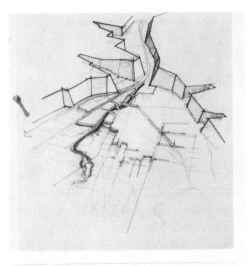

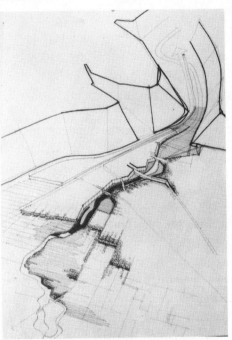

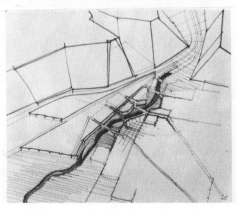

9-3 A,B,C Riveredge Settlement Diagram. The aerial diagram reduces the basic form of the city into built blocks and relates them to the spatial shape of the flood plain that is created along the course of the river through the city. These drawings are the first step in identifying a river corridor master plan.

flooding, has carved along its course a natural flood plain through the city. The flood plain pattern, a distinct boundary between river and city, organizes the visual studies of the river corridor district and is repeated throughout drawings, carried down from scale to scale, until it becomes a pervasive theme organizing detailed study site proposals. The two-and three-dimensional diagrams depict the city's river corridor as an artery running through a larger system with the course of the river moving completely across the paper. The plan diagram emphasizes the relationship of Missoula's city center to the course of the river as resembling a cross, one leg being the city's main street, the other leg, the river corridor. Both study sites are located along the river, the downtown site being at the section of the two legs of the cross.

Drawing Value

The drawing treats the value of built patterns differently, establishing a hierarchy of the darkest value of buildings fronting and forming main street. The next order of value is given to the buildings a block away from Main Street and to those both proposed and existing along the river corridor. A series of circles is superimposed on the existing river corridor to suggest a sequence of open spaces, already formed in part by the meeting of the flood plain and the built edge of the city. New building in-fill is suggested to further define the edges of these areas as a series of large outdoor rooms along the river corridor.

Conceptual Open-space Framework

Development of the open-space system is advanced in the aerial perspective of the river corridor through the city. The river, snaking through the drawing before disappearing into the Bitteroot Mountain Range at the top of the drawing, provides inherent continuity. The river surface and its edges receive the strongest value with the floor texture of the river places and their edges receiving the next value. The city grid is only suggested, receiving less value than the river or river room surface. Connections between the river places and the city grid are emphasized in strings of existing and proposed vegetation, edged in

black. Establishing a spatial boundary that defines the proposed open space system is the overriding consideration of this visualization.

Project Sites Within the River District

The river corridor design is developed in further detail through drawings that carry down the form and dimension of the larger river system into the development of two project sites along its course: one at the intersection of main street and the river, the other at the next bridgehead fronting the University of Montana campus. The plan reiterates the basic principals of earlier drawings and begins to develop the idea of a series of distinct yet connected places along the river corridor. The drawing focuses on informational aspects of use, rather than natural and built elements. For purposes of reference and communication, the diagram gives names to the proposed places to be developed in the master plan, and identifies uses that might support such spaces. The series of places designated by the large circles are called McCormick Place, Rivertown Place, Rivergreen Place and Riverstadium Place. Flood problems, railroad development, and topographical differences allowed the settlement pattern to touch the river in only a few places and each proposed "riverplace" is viewed as a different opportunity to connect citizens directly to the varied amenities of the river. Pedestrian and bikeways parallel the river on both its banks, linking the system of riverplaces into a continuous network of public space. At this conceptual stage, the riverplaces are defined with heavy line weight as a circle with paths corresponding to the surrounding street system leading to it. The boldest directional arrow is the crossing of Main Street and the river at Rivertown Place, one of the study sites to be developed in further detail.

Carryover from Diagram to Development

The intention of this diagram is to simplify, introduce, and communicate a complex, large-scale planning proposal to the public. The visualization creates a framework of place locations and connections that

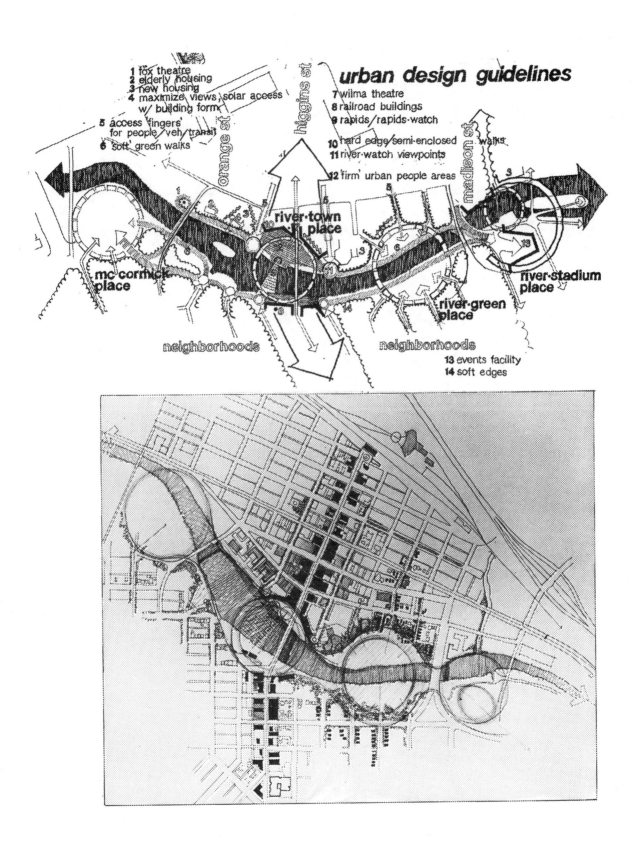

1 fox theatre
2 elderly housing
3 new housing
4 maximize views/solar access
w/ building form
5 access 'fingers'
for people/veh/transit
6 soft green walks

urban design guidelines

7 wilma theatre
8 railroad buildings
9 rapids/rapids·watch
10 hard edge/semi·enclosed
11 river·watch viewpoints
12 'firm' urban people areas

higgins st

orange st

madison st

river·town place

mc cormick place

river·stadium place

river·green place

neighborhoods

neighborhoods

13 events facility
14 soft edges

9-4 River Plan Diagrams. The two plan diagrams of a riverfront design proposal emphasize different information. The first relates a sequence of two-dimensional "rooms" along the river corridor to existing building patterns. The second is more informational and includes the names of proposed spaces and the activities that surround them.

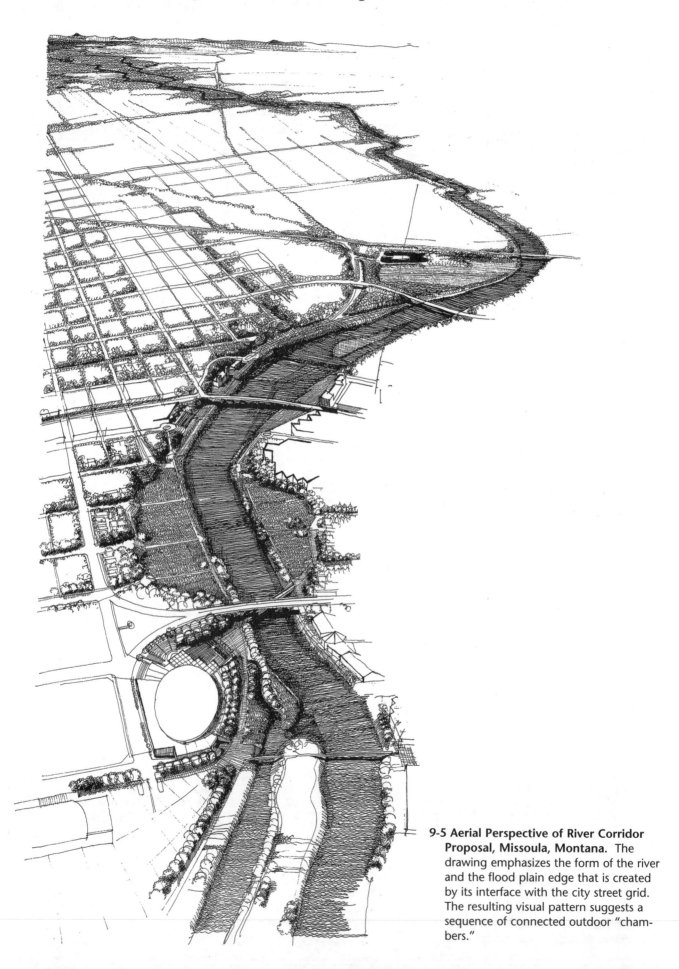

9-5 Aerial Perspective of River Corridor Proposal, Missoula, Montana. The drawing emphasizes the form of the river and the flood plain edge that is created by its interface with the city street grid. The resulting visual pattern suggests a sequence of connected outdoor "chambers."

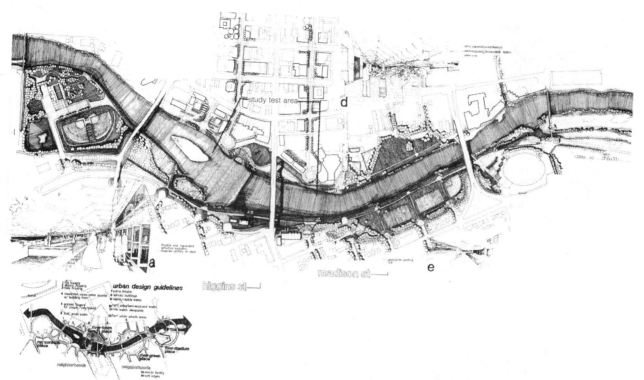

9-6 Plan Diagram of River Corridor Proposal. The rendered plan of the river corridor proposal repeats the same value system of the aerial perspective. The water surface of the river receiving the highest value and the treed outline of the floor plain edge the next. The city grid and design proposals remain line drawings, an order under the natural forces that shape them.

will guide the city's reconsideration of its urban river corridor, acting as a policy diagram rather than describing a physical place. The basic principles described in the framework are elaborated upon in the river corridor plan, which begins to deal with the physical and political realities of the site. The river places are no longer abstract circles connected by arrows, and their shapes are adjusted to existing contours and other site constraints. Nonetheless, the principles implied in the shapes of the earlier diagrams are carried into this more developed drawing. For example, the inherent characteristics of the circular enclosure, centering and focus, are carried into the development of individual river places. Characteristics of the connections described in previous diagrams, linearity and directionality, are also key principles in the following level of design development.

Value

In this more literal visualization of the proposed river corridor design, realistic graphic image is used to emphasize the surfaces of the river and river places with closely spaced parallel lines and dense scribble techniques. Existing tree patterns that surround the river places and act as potential boundaries are infilled with new plantings and pulled out of the visualization with edge shadows. These planting patterns surrounding the river places also lead away from the river and become connected to the city grid system. Starting from the west, McCormick Place is recognized as an existing city park with the surface of playing fields rendered as a point of focus. Next, Rivertown Place, the one place along the river's edge where direct hard surface contact with the river could occur, contains the beginning of a design proposal that will reconnect the city's downtown to its riverfront. The city and university have programmed several uses for this area and it is the first phase to be implemented by the competition work. The next place along the proposed river corridor system is Rivergreen Place. It is framed by two bridge crossings, bordered by two neighborhoods and is the softest and most natural of the river places. The south side of Rivergreen Place is defined by a bluff in the

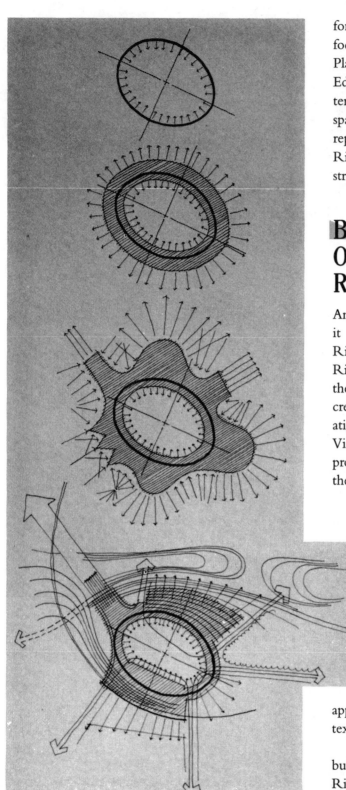

9-7 A,B,C Evolving Form Diagram. The sequence of diagrams traces the steps of a complete "internalized" stadium form responding within a context of varying external site forces. A transitional layer (shaded zone) ultimately resolves the predetermined stadium form into a single-site composition.

form of dish containing former railroad yards. The focus and definition of this place, like McCormick Place, is brought out by rendering grass surface. Edges, lined with existing and proposed tree patterns, are given a dark value to heighten the sense of spatial enclosure. Linear tree patterns, that have replaced the arrows in the previous diagram, connect Rivergreen Place north and south in neighborhood streets.

Building Organization Opportunities: Riverstadium Place

An objective of the design competition was to solicit and communicate ideas for two study sites: Rivertown Place and Riverstadium Place. Riverstadium Place, adjacent to Rivergreen Place, is the fourth place along the river corridor system. Its creation was initiated by a proposed multi-use recreational facility for the University of Montana. Visualizations explore the conceptual design of this proposal within the previous framework defined in the river corridor master plan of connected places.

Internal Building Organization vs. External Contextual Connections

The design of the large multi-use facility poses a recurring conflict between the internalized needs of large-scale building proposals and their ability to respond to the exterior context in which they occur. Many times, large-scale building proposals have little apparent opportunity to relate to an external context, either built or natural.

In the first diagram, the major internalized building piece of the multi-use proposal for Riverstadium Place is represented by a singular and totally complete oval form with inward-pointing arrows. The second diagram adds a shaded zone that straddles the boundary of the oval, relating to both its inside functions and the external forces surrounding the building. The varied, external forces are represented by free-flowing patterns with arrows flowing in outward random directions. This diagrammatic

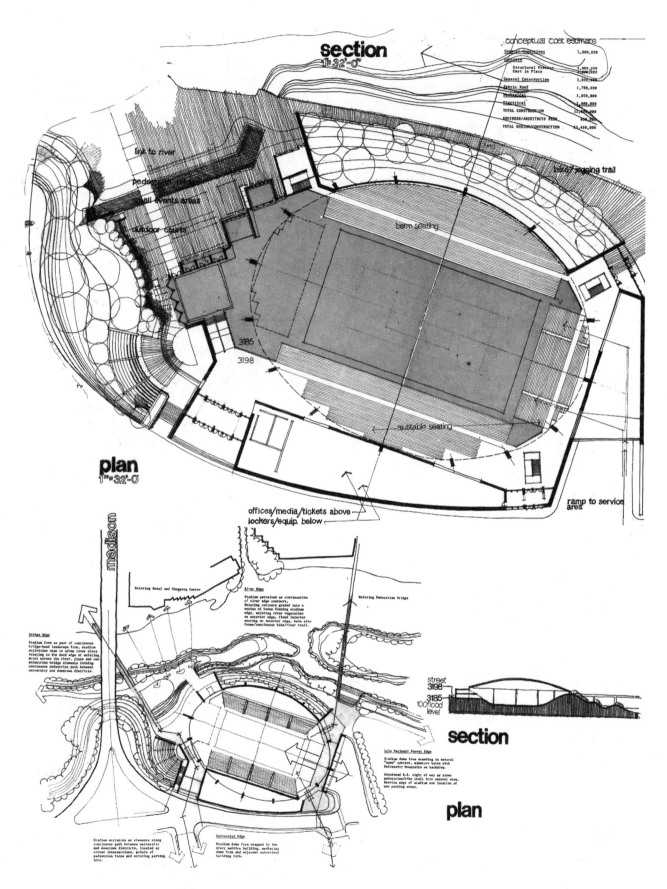

9-8 A,B Stadium Form Organization, Missoula, Montana. The plan and section diagram define in more specific terms the two- and three-dimensional organizational form of stadium "parts" within the river front context.

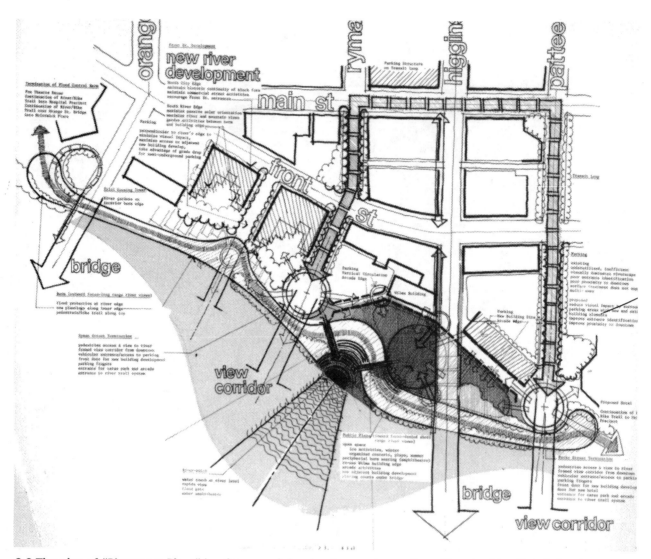

9-9 The plan of "Rivertown Place" is a framework for development over time. The plan identifies design issues regarding river access, the incorporation of the historic Wilma Building, street view corridors, and basic design guidelines for the creation of new housing blocks along the river corridor.

concept of a major internalized building element surrounded by a secondary zone that can respond to both internal building functions and connect to external site forces is carried into the development of the proposed building organization within Riverstadium Place.

Building Elements. The size and shape of the major building piece, the dome containing the playing field and seating, are predetermined by the program. The surrounding pieces that serve the dome, the locker rooms and storage, are less rigidly defined and represented by the shaded area of the last diagram. The diagram depicts the integral relationship

between the major fixed piece and these surrounding pieces that both serve it and fit into the surrounding context. The locker-shower and outdoor seating amphitheater are fit into the curve of Madison Avenue Bridgehead at the entrance to the University Campus. Along the riveredge, a seating/storage berm forms the edge of the pedestrian river trail and irrigation canal entrance. The spaces between these building elements create pedestrian and service building entrances that are extensions of the pedestrian system linking all river places. The final diagram summarizes the design objectives of the building proposal and adds statements to the drawing that turn the visual organization into preliminary

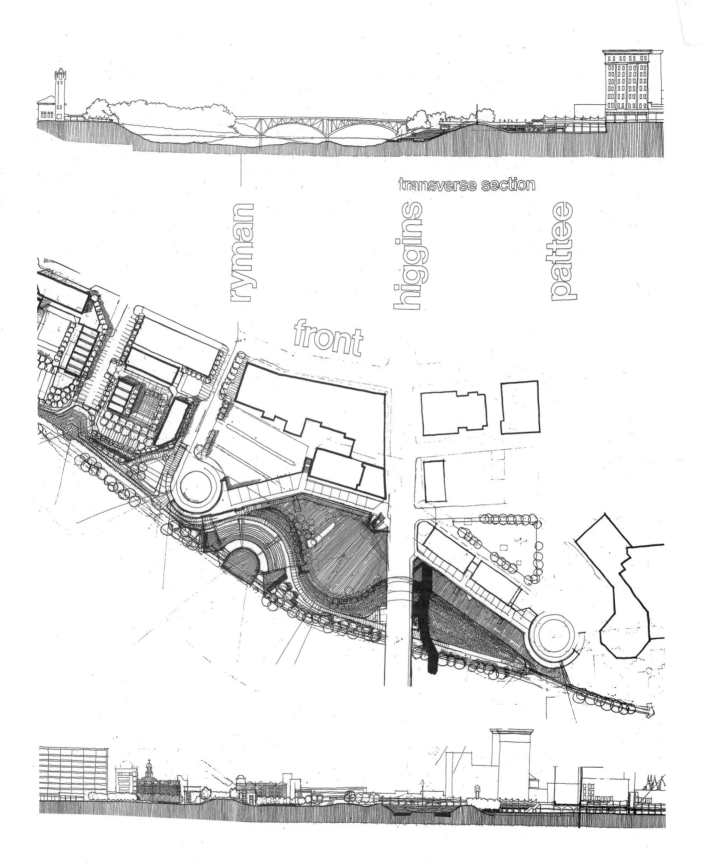

transverse section

ryman

higgins

pattee

front

9-10 Preliminary Test of Riverfront Project Plan/Section, Missoula, Montana.

design guidelines. The integration of predetermined, internalized building form and several natural systems of the riversite become the basis for the design proposal.

Building Organization Opportunities: Rivertown Place

Rivertown Place, located at the intersection of Main Street and the river, is the second site studied in further detail. The diagram reiterates this position within the river corridor framework as a focus of urban activity connected to the downtown. The following framework diagram adds specific programmatic information, site constraints, and policies for implementation to the previous diagram. Programmatic elements in the diagram include a level space to erect theatrical tents, an outdoor amphitheatre, a "river touch" place, more efficient parking, and sheltered space for vendors and storage. All programmatic elements are organized within a framework of connections to both the river corridor and the downtown commercial district. The major site constraint is the existing flood protection berm that prevents easy access to the river. The serpentine shape lining the river's edge represents a proposed extension of the existing flood berm. The new riveredge form increases flood protection while defining, with the bridgehead and the historic Wilma Building, a public space.

Value

The diagram allocates the greatest value to the surface and elements that define the proposed open space at the foot of the bridge. These defining elements are: the ground floor of the historic Wilma Building activating the north edge of the space; the underside of the Higgins Bridge providing cover along the east side of the space; the proposed riveredge berm incorporating an amphitheater that would flood during high water; and an open building arcade along the west edge of the place. Existing building is given a dark value and proposed building

and river berm form that would help define new spaces and connections are shaded. Building elements in the diagram occur within a framework of pedestrian paths, view corridors, and a potential transit loop between the riveredge and the downtown. Selected streets, namely Ryman and Pattee, are designated as important view corridors with brackets. New plantings are suggested along these streets and abstract circles designate their ends as transit stops and entrances. The proposed block patterns along Front Street immediately west of Rivertown place are not buildings, but conceptual organizations of new housing blocks that both define city streets and take advantage of the south facing river frontage.

Three-Dimensional Form and Value

The rendered plan, model, and perspectives give the diagrammatic planning framework three-dimensional expression and allow it to be more fully understood by the public. In the drawing, the surface of the river, the organizing element carried down the scale ladder, is given the darkest black. Proposed building blocks west of the study site and the linear arcade element are both new defining elements and are given rendering around their edges.

The three-dimensional model interpretation of this framework plan is both a study and a presentation tool. Surface structure is given a detailed pattern and the roof of the arcade is removed to exhibit and study the structure and scale of this new building edge. Perspective development of the Rivertown proposal gives the plan a three-dimensional reference that the public can readily understand. The first perspective sketch, done with the aid of a traced city backdrop, is framed by the river and Main Street. The drawing is primarily a study, done in line, with some rendering emphasis on the river and the surface of Rivertown Place. The second drawing is more for presentation purposes and builds in more fine detail in the Wilma Building, the landmark of downtown. The surface of the proposed Rivertown Place is developed in more detail with plantings, activity, and a grid and grass texture.

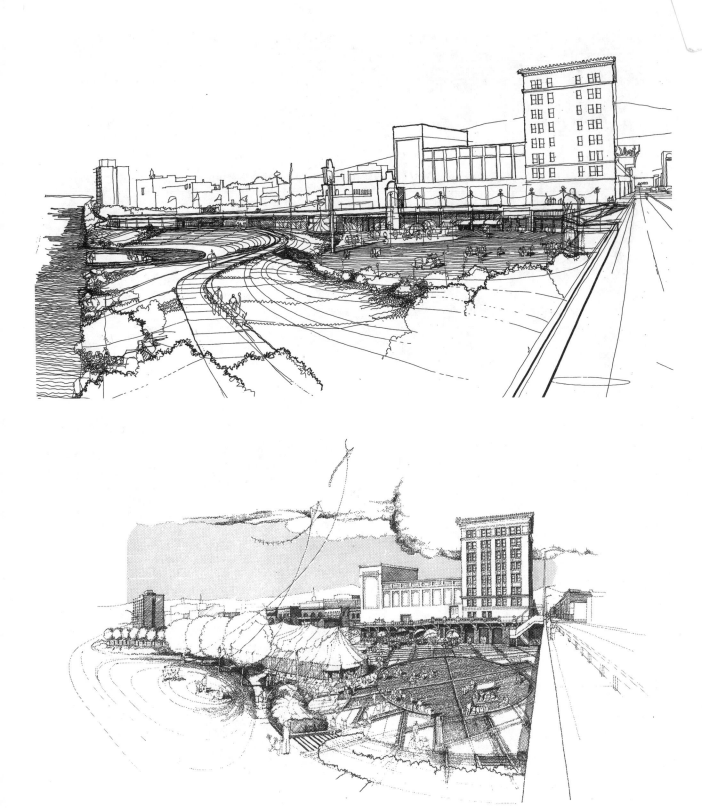

9-11,12 Riverfront Project Perspectives. The perspectives are site sketches that place the riveredge place in the foreground and the city skyline (specifically the Wilma Building) as background references. Rendering value is built on the surface of the proposed public space and the Wilma Theater, the main building edge of the space.

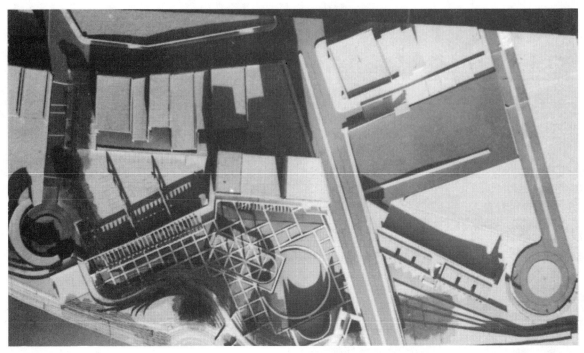

9-13,14 Riverfront Project Model, Missoula, Montana.

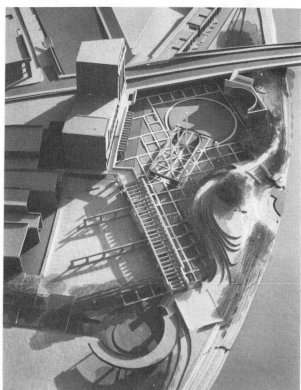

9-15 River Place Arcade Elevation.

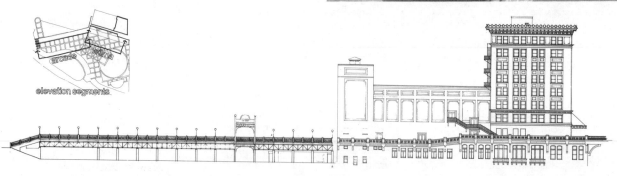

INDEX